How to
Make Your
Advertising
Make Money

How To Make Your Advertising Make Money

John Caples

Vice President
Batten, Barton, Durstine & Osborn, Inc.

Prentice-Hall, Inc.
Englewood Cliffs, New Jersey

Prentice-Hall International, Inc., *London*
Prentice-Hall of Australia, Pty. Ltd., *Sydney*
Prentice-Hall Canada Inc., *Toronto*
Prentice-Hall of India Private Ltd., *New Delhi*
Prentice-Hall of Japan, Inc., *Tokyo*
Prentice-Hall of Southeast Asia Pte. Ltd., *Singapore*
Whitehall Books, Ltd., *Wellington, New Zealand*
Editora Prentice-Hall do Brasil, Ltda., *Rio de Janiero*

© 1983 by

John Caples

Library of Congress Cataloging in Publication Data

Caples, John.
  How to make your advertising make money.

  Includes index.
  1. Advertising.   I. Title.
  HF5823.C179   1983   659.1   83-4455
  ISBN 0-13-423608-4
  ISBN 0-13-423590-8 {PBK}

Printed in the United States of America

How This Book Will Benefit You

This book tells you the most important secrets of successful advertising that have been discovered in the last fifty years.

Many of these secrets have been discovered by mail order advertisers.

Every mail order ad is a sales test. For example, if the Book-of-the-Month Club publishes an ad in a Sunday newspaper, the Book Club finds out in a few days, by counting coupon returns, whether the ad is a success or a failure.

If an ad gets poor results, it is dropped. If an ad gets good results, it is run again and again.

Every decision regarding advertising is based on facts. No decisions based merely on opinions are tolerated.

The legendary Claude Hopkins said: "Every ad writer should have some mail order experience because mail order advertising is scientific advertising."

In the pages of this book you will find:

- A list of the most persuasive words and phrases you can use in writing ads. Hundreds of examples.
- How to make your ads get attention.
- Famous advertising case histories.
- A list of 106 ads that made money.

- How mail order advertising techniques can help general advertisers make money.
- How you can use stories to sell products and services.
- How editorial-style ads can bring increased results.
- How to write ad headlines that make money. Scores of examples.
- A list of 106 successful ad headlines.
- How to write small ads that make money.
- How to make classified advertising pay.
- How to write sales letters that make money.
- Ten ways to begin a sales letter.
- Six ways to end a sales letter.
- One of the most successful sales letters of all time.
- How to write radio commercials that get action.
- How to write effective TV commercials.
- Tips on copywriting: Ten ways to get started. Eleven ways to keep going.
- Fourteen ways to improve your copy.
- Sales appeals that last forever.
- Success secrets of famous ad men.

This book gives you the results of millions of dollars spent in testing the sales effectiveness of hundreds of different kinds of ads, plus the author's more than fifty years' experience in writing and researching advertising for du Pont, General Electric, U.S. Steel, Lever Brothers, Johnson & Johnson, Rexall, United Fruit, Hormel, Phoenix Mutual Insurance, *Reader's Digest, The Wall Street Journal,* Western Airlines, U.S. Navy Recruiting and many others.

John Caples

Contents

Illustrations

How to
Make Your
Advertising
Make Money

1

Secrets of
Successful
Advertising

The purpose of this book is to give you the secrets of successful advertising that have been discovered in the last fifty years.

These proven methods are not theoretical. They are based on actual sales results—on evidence that can be measured and weighed.

Everybody who is interested in advertising, either as a producer of goods, writer of copy, publisher, broadcaster, teacher of advertising practice, or student can take these methods and use them to multiply their sales.

This brief first chapter gives you a quick preview of some of the methods. Many more are revealed in the chapters that follow.

A FEW OF THE SECRETS

1. First of All, There's the Importance of Headlines

Headlines make ads work. The best headlines appeal to people's self-interest, or give news.

Long headlines that say something outpull short headlines that say nothing. Every headline has one job. It must stop your prospects with a believable promise.

All messages have headlines.

In television, it's the start of a commercial.

In radio, it's the first few words.

In a letter, it's the first paragraph.

Even a telephone call has a headline.

If you can come up with a good headline, you are almost sure to have a good ad. But even the greatest writer can't save an ad with a poor headline. You can't make an ad pull unless you can make people read your copy.

2. What Kinds of Words Are the Most Powerful?

Simple words are powerful words. Even the best-educated people don't resent simple words. But they are the only words many people understand.

Remember, too, that every word is important. Sometimes you can change a word and increase the pulling power of an ad.

For example, the headline of an ad for an automobile repair kit was "How To Repair Cars." The headline was changed to "How To *Fix* Cars." The ad pulled twenty percent more.

3. How Long Should Your Copy Be?

Write more copy than you need. If you need a thousand words, write two thousand. Then trim it down.

Ads with lots of facts are effective. And don't be afraid of long copy. If your ad is interesting, people will read all the copy you can give them. If the ad is dull, short copy won't save it.

4. Get to the Point in Your Copy.

Direct writing outpulls cute writing. Don't save your best benefit until last. Start with it. You will have a better chance of keeping your reader with you.

Don't stop by just telling people what benefits your product or service offers. Tell them what they will miss if they don't buy it.

If you have an important point to make, make it three times—in the beginning, in the middle, and at the end. At the end, ask for action. If people are interested enough to read your ad, they want to know what to do. *Tell* them what to do.

5. Should You Use Humor in Advertising?

Avoid humor. What is funny to one person is not funny to millions of others. Copy should sell—not just entertain. Remember, there is not one funny line in the two most influential books ever written—the Bible and the Sears, Roebuck Catalog.

6. Is It Okay to Repeat Ads?

Advertisers get tired of their ads before the public does. Advertisers who can't measure results almost always change campaigns too often. Mail order advertisers know what works and they stick with it.

Of course, you should try to write ads that work even better. That is why I have enjoyed writing sales-tested advertising. You are always trying to beat the ads that do work—to beat the proven winner.

When you try to develop a new winner, test ten ads, not just one. If you lose, you will learn something from your experience.

7. What Effects Do Changing Times Have on Advertising?

Times change but people do not change. Words like *free* and *new* are as effective as ever.

Ads that appeal to the reader's desire for self-improvement still work. People may disagree about what kind of self-improvement is important, but we all want to improve ourselves.

Ads that offer news still work. Subjects that make news change, but the human curiosity to know what is new does not change. These appeals worked fifty years ago. They work today. They will work fifty years from now.

8. How Important Is Testing?

Every element in an advertising campaign should be tested. For example: which ads sell best, which media pull best, which positions in publications are most effective, what time of day is best for broadcasting, which seasons of the year get the most sales.

By running the best ads in the best positions, in the best media and in the best seasons, you can make one dollar spent in advertising do the work of five or ten.

Which Ad Made the Most Sales

Seven ads were tested in the Sunday Magazine Section of *The Los Angeles Times*. Each ad had a different headline. Each ad had a coupon offering home-delivery of the *Times*. The ad "How to Get *The Los Angeles Times* Delivered to Your Home" pulled more than three times as many orders as the ad "This is the paper for you." This test was run more than 20 years ago. The *Times* is still using this same ad. A better one has never been found. Other newspapers, including *The New York Times* and *The Wall Street Journal,* are now using adaptations of this ad.

Ladies:
Here are 14 articles of interest to you.
Which 3 do you want FREE?

HERE'S HOW TO GET THEM. We'd like to know the type of article that you're most interested in. And if you'll help us find out we'll send you those articles *free*.

All you have to do is look over the titles of the articles listed below. Pick the three that you'd most like to read. Circle the numbers of those three articles on the coupon we've provided. Then cut out the coupon and mail it to us together with your name and address. We'll send you the 3 articles you choose absolutely *free* —without any obligation to you.

This offer is good for *seven days only*. So pick out your *favorite* articles and send in your coupon *today.*

1. How to Mix Furniture Styles Tastefully.

2. Dr. Ginnot: Five Techniques to Win Your Children's Cooperation.

3. Kitchens of the Food Experts: Julia Child, Peg Bracken, etc.

4. Angela Lansbury Says:"Eat Six Meals a Day—And <u>Lose</u> 20 Pounds!"

5. Special 8-Page Camping Guide.

6. What the Sex Doctors Are Up to Now.

7. "Action" Hairdos.

8. Grace Kelly: What Being a Mother Means.

9. The 10 Most Common Home Improvements and What They Cost.

10. Magic. New Ways With Outdoor Foods.

11. Natural Estrogen—Preventative for Breast and Pelvic Cancer?

12. Quick-Knita Poncho or Shawl—Complete Instructions Included.

13. Picture Recipe For Exotic Duck A L'Orange.

14. Miracle Clothes That Travel Neatly.

CIRCLE NUMBERS OF 3 ARTICLES YOU WANT*

Cut out coupon and mail today!

*Note: Only one set to a reader

To: Article Agency, Reader Service Dept.
Box 1518, Grand Central Station, New York, N.Y. 10017

Gentlemen: Please send me FREE the 3 articles I have <u>circled below</u> by number.

1 5 9 13   Mr. / Mrs. / Miss
2 6 10 14   Name Mrs. _____ (Please Print) _____ Age _____
3 7 11   Address _____
4 8 12   City _____ State _____ Zip _____

I regularly read the following magazines:
☐ American Home   ☐ Family Circle   ☐ Good Housekeeping
☐ Ladies' Home Journal   ☐ McCall's

Which Magazine Articles Are Most Popular?

Magazines have to be sold the same as other products. And so, some magazine publishers run ads that talk about the articles in their issues. But which articles are most likely to induce people to buy magazines? The above ad shows a way to find out. This ad was published in a newspaper a few weeks before a certain well-known magazine was put on newsstands. The titles of fourteen articles are listed. Readers are invited to send for three articles free. The articles that get the most requests are then featured on the cover of the magazine and in ads selling the magazine.

HAND WOVEN

BY THE MOUNTAIN PEOPLE
OF NEW MEXICO

New Christmas patterns in these unique ties.

Wearers say an exceptional value.* Sold only direct

from weavers to you.

For over 200 years the Spanish people who settled New Mexico have been raising sheep and weaving wool. Their looms and their craft have been handed down from father to son. And the colorful landscape in which these people have lived and worked has made natural artists of them.

Today I take the lovely fabrics these people weave and have them made up into such stunning ties as are shown here. These are as true reproductions as the modern color camera can get, made direct from the ties.

Well dressed men from all over America now send to me for these ties, because they say they can find no others, anywhere, so beautiful, unique, and durable at so low a price.

Fascinating texture

These ties are all wool—every thread of them—except an invisible silk seam along the fringed edge. That is what gives them their fascinating texture. And that is what gives the man who wears them that tweedy, out-of-door look.

That, too, is why these ties wear so well. When men learn by experience that these ties are cut and sewn so as always to tie right and hang right; when they learn that they can rumple them all they please and the wrinkles come right out; and when they find they can be sent to the cleaners again and again without showing wear—then they become fans for these ties.

My Christmas Offer

Yet—by selling direct from the weavers to you—I am able to give you these fine ties for only $1.00 each, postpaid. And for Christmas (until December 15th) I will send you any six of these ties for only $5.00, postpaid.

Can you think of any other gift so unique, so acceptable, so reasonable? Why not simplify your whole Christmas shopping by making selections for every man on your list now?

And you take no risk! For I sell every tie with this unqualified GUARANTEE! If any tie doesn't please you (or the one you give it to) for any reason what-soever, send it back for exchange or get your money back without quibble. I must have satisfied customers, who repeat, to make this business successful.

How to order

Order by the number opposite each tie. Give me one or two second choices, in case I run out of some pattern you want.

Send payment by personal check, postal money order, or bank draft. *I cannot accept stamps.*

Orders from foreign countries cannot be filled—except Canada and Mexico—and of course all U. S. possessions and territories. Foreign customers must pay customs duties.

For Air Mail Service in U. S. (sent within four hours after your order is received) add extra postage as follows: 1 tie 18¢; 2 ties 24¢; 3 ties 30¢; 4 ties 36¢; 6 ties 54¢; and 6¢ for each tie above six.

Ties packed in an attractive gift box and wrapping for 5¢ extra. Mailed direct to recipient, if you wish, with your card or your name on our own unique card, without additional cost.

Please *print* all names and addresses. I am not much of a handwriting expert.

But order quickly, please

I must tell you that these weavers, in true Spanish style, start celebrating *El Natividad* pretty early in the month. So please send your order quickly if you want to be sure of Christmas delivery. I try to fill every order the day it is received, and usually do; but you know what the postal people are up against. For eastern states, in particular, let me have your order not later than Dec. 12th.

And remember: Every order filled with my GUARANTEE that if any tie I send you doesn't please you, for any reason whatsoever, return it for exchange or get your money back without quibble. Could I speak fairer than that?

SPECIAL NOTE: Tie No. 1006, in addition to maroon, can also be had in plain brown, rust, forest green, pearl grey, turquoise blue, light tan, black, blue-green, and light blue. Use this number and add the color you want.

WEBB YOUNG, Trader

203 Canyon Road, Santa Fe, New Mexico

* For instance, George W. Engelmann, well known Chicago business man, writes:—"Enclosed is my order for some of your ties. I would like to take this opportunity to tell you how well I like your ties. When I wear them they never fail to attract favorable comment. They are also the most durable ties and the best value I have ever seen."

Don't Be Afraid to Write Long Copy

In addition to the headline and photos of twenty-seven necktie patterns, this ad contains over 700 words of copy. The ad was written by James Webb Young, former vice president of J. Walter Thompson. The ad sold more than 26,000 neckties from one page in a national magazine. The ad helped to found Young's successful necktie business.

"The most complete and most scholarly dictionary of the English language."

—The Christian Science Monitor

The Compact Edition of the Oxford English Dictionary.
Yours as an introduction to membership in the BOOK-OF-THE-MONTH CLUB®

YOURS FOR ONLY
$19⁹⁵

(PUBLISHER'S LIST PRICE: $125)
You simply agree to buy 4 books within a year.

FOR the price of an average dictionary, you can now treat yourself and your family to the world's best dictionary of the English language. The contents of this two-volume edition are identical to those of the original thirteen-volume set, priced at $495.

FEATURES
- Boxed set of two volumes, 9¾" by 13½" each.
- All 16,569 pages of the 13-volume original included in 4134 pages of *The Compact Edition* through a photo-reduction process which permits printing of four pages of original on one page of compact edition.
- Paper is 30-pound Special Dictionary White.
- Binding is library buckram reinforced and gold-stamped.
- Bausch & Lomb magnifying glass included in special drawer of slipcase. 2" by 3⅞" lens scientifically designed to make reduced print easily readable.

Book critics call the OED a "miracle." Join the Book-of-the-Month Club and this "miracle" can be yours now. As a Club member, you'll continue to enjoy benefits on the best and most important books published today.

Bookstore Quality at Book-Club Savings You conveniently shop at home at considerable savings. Whether you're adding up your remarkable savings on the introductory offer, or on books you are offered as a member, these are always true savings...because every Club book is as good as, or better than, those sold in stores. You *don't* settle for the altered or inferior editions that some book clubs send their members.

Book-Dividends. When you remain a Club member after the trial period, every book you buy earns Book-Dividend® credits. These entitle you to choose from a wide variety of significant books at hard-to-believe savings of *at least 70%*.

Book-of-the-Month Club, Inc. A8-7
Camp Hill, Pennsylvania 17012

Please enroll me as a member of Book-of-the-Month Club and send me THE COMPACT EDITION OF THE OXFORD ENGLISH DICTIONARY. Bill me $19.95 (in Canada $22.50), plus shipping and handling charges. I agree to buy 4 books during the coming year. A shipping and handling charge is added to each shipment.

Mr.
Mrs.   9-35
Miss.   (Please print plainly)

Address..Apt.......

City...

State..Zip................

Facts About Membership You receive the *Book-of-the-Month Club News*® 15 times a year (about every 3½ weeks). Each issue reviews a *Main Selection* plus scores of Alternates. If you want the *Main Selection* do nothing. It will be shipped to you automatically. If you want one or more Alternate books—or no book at all—indicate your decision on the reply form always enclosed and return it by the date specified. *Return Privilege:* If the *News* is delayed and you receive the *Main Selection* without having had 10 days to notify us, you may return it for credit at our expense. *Cancellations:* Membership may be discontinued, by either you or the Club, at any time after you have purchased 4 additional books.

Effective Use of the Bargain Appeal

Some ads for bargains use headlines set in enormous type with phrases such as "prices slashed." This may be okay in certain situations such as a year-end clearance or a fire sale. But for the Book-of-the-Month Club, a dignified approach is more appropriate. This ad simply says "Yours for only $19.95 (Publisher's List Price $125.)" This is a powerful appeal. This ad has been running successfully for years.

2

Twelve Ways to Find Advertising Ideas

Nothing is more important in advertising than ideas.

Ad men are constantly searching for ideas that will sell goods and services. Sometimes they invent new ideas. Sometimes they reactivate old ones. And sometimes they combine two successful ideas to create a super success.

Where should an ad man look for ideas? Described below are twelve proven methods for finding ideas. All of these methods have produced successful campaigns.

1. CASH IN ON YOUR OWN PERSONAL EXPERIENCE

The first place to look for advertising ideas is inside your own head. Leo Burnett said, "Your best source of information may be you."

Have you had any personal experience with the product or service you are advertising? Do you have any knowledge that relates in any way to the product or service? Some of the best advertising ideas have come from the copywriter's own experience. For example: One time I was assigned to write an ad for a magazine called *Books*, which devoted its space to book reviews of current best sellers. The purpose of the ad was to induce the reader to mail a coupon for a trial subscription.

The ad I wrote came out of this childhood experience. My mother was a lover of literature. When she had friends in, the conversation usually turned to books. I noticed that those persons who had not done much reading were silent at these gatherings. Apparently, they were embarrassed because they could not talk about books. And so I wrote an ad with this headline:

CAN YOU TALK ABOUT BOOKS
WITH THE REST OF THEM?

The ad outpulled all others. It was repeated many times. And recently, a well-known book club used the same theme successfully.

Here is another example from the same source. At one time, my mother taught a course in English literature. She prepared for her students a list of the hundred greatest books. She said, "These books have come down through the centuries—defeating all others."

This remark came to mind during my first year at Batten, Barton, Durstine & Osborn, Inc. (BBDO), when I was asked to write an ad for a famous set of books—*The Harvard Classics*. I wrote the following headline:

> LIKE A CONQUERING ARMY THESE BOOKS
> HAVE MARCHED DOWN THE CENTURIES

The artist illustrated the ad with a picture of a row of famous books, and a row of marching soldiers. This ad ran for years—defeating all others.

2. ORGANIZE YOUR EXPERIENCE

Another of my early assignments at BBDO was to write ads designed to get coupon leads for life insurance salesmen. Every ad was tested for pulling power by running it in *The New York Times Magazine*. New ads were tested at the rate of one per month.

At the end of eleven months, I obtained a set of proofs of all eleven ads. I then wrote on each ad proof the number of coupon replies brought by that particular ad. I took these proofs to the BBDO conference room and laid them on a long table, in order of merit. The ads ranged in pulling power from 191 replies for the poorest ad to 867 replies for the best ad.

I studied the ads to try and learn what qualities the successful ones possessed that were lacking in the unsuccessful ones. It was immediately apparent that the eleven ads could be divided into two groups: successful and unsuccessful.

The unsuccessful group consisted of six ads that ranged in pulling power from 191 replies to 263 replies. These ads featured a variety of miscellaneous appeals.

The successful group consisted of five ads that brought 502 replies to 867 replies—an average of more than double the failures.

I looked at the five winning ads to see what quality they might have in common. The winning quality was instantly apparent. It seemed to actually jump out at me from the conference table.

Every one of the five winning ads featured the words *Retirement Income* in the headline. Not one of the losing ads featured these words. I felt as excited as an astronomer who has just discovered a new planet.

This analysis of winning ads versus losing ads showed me the importance of the idea on which an advertisement is based. A cub copywriter who uses the right idea can beat a professional who uses the wrong idea. I also learned that the winning idea must be in the headline, not merely in the copy.

For thirty years, the insurance company continued to use the "Retirement Income" appeal successfully with ads showing pictures of men and women happily retired on guaranteed incomes.

The above experience happened years ago, but I have been using the following method ever since:

Step One: Test a lot of different ads.

Step Two: Arrange the ads in order of pulling power and observe what quality the winning ads have in common.

This is more than just a philosophy of advertising. It is a philosophy of life. Observe the qualities that successful people have in common and cultivate those qualities in yourself.

3. WRITE FROM THE HEART

At a luncheon meeting with Maxwell Sackheim at the Toots Shor restaurant in New York, I asked: "Max, tell me the secret of the success of your famous ad for a correspondence course in English that had the headline, "Do You Make These Mistakes in English?"

"It was written from the heart," said Max. "I was born in

Russia. When I came to America, I had trouble with English. I knew from experience how embarrassing it is to make mistakes in English. When I wrote that ad, I poured my heart out. My copy touched the hearts of others who had trouble with English. They mailed the coupon and took the course."

Max's ad ran for forty years. In all that time, no one was able to write an ad that equalled it in pulling power.

In my own early years as a copywriter, I had the good fortune to have a similar experience. When I wrote the ad "They Laughed When I Sat Down At the Piano," I wrote from the heart. I could not play the piano myself, but I had always wanted to. All through my childhood, I had enjoyed hearing my father play the piano. I thought how wonderful it would be to sit down at the keyboard and thrill an audience with beautiful music. I put this feeling into my copy. The ad was successful and the appeal in the headline "They Laughed" is being used to this day.

In the book, *100 Top Copywriters and Their Favorite Ads,* there are many stories of how writers produced outstanding copy by writing from the heart. One particularly touching ad in the book was written by Jim Breslov for the American Cancer Society.

> *Illustration:* Picture of a man standing at the bedside of a stricken woman. The man is smiling wistfully at the woman.
> *Headline:*
>
> "GOD: GIVE ME THE STRENGTH TO SMILE"
>
> *Copy:* Smile and hold back your tears. She must not see them.
> Keep secret the voice that is crying inside of you. She must not hear it.
> Smile . . . that she may sense no echo of the voice you heard this morning—the surgeon's voice, gentle and hopeless. "I'm sorry. I'm afraid we're too late." Slogan at the bottom of the ad: Strike Back! Give to Conquer Cancer!

Jim Breslov called this, "The ad I didn't want to write." He said, "You see, I myself am the man in the picture. This is something that happened to me—and this ad, feeble as it may be, was a first effort to strike back."

Benjamin Disraeli, author and one-time Prime Minister of England, said, "The best writing is that which goes from the heart to the heart—from the heart of the writer to the heart of the reader."

4. LEARN FROM THE EXPERIENCE OF OTHERS

You will not always be fortunate enough to have had previous experience with the product you are writing about. In that case, you can seek the help of other people. Talk to friends, family, associates and persons you meet in your daily affairs, or at the luncheon table, or at social gatherings.

Ask questions of people. Have they heard of the product? Where did they hear about it? What do they know about it? What do they think of it? Have they bought it? If yes, why did they buy it? If no, why didn't they buy it? Get their experiences and their viewpoints.

If you can make written notes while interviewing people, do so. If not, you should try to memorize their remarks. And, as soon as possible after the conversation, you should find a quiet spot and write down all you can remember. If you wait half a day, you will forget half of what your respondent said.

Some writers are introverts. They are shy. They tend to be concerned mainly with their own thoughts and feelings. That's why they are writers, not talkers. But they can increase their effectiveness by adding the thoughts of others to their own thoughts.

If you have the time and the money to spend on a survey, your collection of ideas can be broadened even further. You can hire interviewers to ring doorbells, talk to people and record their answers to a set of questions.

You can do a survey by mail. You can send out a questionnaire with a business reply envelope. To stimulate replies, you can enclose a quarter as a token of appreciation for the respondent's cooperation. Or, you can promise a free gift to all who answer the questionnaire.

When I was working on advertising for Murine Eye Drops, I recall that a number of sales appeals were tested. The winning appeal came in a letter from a user who said, "I use Murine when my eyes are tired."

An ad with the headline: "Quick relief for tired eyes" outpulled all other ads tested. This appeal was used for years. It made Murine the largest selling eye drops in the United States at that time.

5. TALK WITH THE MANUFACTURER

Talk with the man who makes the product. He is a prime source of information for finding out how to sell it. Get his answers to these questions:

Who should buy your product?

Why should they buy it?

Where do they live?

What will the product do for people?

How did you happen to invent it?

How is it better than competitive products?

How is it manufactured?

What proof is there that it works?

How many people use the product?

What do they say about it?

Are testimonials available?

Has the product won any awards?

Are sales increasing?

Is there a money-back guarantee?

You should also talk to the manufacturer's salesmen and to his dealers and ask similar questions.

6. STUDY THE PRODUCT

One of the most important sources of advertising ideas is the product itself.

If the product is a car, drive it.

If it's a bicycle, ride it.

If it's a cake mix, bake it.

If it's a candy bar, taste it.

If it's a beverage, drink it.

If it's a book, read it.

If it's a service, try it.

If it's a vacation cruise, go on it.

If you can't drive the car, ride the bicycle or go on the cruise, get pictures of people doing these things. Pictures of the product in use are usually the most effective illustrations you can use in advertisements. Look at the pictures and imagine yourself enjoying the product or using the service.

You can also conjure up mental pictures of your own. One time I was assigned to write copy for a book entitled, *The Cultivation of Personal Magnetism*. I imagined how thrilling it would be to use magnetism in dealing with people in business and in social life. I pictured myself as a leader in business and as the life of the party at social gatherings. This imagining put me in the right mood for writing effective personal magnetism copy.

Another approach is to get from the manufacturer a list of specifications of the product. What materials are used in making it? How is it put together? What are its special features—its unique qualities? How is it tested for reliability?

All the time that you are studying the product, you should be making notes. Write down every idea that comes into your head—every selling phrase, every key word. Write down the good ideas and the wild ideas. Don't try to edit your ideas at the start. Don't put a brake on your imagination. Sometimes a wild idea can be tamed and made useful. But a tame idea will always be a tame idea. Write in haste, edit at leisure.

7. REVIEW PREVIOUS ADVERTISING FOR THE PRODUCT

After studying the product itself, you should review any previous advertising for the product that you can lay your hands on. This includes publication advertising, direct mail letters, package inserts and publicity.

If others have done groundwork before you came on the scene, don't reject the fruits of their labors. In your search for ideas that are new and different, don't reject the results of past research.

A famous adman was assigned to prepare advertising for a cigarette that had long been advertised. In an old ad he found the seed of an idea which, in his skillful hands, blossomed into an entire campaign.

I recall the time I was assigned to handle the circulation advertising for a well-known publication. I asked for, and received from the client, a set of proofs of all ads previously tested, along with the sales results of the tests. I studied these results and compared the successful ads with the failures. This enabled me to avoid using ideas that had proved ineffective in the past. And I was able to add to my own thinking some tested ideas that had done well in the past.

The client was pleased. He said, "You not only showed us how to spend our future appropriation more efficiently, but you got additional mileage out of money already spent."

In some cases, you can read articles and books about the product. The creative head of a large New York advertising agency spent weeks reading medical books in order to find a sales appeal for a patent medicine. Out of this reading came a number of appeals that were sales tested by mail order ads offering samples of the product. The winning appeal became the basis of a campaign that ran for years.

Another example: Gerard Lambert, of the Lambert Pharmaceutical Company, (now Warner-Lambert) discovered the word *halitosis* in medical literature about Listerine. This was the start of one of the most famous campaigns in the history of advertising. It sold millions of dollars' worth of Listerine.

8. STUDY COMPETITORS' ADS

In studying competitors' ads, you will usually find three kinds of ideas:

a. Ideas you have already used.

b. Ideas that do not apply to your product.

c. Ideas you never thought of.

For example, in writing copy for a real estate development, I wrote glowingly about the peace and quiet of the area, the beautiful scenery, the fresh country air. But I forgot to mention the convenient transportation facilities. I found this feature mentioned in a competitor's ad and quickly added it to my own copy.

In writing an ad for a book on engineering, I told about the many ways the book would help professional engineers. But I neglected to say that the book would also benefit students taking engineering courses in school. A competitor's ad showed me my error.

Watch for ads that are repeated again and again. These are usually the successful ads. Pay special attention to repeated mail-order ads. In mail-order advertising, the sales results are known. Only the successful ads are repeated.

For example, a writer of copy for life insurance annuities saw two mail-order ad headlines repeated many times:

Headline 1:

RETIRE IN 15 YEARS (FOR A FINANCIAL SERVICE)

Headline 2:

TO A MAN OF 35 WHO IS DISSATISFIED (FOR A BUSINESS SUCCESS COURSE)

The copywriter concluded that the specific figure "15 years" and the specific age "35" were key factors in the success of these headlines. So he put together an ad with the headline: "How a man of 40 can retire in 15 years." This ad was used successfully for many years.

Remember that your competitors are watching your ads in order to discover any good ideas they never thought of. You will be at a disadvantage if you don't do the same.

9. STUDY TESTIMONIALS FROM CUSTOMERS

Usually the manufacturer has in his files some letters he has received from satisfied customers. Or the manufacturer's salesman may be able to furnish comments from users of the product or service.

Ask the manufacturer for any available testimonials. Sometimes a brief quote from a testimonial letter can be used as the headline of an ad. Or, you may want to quote several testimonials in a box of copy with the subhead, "What Others Say." If the testimonials are not usable in their original form, they may, nevertheless, give you ideas you can translate into effective copy.

One way to get testimonials is to run a contest offering cash prizes for the best letters telling, "Why I Like (Name of Product)."

The prizes need not be large. I was once given the assignment to write an ad selling the idea of tea for breakfast. This assignment came from a British tea concern. They wanted to introduce to America the English custom of drinking tea in the morning instead of coffee.

Since I was a coffee drinker, I had absolutely no idea why anybody should start the day with a cup of tea. So I ran a small ad in the New York *Daily News* offering small cash prizes for the best letters on "Why I Drink Tea at Breakfast." I was amazed at the results. I received more than a hundred letters— many of them excellent. The letters came from folks in all walks of life—housewives, businessmen, factory workers and students. A letter from a truck driver was especially good. I had enough copy ideas for a whole campaign.

Some advertisers have run national ads in large circulation publications offering prizes to people who will send in testimonials. Usually, these ads feature an entry blank containing the following instructions:

> **Finish this sentence in twenty-five words or less: I like (Name of Product) because.......................**
> ....
> ....

Ads like this for various products and services have brought in thousands of testimonials.

10. SOLVE THE PROSPECT'S PROBLEM

There is an old saying: "An ounce of prevention is worth a pound of cure." True enough! But, with human nature being what it is, you will often find that a pound of cure is easier to sell than an ounce of prevention.

Therefore, it is important to discover what problems people have with various products. Don't ask them, "What do you like about this product?" Instead, ask them, "Have you had any problems with this product?"

For example: A survey among cat owners asked, "What quality do you want in a cat food?" The answers received were obvious. Cat owners want a product that the cat will eat. Another survey asked, "Do you have any problems with cat food?" The most frequent answer was "Cat food has a bad odor." This led to an effective campaign featuring odorless cat food.

Here are some advertising ideas based on problems:

SKIN REMEDY: "I WAS ASHAMED TO WEAR A SLEEVELESS DRESS."

CLOROX: THE 4-SECOND SINK STAIN REMOVER.

LEA & PERRINS: PREPARE-AHEAD PLEASERS. DELICIOUS MEALS
WITH NO LAST-MINUTE FUSS.

20 MULE-TEAM BORAX: GARBAGE PAILS DON'T HAVE TO SMELL
LIKE GARBAGE.
NOVELTY MANUFACTURER: DEFEND YOURSELF WITH A POLICE
WHISTLE.

11. PUT YOUR SUBCONSCIOUS MIND TO WORK

In your quest for ideas, don't forget to use your subconscious mind—that great reservoir of mental power that works while you sleep.

After you have studied the product, reviewed previous advertising and explored all other sources of ideas, you should then put the problem entirely out of your mind. Sleep on it. Go to a movie. Read a book. Take a walk. Engage in some other task for awhile. At the end of this period, you will probably get a clearer insight into your problem. You may even get a mental flash that will tell you which idea, of all those you have considered, is the *big idea*.

12. "RING THE CHANGES" ON A SUCCESSFUL IDEA

The Random House Dictionary defines "ring the changes" as follows: "To vary the manner of performing. To repeat with variations."

Examples:

A typewriter manufacturer decided to advertise portable typewriters as Christmas gifts. His first campaign showed a mother giving a portable to her son. The following Christmas, the ads showed a father giving his daughter a portable. A year later, the ads pictured a wife giving a typewriter to her husband.

An insurance company found that ads featuring retirement annuities brought the most coupon replies. So all the ad headlines featured retirement. However, the appearance of the ads was varied by using different illustrations, such as: a man fishing

. . . a couple sitting on the beach under a palm tree . . . an elderly couple embarking on a cruise ship.

A car insurance company tested a number of sales appeals and found that "save money" was the winner. Here are head-lines of some of the ads:

IF YOU ARE A CAREFUL DRIVER
YOU CAN SAVE MONEY ON CAR INSURANCE

HOW TO TURN YOUR CAREFUL DRIVING
INTO MONEY

DID YOU SAVE $89 ON YOUR CAR INSURANCE?

Once you have found a winning sales idea, don't change it. Your client may tire of it after a year or two. He sees all the ads from layout stage to proof stage to publication stage. Explain to him that when he is tired of the campaign, it is just beginning to take hold of the public.

3

Three
Famous
Case Histories

Some writers have said that their best ads were self-portraits. An example is a Christmas gift ad for a Hamilton Watch with the headline, "To Peggy—for marrying me in the first place . . ."

This classic was written by Carl Spier, former copy supervisor at Batten, Barton, Durstine & Osborn, Inc. (BBDO). The ad was published during the Christmas shopping season for more than ten years. The copy was a tender, loving letter written by a man to his wife.

A group of 100 well-known copywriters were asked to name which ad they would most like to have written themselves. The Hamilton Watch ad received the largest number of votes.

Spier said: "I believe the best advertising sounds as though one person were talking to another. I have often addressed a piece of copy to some specific person. After days of struggling to write a Christmas gift ad, this basic truth came to me. If I were writing a letter to my wife, what would I say?

"The first line that popped into my head became the headline of the ad. I think from then on, I wrote the ad in seven minutes. If it is good, it is because it was a searching of my own heart."

Here is Spier's ad:

Illustration:

Picture of a happy woman pressing a letter to her·lips with one hand and holding a Hamilton Watch in the other.

Headline:

TO PEGGY—FOR MARRYING ME IN THE FIRST PLACE . . .

Copy:

for bringing up our children—while I mostly sat back and gave advice.

for the 2,008 pairs of socks you've darned.

for finding my umbrella and my rubbers, Heaven knows how often!

41

for tying innumerable dress ties.

for being the family chauffeur, years on end.

for never getting sore at my always getting sore at your bridge playing.

for planning a thousand meals a year—and having them taken for granted.

for constant tenderness I rarely notice but am sure I couldn't live without.

for wanting a *good* watch ever so long . . . and letting your slow-moving husband think he'd hit on it all by himself.

for just being you . . . *Darling, here's your Hamilton with all my love!*

Jim

Panel Copy:

> **This Christmas—give a Hamilton—America's most beautiful watch. Hamilton makes only high-grade watches, $37.50 to $5000. See the new models at your jeweler's, or write for folder. Hamilton Watch Company, 423 Columbia Ave., Lancaster, Penna.**

A FAMOUS AD BY VIC SCHWAB

Another self-revealing ad that became famous was written for the Pelman Institute by Vic Schwab, former head of a New York advertising agency and author of the book *How to Write a Good Advertisement*.

The headline of the ad was "The Man with the Grasshopper Mind." This advertisement was designed to induce people to send for a booklet titled *Scientific Mind Training*. The ad pulled so many coupon replies that it ran for many years.

Schwab named this his favorite among all the ads he ever wrote. He said: "It was a self-portrait. It shows to what lengths a mail-order man will go in order to pull a large quantity of coupons. Its general format was copied from that of the famous Arthur Brisbane editorial pages. These pages were characterized by short sentences, with many of the key words and phrases printed in full caps, and with line-drawing pictorial treatment. My ad for Pelman imitated the Brisbane technique."

Here is Schwab's advertisement:

Illustration: A drawing of a man with a puzzled expression on his face. His hand is pressed to his head. He is gazing at a list of sentences that are displayed on the background of the illustration. These sentences are the thoughts that are running through his mind. Here they are:

I guess I'll take up $elling.
Think I'll try to make my evenings worth Something
Ought to put over that Money-Making Idea
Believe I'll do Some Good Reading
Some Day I'm going to Start Out for Myself!
Think I'll change my Job.

Headline:

THE MAN WITH THE GRASSHOPPER MIND

Copy: YOU know this man as well as you know YOURSELF. His mind nibbles at EVERYTHING and masters NOTHING. He always takes up the EASIEST thing first, puts it down when it gets HARD, and starts something else. JUMPS from ONE THING TO ANOTHER all the time!

There are thousands of these PEOPLE WITH GRASSHOPPER MINDS in the world and they do the world's MOST TIRESOME TASKS—get but a PITTANCE for their work.

If YOU have a "Grasshopper Mind" you know that this is TRUE—and WHY. Even the BLAZING SUN can't burn a hole in a little piece of TISSUE PAPER unless its rays are concentrated ON ONE SPOT!

Yet you KNOW you have intelligence and ability. WHAT'S holding you back? Just one fact—one SCIEN-

TIFIC fact—PROVEN and stated by the world's foremost scientists and psychologists. You are using only ONE-TENTH of your real BRAIN-POWER! The mind is like a muscle. It grows in power through exercise and use. It weakens and deteriorates with idleness. Increase your BRAIN-POWER and you will increase your EARNING POWER.

But HOW? Merely gamble a postage stamp. Send the coupon at the right for a copy of *Scientific Mind Training.*

This little book will tell you the secret of self-confidence, of a strong will, of a powerful memory, of unflagging concentration, of keen imagination—showing you how to banish negative qualities like forgetfulness, brain fatigue, indecision, self-consciousness, lack of ideas, mind wandering, lack of system, procrastination, timidity.

Men like Sir Harry Lauder, Prince Charles of Sweden, Frank P. Walsh, former Lieutenant Governor Lunn of New York, and hundreds of others equally famous, praise the simple method of increasing brain-power described in this free book about Pelmanism. It has helped over 750,000 OTHERS during the past 25 years!

You have only A POSTAGE STAMP to lose by writing for your copy. You may GAIN thousands of dollars, peace of mind, happiness, independence! Don't wait. Mail the coupon NOW.

THE PELMAN INSTITUTE OF AMERICA
Suite 112B, 71 West 45th Street, New York City

Please send me your free booklet, *Scientific Mind Training*. This does not place me under any obligation and no representative will call upon me.

Name..

Address.......................................

City.................. **State**....................

AN AD THAT STARTED AN INDUSTRY

Oregon fruit growers Harry Rosenberg and his brother David, had for years exported Royal Riviera Pears to France, England and Italy. The pears were highly esteemed and sold at high prices.

One time, in November, Harry brought fifteen boxes of pears to New York and asked ad man G. Lynn Sumner, how to induce executives to send boxes of this rare fruit as Christmas gifts instead of the usual liquor.

Sumner wrote a sales letter that was delivered by messenger to fifteen top executives in the Grand Central area. Then the fifteen boxes of pears were delivered to the executives by messenger. Each recipient was invited to take a bite of one of the pears, then to think what joy this gift would bring to customers and prospects.

Harry received orders for more than 400 boxes from eleven out of the fifteen men

The next step was to send out direct mail to selected lists. About 6,000 boxes were sold. The following year 15,000 boxes were sold by direct mail.

Then David Rosenberg came to New York to discuss future sales plans. Sumner told him that the time had come for national advertising, and that the first ad should be a full page in *Fortune* magazine.

David was astounded at this idea. He said, "Imagine Harry and me advertising our pears in *Fortune.*"

Sumner used this remark as the headline. The copy was based on the direct mail letter that had worked so well. The ad ran in *Fortune* and was extremely successful. It won an advertising award as the best magazine ad of the year. More importantly, it marked the beginning of a new industry in America— selling fruit by mail.

Here is the ad. It is a model for any writer who has been assigned the task of introducing a new idea.

Headline:

IMAGINE HARRY AND ME ADVERTISING OUR PEARS IN FORTUNE!

Copy: Out here on the ranch we don't pretend to know much about advertising, and maybe we're foolish spending the price of a tractor for this space; but my brother and I got an idea the other night, and we believe you folks who read *Fortune* are the kind of folks who'd like to know about it. So here's our story:

We have a beautiful orchard out here in the Rogue River Valley in Oregon, where the soil and the rain and the sun grow the finest pears in the world. We grow a good many varieties; but years ago we decided to specialize on Royal Riviera Pears, a rare, delicious variety originally imported from France, and borne commercially only by 20-year-old trees. And do you know where we sold our first crop—and the greater part of every crop since?

In Paris and London, where the finest hotels and restaurants know them to be the choicest delicacy they can serve to discriminating guests. And they serve them at about 75 cents each! Our Royal Riviera Pears went to other distinguished tables too—to the kings and queens and first families of Europe. We got a great kick out of wrapping big, luscious, blushing Royal Riviera Pears in tissue and knowing they were going to be served on golden plates and eaten with golden spoons.

AMERICA'S RAREST FRUIT— SHALL WE SHIP IT ABROAD?

But I'm getting away from my story. The idea that kept coming to Harry and me was this: Why must all this fruit go to Europe? Aren't there people right here in America who would appreciate such rare delicacies just as much as royalty? Wouldn't *our* first families like to know about these luscious, golden pears, rare as orchids, bursting with juice, and so big you eat them with a spoon? Wouldn't folks here at home like to give boxes of these rare pears to friends at Thanksgiving and Christmas?

So we made an experiment. We packed a few special boxes of these Royal Riviera Pears and took them down to some business friends in San Francisco. You should have seen their faces when they took their first taste of a Royal Riviera. They didn't know such fruit grew anywhere on earth.

Well, a banker wanted not only a box for home, but 50 boxes to be sent to business friends to arrive just before Christmas. A newspaper publisher wanted 40 for the same purpose, and a manufacturer asked for 25. And that gave us another idea. We sent 11 sample boxes to important executives in New York, and back came orders for 489 Christmas boxes for *their* friends.

A NEW CHRISTMAS GIFT IDEA

That seemed to indicate there were plenty of men looking for something new as a Christmas remembrance for friends who "have everything." The next year, orders came in for several thousand boxes of these rare pears, and you never read such letters as we got afterward—not only from the men who had *sent* the pears and made such a hit, but from folks who *received* them and wanted to know if they could buy more.

Well, that's how Harry and I got the idea that there must be *enough* discriminating people right here in the U.S.A. who'd like to do the same thing. So we talked it over the other night and said, "Let's put an ad in *Fortune*—and see." We got a shock when we found what it would cost us to do it, but here we are—and *you* are going to be the judge.

Right now as I write this, it is late September, and out here in this beautiful valley our Royal Riviera Pears are hanging like great pendants from those 40-year-old trees. We'll have to watch them like new babies from now until picking time—not a leaf must touch them toward the last— trained men will pick them gently with gloved hands and lay them carefully in padded trays. They'll be individually wrapped in tissue, nestled in cushion packing, and sent in handsome gift boxes lithographed in colors, to reach you— or your friends—firm and beautiful, ready to ripen in *your* home to their full delicious flavor.

I envy you *your* first taste of a Royal Riviera—every spoonful dripping with sweet liquid sunshine. And you can just bet that everyone who receives a box is going to have the surprise of his life.

We hope that right now you'll make up your list of business and social friends and let us send them each a box with your compliments. We'll put in an attractive gift card with your name written on it, and we'll deliver anywhere in the United States proper, wherever there is an express office, express prepaid, to arrive on the date you name. And don't forget to include a box for yourself! A "Medium Family" box (10 pounds) is only $1.85. A "Large Family" box (double the quantity) is $2.95. At these low prices these pears cost a mere fraction of what you would pay for them in fine restaurants and hotels. And here's how sure we are you'll be delighted. If, after eating your first Royal Riviera, you and your friends don't say these are the finest pears you ever tasted, just return the balance at our expense and your money will come back in a hurry. Harry and I have agreed you are to be the final judge—*and we mean it.*

Just one more thing—there are far more folks reading *Fortune* than there will be boxes of Royal Riviera Pears this year. So, if you want to be sure to get some, we hope you'll send your order right along. We are putting a coupon down below, but a letter is just as good. Only, if you write, please say you saw this in *Fortune*.

HARRY and DAVID
Bear Creek Orchards, Medford, Oregon

OTHER CASE HISTORIES

Some outstanding ad campaigns have been the result of inspiration, and some the result of research. At one time Murine eyedrops were advertised as a remedy for bloodshot eyes. Sales were not good. Users of Murine were interviewed and several possible sales appeals came out of the interviews. The appeals were tested by mail-order sales tests. The winning ad showed a pair of eyes with the headline "Quick relief for tired eyes." A campaign of frequently repeated small ads based on this appeal made Murine the best selling eyedrops in the United States.

A number of writers have said that their best ideas have come to them suddenly and, apparently, from out of nowhere. Said Walter O'Meara, regarding one of his favorite pieces of copy: "The whole thing just came to me in a blinding flash." Another writer said, "The idea turned up, uninvited in my head. It seemed a happy thought." Another said, "Ideas often occur at unexpected moments, for example, while shaving. But these ideas usually follow hours and days of searching."

Most copywriters seem to agree that ad ideas are usually the result of long periods of hard work, punctuated by occasional flashes of inspiration.

One writer said: "Searching for ideas is like digging for gold with a pick and shovel. You labor for days and weeks without success. Scores of times, you dig into the dirt and turn up nothing. Then suddenly, when you least expect it, you strike pay dirt—gold for your client, and gold for you. This is the most exciting moment of an ad man's life—the discovery of an idea that pays off."

4

How to Get Advertising Ideas from Brainstorming

Briefly stated, brainstorming is group thinking. It is a meeting in which a group of people use their brains to storm a problem and to create ideas that will solve the problem.

Brainstorming is based on the age-old belief that two heads are better than one—that the general staff of an army is wiser than any individual commander.

The term "brainstorming" was first popularized in the book *Your Creative Power* (Scribners, 1948) by Alex Osborn, former vice chairman of Batten, Barton, Durstine & Osborn, Inc. (BBDO).

ORGANIZATIONS THAT HAVE USED BRAINSTORMING

During the last twenty-five years, brainstorming has been used by ad agencies, department stores, universities, government agencies and various industries. Here are some who have used brainstorming successfully:

General Motors

General Electric

I.B.M.

Aluminum Corporation

B. F. Goodrich

Sears, Roebuck

U.S. Steel

Harvard Business School

M.I.T.

Army Command Management School

Naval Ordnance Units

U.S. Air Force ROTC Units

WHY BRAINSTORMING WAS INVENTED

Brainstorming was invented in order to increase the output of creative meetings. In the past, many creative meetings failed to produce ideas. Here is why:

a. No advance notice was given regarding the subject matter of the meeting. Thus the members arrived unprepared and empty-handed.

b. Too many subjects were discussed in the same meeting. The meeting drifted aimlessly, and the conversation wandered.

c. Creative thinking was hampered by judicial thinking. The participants tried to create ideas and evaluate ideas at the same time. This was wrong. Osborn said: "If you try to get hot water and cold water out of the same faucet, you will get only luke-warm water. The judicial evaluation of ideas should come later."

d. Most meetings contained two kinds of people—talkers and non-talkers—extroverts and introverts. As a result, two or three talkers would often dominate the entire discussion. Thus the ideas of the non-talkers were never expressed. Yet the non-talkers were sometimes the most creative thinkers—the most likely to have novel and original ideas. Speaking of compulsive talkers, Benjamin Franklin said, "The empty wagon makes the most noise."

e. If a senior executive was present at a meeting, the junior members confined their suggestions to ideas designed to please the boss. Thus some good but unorthodox ideas were withheld. Therefore it is wiser to omit the "brass," or have the meeting consist of all "brass."

The tendency of the juniors to try to read the minds of the seniors is recognized in military life at court martial proceedings. At the conclusion of a court martial, the lowest ranking officer is required to give his verdict first, so that he will not be swayed by the verdicts of the senior officers. The highest ranking officer gives his verdict last.

f. No records were kept of the ideas expressed in the meeting. Hence, most of the ideas were soon forgotten.

g. No action was taken on any of the ideas.

Brainstorming overcomes these handicaps and increases the production of ideas.

OSBORN'S RULES

Osborn gave four rules for a successful brainstorm meeting. He said that the leader or chairman should announce these rules at the beginning of the meeting:

1. No judicial judgment of ideas is permitted in the meeting. No member of the group is allowed to criticize any idea proposed by another member.
2. Wildness is encouraged. The crazier the idea, the better. It is easier to tone down than to think up.
3. Quantity of ideas is desired. The more ideas that are proposed, the greater the chances of finding winners.
4. Improvement of ideas is sought. In addition to contributing ideas of their own, the group members are encouraged to suggest how another member's idea can be made better, or how two ideas can be combined into a super idea.

THE SECRET OF SUCCESSFUL BRAINSTORMING

The principal secret of success in a brainstorm session is: *No criticism of anybody's ideas is allowed.*

Ideas are precious things. Good ideas are often left unspoken in meetings because the speaker fears criticism. It is worthwhile to propose a dozen ideas in order to get one good one. The time spent in writing a dozen headlines for an advertisement is not wasted if one of the headlines is a winner.

Too often the free flow of ideas in creative meetings is stifled by "killer" remarks such as:

Aw, that won't work.

You'll never sell that to management.

It's against regulations.

It's too modern.

It's too old-fashioned.

We tried that ten years ago.

Customers won't stand for it.

It's too expensive.

It will mean more work.

It will offend people.

As previously mentioned, creative people are apt to be sensitive and shy. If a creative person is slapped down by a "killer phrase," he may not open his mouth for the rest of the meeting.

HOW TO ORGANIZE A BRAINSTORM MEETING

Here is a step-by-step outline showing the time-tested methods for conducting a successful brainstorm session.

Step 1: The Problem

Choose a problem. It should not be a general problem such as—how can we promote the sale of a new product? It should be a specific problem such as:

- What name should we give to a new product?
- What would be an effective package design?
- What product benefits can we think of?

Step 2: The Invitation

A week in advance of the brainstorm meeting, the leader or chairman should telephone the people he wants to have in the meeting, in order to make sure they are available. He should state the problem briefly and say: "We would like to get your ideas."

This advance notice enables the members to start thinking. It gets their subconscious minds working on the problem.

Two days before the meeting, the participants should receive a written invitation on a single sheet of paper, which can be worded as follows:

To: Name of participant

You are invited to attend a brainstorm meeting on *(date)* **at** *(place)* **at** *(time).*
The problem is: What new product benefits can we think of in regard to Product X? Here are some benefits that are now being featured in the ads:
(Include a list of benefits.)

John Doe
Chairman
Telephone Extension 714

When brainstorming is new to the participant, it is good to attach to the invitation an explanation of what brainstorming is and how it works.

Step 3: Choosing the Time and Place

Meetings that are held early in the day are usually preferred. In the hours before lunch, people are more cheerful, alert and creative.

The meeting can be a coffee break, if desired. Some chairmen have obtained good results by making the meeting a soup and sandwich lunch break. Another alternative is an evening meeting.

Choose a meeting place where you can get away from phone calls and interruptions.

Set a time limit and end the meeting on time, unless the ideas happen to be coming fast. It is best not to have the meeting drag on and on to a slow finish.

For people who are new to brainstorming, a twenty-minute meeting is about right. Experienced brainstormers can keep going for thirty to forty-five minutes. A soup and sandwich lunch meeting can take an hour.

Step 4: The Chairman's Duties

At the beginning of the meeting, the chairman should explain how brainstorming works. He should insist that no criticism of any idea is permitted; not by word of mouth, by look, or by gesture.

The chairman should try to make the meeting fun. Thinking up ideas is one of the most exciting and rewarding features of the advertising business. Even a crazy idea can help to brighten a meeting by getting a laugh.

A good way to begin the meeting is for the chairman to read aloud the four rules of brainstorming, as follows:

a. Judicial judgment is ruled out. Criticism of ideas will be withheld until the next day.

b. Wildness is welcomed. The crazier the idea, the better; it's easier to tone down than to think up.

c. Quantity is wanted. The more ideas we pile up, the more likelihood of having winners.

d. Combination and improvement are sought. In addition to contributing ideas of our own, let's suggest how another's idea can be turned into a better idea; or, let's see how two or more ideas can be joined into still another idea.

The chairman should moderate the meeting by preventing the habitual talkers from doing all the talking. He can say: "Charlie, your ideas are not to be sold or defended—just tossed on the table to be sorted out and discussed later."

Some chairmen keep a bell on the table. The bell is rung when a member talks too long or makes a critical remark such as "Oh, that won't work," regarding an idea proposed by another member.

The chairman should encourage the shy, non-talkative members with remarks such as: "Joe, we haven't heard from you," or "Margaret, can you add anything we haven't thought of?"

Step 5: Stimulating the Flow of Ideas

If there is a lull in the flow of ideas, the chairman should get things going again. He can restate the problem. He can propose an idea of his own that he has been saving for this occasion. He can restate some of the ideas already proposed. He can go around the table, calling each member by name and saying: "Dick, what else can you think of?" . . . "Tom, are there any angles we haven't covered?" Toward the end of the meeting he can say: "Let's see if everybody can give us one more idea."

Step 6: Encourage the Hitchhiking of Ideas

Hitchhiking occurs when a member adds a plus or an alternative to another member's idea. The chairman should encourage hitchhiking.

Here are examples of hitchhikes from a brainstorm meeting held at Direct Marketing Day in New York. Ways to increase direct response were being discussed.

Member A:	"Offer ten days' free trial."
Hitchhike by Member B:	"If your product is a good one, you could offer thirty days' free trial."

*   *   *

Member C:	"We had a quarter-page ad that did well. We enlarged it to a full page and it did even better on a cost-per-inquiry basis."
Hitchhike by Member D:	"It can work the other way. We had a full-page that was working effectively. We found we could narrow it by one column. Our response held up and our space cost was down."

*   *   *

Member E:	"If you are running an ad looking for inquiries, try increasing replies by adding a lot more description of the offer."
Hitchhike by Member F:	"If you have an interesting free booklet to offer, try an ad built entirely around the offer."

*   *   *

Member G:	"Include a money-back guarantee."
Hitchhike by Member H:	"If you are advertising a low-cost item, you could offer double your money back."
Additional Hitchhike by Member J:	"Make the guarantee dramatic. An American Express promotion offered a guarantee to repurchase the full set of art medals at full price after the buyer had completed his collection."

Step 7: Keep a Record of Ideas

A secretary should be present at the brainstorm meeting to record in shorthand all the ideas proposed. The ideas should be typed, triple-spaced, in the same order as they were proposed at the meeting. Copies of the list of ideas should be sent to every member, with a request to send any additional ideas to the chairman. It is not unusual for a brainstorm meeting to produce 50 to 100 ideas.

Step 8: Appoint a Committee of Judges

A committee should be appointed to select the best ideas. Perhaps ten percent of the ideas will be usable. The other ideas can be ruled out because they are against policy, too expensive, or impractical for one reason or another. The committee can consist of the two or three persons most concerned with the problem.

Step 9: Promote Action

A list of the best ideas should be given to the client, the concerned department head, or the company president for *action*.

SUMMING UP

Here are factors that contribute to a successful brainstorm meeting:

1. Give advance notice regarding the problem to be discussed.
2. The discussion should be limited to a single problem.
3. "Wild" ideas are encouraged.
4. Quantity of ideas is sought.
5. No criticism is permitted.
6. The chairman of the meeting should draw out the thoughts of all the participants.
7. A secretary should be present at the meeting to record all the ideas.
8. A typed record of the ideas should be prepared and distributed to a judicial committee, whose members select the ideas that can be acted upon.

5

303 Words and Phrases That Sell

One day at my office in New York, I received a telephone call from a public relations counsel in Washington, D.C.

"Will you tell me the ten most frequently used words in advertising?" he said.

I gave him some words off the top of my head: "New . . . free . . . you . . . how . . . wanted." Then I said: "What is the purpose of your inquiry? How are you going to use the words?"

"I'm writing titles for political speeches. It seems to me that words that are used in advertising would be effective in politics."

I gave him some more words. Then I said: "Here is an idea for you. I recall an advertisement that was published some years ago that drew a large response. It was a couponed ad for a correspondence course in business training. The headline of that ad would be a good title for a political speech." Here is the headline:

WANTED . . . SAFE MEN FOR DANGEROUS TIMES

The caller thanked me. That was the end of our conversation. But it was not the end of my thoughts regarding his question.

WHAT ARE THE TEN MOST FREQUENTLY USED WORDS IN ADVERTISING?

How does one go about finding the words most often used in the advertising business? Is this a job for a computer? Or should the task be turned over to a researcher or to a Ph.D. student who is looking for a subject for his or her doctoral dissertation?

Some preliminary questions would have to be answered first. What kind of advertising should be analyzed? A study of department store ads would yield a set of words that would be somewhat different from classified advertising. Corporate image advertising would contain some words that would be different from supermarket advertising, and so on. Financial advertisers,

65

industrial advertisers and drug product advertisers all have special words of their own.

Direct marketing advertising is the field I would prefer to study. Why? Because the direct marketers know the sales results of every ad they publish. The words used by direct marketers would be the most effective tool for producing immediate sales.

How should such a word study be undertaken? Should I count the words in a hundred successful direct marketing ads? That would be a time-consuming task. Direct marketing ads often contain a thousand words or more.

Is there a shorter way to solve this problem? Yes, there is. Where do direct marketing copywriters put their best words? They put them in the headlines of their ads. Why not analyze the headlines of successful direct marketing ads? That would reduce the task to practical dimensions.

So I turned to the chapter on headlines in Vic Schwab's direct marketing book *How to Write a Good Advertisement*. In this chapter, Schwab lists "100 Good Headlines and Why They Were So Profitable." This same list of 100 good headlines is quoted in Maxwell Sackheim's book *My First Sixty Years in Advertising*. Now we have two famous direct marketing authorities who endorse this list of 100 headlines.

I underlined every meaningful word in the 100 headlines. I omitted such words as *and, the, an, but, this, these.* Then I tabulated the words and wrote after each the number of times it was used.

Here is the list of the ten most frequently-used words in Schwab's 100 good headlines. Following each word is a figure showing the number of times the word was used.

The Top Ten Words

you	31	money	6
your	14	now	4
how	12	people	4
new	10	want	4
who	8	why	4

I found some surprises in this list. I knew from experience that the word *you* is one of the most frequently used words in advertising, but I did not realize that it would be the winner by such a wide margin.

If we combine the score of the word *you* (thirty-one mentions) with the score of the similar word *your* (fourteen mentions), we get a total score of forty-five mentions in the *you/your* category. This score is almost as great as the combined scores of all the other eight words.

How about words in the *new/now* category? If we combine the score of the word *new* (ten mentions) with the score of the similar word *now* (four mentions), we get a total score of fourteen mentions in the *new/now* category. This puts the *new/now* category in second place.

I was surprised that such words as *free, save, quick,* and *easy* did not appear in the top ten. But I was not surprised at the high score of the word *how*. This word, and the combinations *how to* and *how you,* have been used in successful advertising for as long as I can remember.

EXAMPLES OF WORD USAGE

Let's take a look at the manner in which these top ten words are used in Vic Schwab's list of 100 good headlines. Maybe we can find some clues to effective copywriting. In the following list, the winning words are capitalized for easy identification.

The secret of making PEOPLE like YOU

HOW a NEW discovery made a plain girl beautiful

HOW to win friends and influence PEOPLE

WHO else WANTS a screen star figure?

WHY some foods explode in YOUR stomach

WHY some PEOPLE almost always make MONEY in the stock market

To men WHO WANT to quit work someday

NOW own Florida land this easy way

Suppose this happened on YOUR wedding day!

YOU can laugh at MONEY worries if YOU follow this simple plan

161 NEW ways to a gourmet's heart in this fascinating book for cooks

This is not a large-scale study, but the chief findings are significant; namely, the words *you, new* and *how* are outstanding.

Every copywriter should remember the value of hammering away at *you, you, you,* both in headlines and in copy.

Regarding *new,* David Ogilvy said: "If you try hard enough, you can almost always use *new* in your copy."

Then there is the word *how,* which is in third place on the list. People want to know how to solve problems, how to get ahead, how to be attractive, how to win friends and how to end money worries.

So, the next time you write an ad or a direct-mail letter or a TV commercial, try to give your copy the benefit of these three important words: *you . . . new . . . how.*

WHAT ARE THE MOST PERSUASIVE WORDS IN ADVERTISING?

Now I would like to tackle the question: "What are the most persuasive words in advertising?"

David Ogilvy, in his book, *Confessions of an Advertising Man,* said that words that work wonders are:

suddenly	miracle
now	magic
announcing	offer
introducing	quick
improvement	easy
amazing	wanted
sensational	challenge
remarkable	compare
revolutionary	bargain
startling	hurry

Ogilvy also said: "Don't turn up your nose at these clichés. They may be shopworn, but they work. That is why you see them turn up so often in the headlines of mail-order advertisers and others who can measure the results of their advertisements."

Max Sackheim seconded this advice by reprinting Ogilvy's list of words in his book *My First Sixty Years in Advertising.*

AN ENLARGED LIST

I would like to enlarge on Ogilvy's list and give the aspiring copywriter an even greater range of words to choose from. In order to do this, I turned to the following:

Successful direct marketing ads

Successful direct-mail letters

Mail order catalogs

Textbooks on advertising

Direct response classified advertising

I reviewed these and other sources, and tabulated the persuasive words that occurred most often. Listed below are the results of this analysis. For easy reference, the words are grouped under ten headings.

1. Words That Denote News

If you have news to tell, here are a number of ways to present it:

announcing	novel
introducing	modern
presenting	recent
today	latest
new	suddenly
now	revolutionary

2. Approval

People are more apt to buy if you can furnish evidence of the value of your product or service.

approved	commended
proven	recommended
accepted	honored
guaranteed	acclaimed
endorsed	complimented
certified	popular
tested	lauded
praised	admired

3. Large Size

Here are words you can use if large size is a feature of your product:

big	tremendous
large	massive
sizable	gigantic
huge	voluminous
vast	mammoth
enormous	great
spacious	colossal

4. Surprising

The element of surprise or unusualness is an attractive feature in some cases.

amazing	fantastic
astonishing	extraordinary
astounding	exceptional
startling	notable
surprising	noteworthy
singular	striking

sensational	strange
uncommon	stunning
unusual	magic
remarkable	miracle

5. Quality

Every reader or listener is concerned with the quality of your product.

good	first-rate
better	choice
fine	unparalleled
valuable	unsurpassed
remarkable	unique
exclusive	terrific
imported	selected
rugged	special
durable	personalized
improved	limited
excellent	rare
top	genuine
superior	authentic
greatest	outstanding
famous	wonderful
noted	surpassing

6. Interest

The following words denote interest and apply mostly to books, booklets, pamphlets, etc.:

absorbing	stirring
instructive	entertaining
informative	enlightening
interesting	fascinating
revealing	exciting
secrets	profusely illustrated

7. Appearance

Sometimes the appearance of a product is its most important feature.

beautiful	classic
elegant	distinctive
attractive	fashionable
flattering	appealing
handsome	fascinating
glamorous	exquisite
dramatic	scenic
captivating	colorful
charming	lavish
spectacular	magnificent

8. Utility

There are times when the utility of a product is the important consideration.

handy	reversible
helpful	serviceable
useful	workable
usable	versatile
practical	powerful
washable	reliable

9. Money

Making money and saving money are topics of universal concern.

wealth	liberal
fortune	reduced (price)
profitable	lowest (price)
bargain	discount (price)

10. Miscellaneous

Here are useful words that apply in a variety of categories:

quick	successful
quickly	gift
easy	complete
easily	lifetime
immediately	absolutely
hurry	only (price)

The next time you write an ad, you may find it helpful to review these word lists. For example, if you have news to tell, take a look at the list of words that denote news. Do the same with the other lists.

Your copy will be improved if you include some of the persuasive words that have sold millions of dollars' worth of goods and services.

WHAT ARE THE MOST PERSUASIVE PHRASES IN ADVERTISING?

What are the persuasive phrases that are used again and again by direct marketing advertisers? Here are examples:

1. Free Offers

A review of direct marketing ads, letters, catalogs, etc., reveals that the most frequently used phrases are free offers.

Yours free	Free trial lesson
Free gift	Free to new members
Booklet free	Free examination
Ask for free folder	Free demonstration
Free guide book	Free cost estimate
Literature free	Free consultation
Moneymaking facts free	Try it ten days free

Thirty-two-page catalog
free   Yours for the asking
Free plans for _____   Test lesson free
Free sample   Free gift if you act at once

2. Charge Offers

Some advertisers charge a fee or require a postage stamp.

Moneymaking facts free   Free gift if you act at once
Free lesson, $.50   Stamped envelope
                                 brings _____
$.25 brings details   Send $.25 to help
                                 cover postage
Stamp brings details   and handling
$1.00 brings complete
_____

3. News

If you have news to tell, it should be given prominence. It will increase response.

Just arrived   New method of _____
New here   New modernized _____
It's here   Latest findings
New discovery   Just off the press
New, improved   Just published
New invention   Just out
Important development   Beginning (date)
The world's
first _____   At last

4. How-To

People want to know how to do things—how to get ahead—how to solve problems—how to make money—how to enjoy life. In each of the following *how* phrases, you can complete the phrase with your own solution to the prospect's problem.

How to _____   How to get the most
                          out of _____
How to get _____   How to avoid _____
How to have _____   How to end _____
How to keep _____   How to get rid
                          of _____
How to start _____   How to conquer _____
How to begin _____   How I _____
How to become _____   How I improved
                          my _____
How to improve
your _____   How to enjoy _____
How to develop _____   How you can _____

5. Information

People buy magazines and newspapers and listen to broadcasts to get information. You can successfully compete for attention by telling your prospects the things they want to know.

Seven ways to _____   The truth about _____
The one sensible way
to _____   Plain talks with _____
Profitable tips for _____ Confidential chats
                          with _____
Twenty tips for _____   The common sense
                          of _____
Your one sure way
to _____   Advice to _____
Guide to _____   What you should know
                          about _____
Helpful hints on _____ Facts you should know
Practical hints on _____ Mistakes you can avoid

6. Confidence Building

No matter how attractive your offer is, you must build believability into your ad. Here are phrases that will help.

Award winning	Make this test
Seal of approval	Over _____ thousands sold
Founded *(year)*	What others say (include testimonials)
Established _____ years	See before you buy
You risk nothing	Money back if not delighted
Proved in laboratory tests	If not delighted, just write *Cancel* on the bill.

7. Price

People are always looking for bargains. Here are some phrases that deal with price:

Sale priced	Fantastic saving
Only ten percent above wholesale price	Price going up
	Price goes up (date)
Save up to $_____	Order before the price goes up
Less than half price	Never again at this price

8. Miscellaneous Phrases

Here are frequently used phrases that can work in a number of situations:

Send no money	The key to _____
No obligation	Only $.25 a day
No salesperson will call	Now you can _____
Special offer	You don't have to be rich to _____

Money-saving offer	From manufacturer to you
The secret of _____	Buy direct and save
Yours if you can qualify	For quick information, telephone _____
Do you have these symptoms of _____?	Easy payment plan
	Orders shipped within forty-eight hours
Who else wants _____?	

9. Immediate Action

Most folks tend to delay action. Urge them to act quickly. Or better still, give them a valid reason for quick action.

Act now	Investigate today
Don't delay	Act fast
Order now	Be the first
Order today	Rush name for details
Order now, pay later	For a short time only
Delay may be serious	While the supply lasts
Don't put it off	Price going up
Send today	Supply limited
Send post card today	Last chance
Get started today	

SUMMING UP

In writing your copy, do not neglect the tested words and phrases that are used in direct marketing advertising. Keep the lists in this chapter handy. Look them over before you write. Refer to them often. Put some *you, new* and *how to* into your ad, letter or commercial. And before you write your *Act now* paragraph, review the action phrases that experienced ad writers have found helpful in promoting the thing that every advertiser wants . . . *action.*

Free! Our latest opinion on any 3 of 1,200 widely held stocks

Merrill Lynch offers up-to-date research reports and opinions (called QRQ's) on each of over 1,200 widely traded important stocks.

They are yours free at any time upon request—and are excellent briefing tools whenever you are considering an opportunity, reviewing your holdings, or making a decision.

These free QRQ reports include recommendations on the stock's suitability for different investment objectives. A review of company developments. Plus specific buy and sell recommendations. Both intermediate and long term.

This is backed up by data on reported and estimated future earnings. Annual dividend projections. Whether or not options are available on the issue. Industry trends or corporate news that may affect trading. And more.

For Free reports on up to any 3 widely traded stocks—from our computerized information research center—just mail the coupon below.

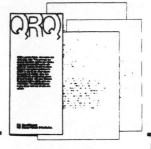

┏ ━ Mail today—for Free reports ━

Write to: Merrill Lynch Service Center, P.O Box 6514, Chicago, Ill. 60680.

☐ YES, I am interested in knowing the vital facts before I make a decision. Please send me your current QRQ opinions on the following stocks. I understand this involves absolutely no charge or obligation on my part.

1. _____ 2. _____ 3. _____

Name _____ Address _____

City _____ State _____ Zip _____

Business Phone _____ Home Phone _____

Merrill Lynch customers, please give name and office address of Account Executive:

_____

NWS05100RQ

🐂 Merrill Lynch Pierce Fenner & Smith Inc.

The Best Word in the English Language

Max Sackheim, author of *My First Sixty Years In Advertising* and dean of mail-order copywriters said: "Sixty years ago the best word in the English language for getting attention was the word FREE. And today, the best word for getting attention is still the word FREE."

When *Doctors* "Feel Rotten"
–This Is What *They* Do!

ARTIE McGOVERN

Formerly Director of New York Physicians' Club. National Amateur Champion Boxer at 16! Learned science of training in prize ring days, but realised after opening first gym, he should know more about workings of human body. So he studied at Cornell University Medical Clinic, where he was also physical director for 8 years. Today, at 44, is a model of physical perfection—stronger and more active than the average college athlete.

HOW can many of New York's busiest physicians stand up under their grueling duties? Why are their nerves so steady, their minds so clear after nights of broken sleep and days of fatiguing work?

The answer is simple. They follow rules for health described by Artie McGovern in his new book. Many not only go to McGovern's famous gymnasium in New York, but asked him to become Physical Director of the former New York Physicians' Club.

These doctors are too wise to fall for work-outs that leave the "patient" gasping, dizzy, exhausted, the kind of exercise that does more harm than good. And not only doctors have benefited by McGovern's safe, sane methods. Among the nationally known people who have used them are: Grover Whalen, Walter Lippmann, Vincent Richards, Babe Ruth, Gene Sarazen, Rube Goldberg, Frank Sullivan, Paul Whiteman.

The exercise shown above, which may be done while you are lying in bed, is one of the best you can do! On the other hand, such stunts as bending over and touching your feet with your hands are some of the WORST you can do—on a par with such food fads and crazy diets. McGovern's book shows you how to keep fit WITHOUT such drudgery or exhausting exercise!

smoking, cocktails, juggle calories or vitamins. He has no pills, trick reducing salts, tonics or apparatus to sell you. His famous Method is based upon sound scientific principles, the result of 20 years' experience in planning physical culture programs for people in all walks of life. Thousands have paid up to $500 for the McGovern course — now so clearly described and illustrated in this great new book, "The Secret of Keeping Fit"—the very same Method relied upon by thousands of doctors and men important in public life.

America's Greatest Trainer at Last Reveals His Secret of Keeping Fit!

In his new book Artie McGovern gives you "de-bunked" truth about exercise. He explodes fallacies. He shows you how to increase vigor, feel better, relieve constipation, either lose weight or put on solid pounds—how to get more enjoyment out of life. Your particular problem (depending upon the type of person you are) is treated as such.

Here is a book of unvarnished truth about *your* body, *your* health, *your* living habits. It shows a safe way to control weight (the way *doctors* and *athletes* do); how to eliminate nervousness, sleeplessness; how to correct constipation without laxatives; how to tone up your entire system, and build reserve vitality to resist sickness. And all with simple, easy exercises you can do *at home*—without apparatus!

Are You Overweight— Run-Down—Constipated?

Do you feel run-down? Are your muscles flabby? Are you overweight or underweight? Do you take laxatives? Do you sleep poorly? Do you wake up tired? If your answer to one or more of these is Yes then you owe it to yourself and family to try the McGovern Method.

Artie McGovern doesn't make you give up

SEND NO MONEY
TRY THE McGOVERN METHOD ON THIS 30-DAY DOUBLE GUARANTEE

The McGovern Method has worked for thousands and can therefore be sold on these terms:

1. Send no money with the convenient coupon below. When postman hands you your copy of Artie McGovern's new book, THE SECRET OF KEEPING FIT, deposit with him the Special Offer price of only $1.98, plus a few cents postage. If, after five days' reading, you are not convinced that the McGovern Method is just what you need and want—you may return it and your money will be refunded at once.

2. If, after applying for 30 days the principles clearly given in Mr. McGovern's book, you don't feel like a new person, vibrant with glowing health and new found "pep" if you aren't thoroughly convinced by actual RESULTS that it is working wonders for YOU, you may even then return the book for a full refund.

Clip and mail this coupon — without money — NOW! SIMON AND SCHUSTER, Inc., Dept. 1011, 386 Fourth Ave., New York City.

PRICE $1.98 *—if you double it home*

The Secret of Keeping Fit!

SIMON and SCHUSTER, Inc., Dept. 1011 386 Fourth Ave., New York City

Send me a copy of Artie McGovern's new illustrated book, "The Secret of Keeping Fit," which tells in complete detail the methods that individuals use in keeping doctors and famous men and women in all walks of life up to par. When postman delivers it, I will pay $1.98, plus few cents postage charges.

It is distinctly understood that if I care to, I may return the book within 5 days. It is also understood that if putting Mr. McGovern's methods into practice does not, within one month, produce the actual results I want, I am to have the privilege of returning the book. In either case my $1.98 is to be refunded at once.

Name ....

Address ....

.... State ....

Check here if you are enclosing $1.98 herewith, thus saving postage charges. Same refund privilege apply, of course.

BABE RUTH
—What the McGovern Method Did for Him

	Before	After
Weight	256	216
Neck	17½	16½
Chest	43	45
Expanded	46½	47
Waist	48½	38
Hips	43	38
Thigh	26	23
Calf	16½	15

GENE SARAZEN Says:

"McGovern's Course of Health building exercises is most effective. His valuable exercise systems I have now experienced. In previous years I have tried various methods to keep in good trim, but none compares with yours for getting results.

"Your health-building program has been of untold value to me. I heartily recommend it to golfers, both professional and amateur, and I am also convinced that it will prove a blessing for any average man or woman."

Colloquial Words Get Attention

If you write copy that sounds like the way people talk, you can often get more attention than by using formal grammar-school English. The catchy slogan: "Winston tastes good like a cigarette should" is more effective than "Winston tastes good as a cigarette should." The words *feel rotten* are more effective than the more formal *feel indisposed*. A copy chief said to a young Harvard graduate who wrote correct but stilted English: "You are not writing for the Harvard Yard. You are writing for the backyard." The above ad headline has three advantages. It quotes doctors. It offers information. The words *Feel Rotten* are attention-getters. The ad was repeated many times.

6

How to Write Sentences That Sell

$\mathbf{M}$y first lessons in writing sales copy came when I was a cub copywriter working for Everett Grady, the copy chief of a large, New York mail-order ad agency.

He asked me to write an ad for a book on personality development entitled: *Instantaneous Personal Magnetism.* I wrote this headline:

THIS SINGULAR BOOK WIELDS A
STRANGE POWER OVER ITS READERS

I felt that the words *singular* and *strange power* were sufficient to induce people to read the copy.

Grady liked the headline, but he added a phrase which promised a benefit. The revised headline read:

THIS SINGULAR BOOK WIELDS A
STRANGE POWER OVER ITS READERS
GIVING THEM A MAGNETIC PERSONALITY
ALMOST INSTANTLY

The ad with this headline turned out to be extremely successful in getting mail-order sales.

Over the years I have tried to apply the method taught me by Everett Grady for strengthening sales sentences by spelling out the benefits.

RECENT CASE HISTORIES

Here are some examples of how various copywriters have used this technique. The first two examples are taken from a luggage ad.

Example 1:

Compare these two sentences:

Sentence 1: The big two-suiter has dome-shaped construction.

Sentence 2: The big two-suiter has dome-shaped construction that provides plenty of wrinkle-free space for your suits.

Sentence 1 merely mentions dome-shaped construction. The reader must use his imagination to visualize the advantage of this type of construction.

However, Sentence 2 spells out the advantage with the words *provides plenty of wrinkle-free space for your suits.*

Now read a third sentence, which spells out still more advantages.

Sentence 3: The big two-suiter has dome-shaped construction that provides plenty of wrinkle-free space for your suits . . . plus shirts, slacks, underwear, shoes, and toilet kit.

A skillful copywriter does not depend on the reader's imagination to visualize all the possible benefits of various product features. Instead, the writer elaborates. He creates a word-picture that makes crystal-clear the specific advantages of every feature.

Example 2:

Here is another example from the same luggage ad:

Sentence 1: The two-suiter has handy side pockets.

Sentence 2: The two-suiter has handy side pockets that keep socks and other small items at your fingertips.

This expansion of sentences, if applied to an entire ad, may triple the length of your copy. Does this make the copy too long? Not at all. It increases your chances of making a sale.

It has been said that people will not read long copy. This applies only to non-prospects. A non-traveler may not bother to read a luggage ad. But that doesn't matter. A person who does not travel is not going to buy luggage anyway.

On the other hand, the prime prospect, the traveler, who needs new luggage, will read every word of your luggage copy, as long as the copy keeps on telling him things he wants to know.

DOUBLE-BARRELED SENTENCES

Sentences such as the preceding examples, which name a product feature and then tell the advantages of that feature, can be appropriately called "double-barreled" sentences. Here's why: These sentences are like a double-barreled shotgun that fires not once but twice, and thus doubles the chances of hitting the target.

When you receive an assignment to write an ad for a product, your first step should be to study the product's features as follows:

1. What are the dimensions of the product?
2. What materials is it made of?
3. What features does it have that make it new, different or better than competitive products?

In writing your copy, your job is to translate these features into benefits.

AN EXERCISE IN WRITING SENTENCES THAT SELL

Listed below are a number of sentences that describe a product feature. Immediately following each sentence is a longer one that not only describes the feature, but also elaborates on the advantages of that feature.

Read the first sentence. Then pause and visualize in your own mind how you would expand that sentence in order to make it into a sales sentence. Then read the second sentence and see how the copywriter did it.

Ad for Stainless Steel Cookware:

Sentence 1: The covers fit snugly.

Sentence 2: The covers fit snugly to seal in moisture and health-building vitamins and minerals.

Sentence 1: These utensils have a hard surface of stainless steel.

Sentence 2: These utensils have a hard surface of stainless steel for easy cleaning and lasting beauty.

Sentence 1: These utensils have molded, heat-resistant handles.

Sentence 2: These utensils have molded, heat-resistant handles that won't turn or loosen or burn the hands of the user.

Ad for a Folding Cot:

Sentence 1: This cot has a rigidly braced, tubular aluminum frame.

Sentence 2: This cot has a rigidly braced, tubular aluminum frame that provides strength without weight . . . can't rust.

Ad for a Traveling Bag:

Sentence 1: This bag has a cover of grained vinyl laminated to cotton.

Sentence 2: This bag has a cover of grained vinyl laminated to cotton that is easy to care for . . . just wipe clean.

Ad for a Book on Memory Training:

Sentence 1: This magic key opens up the memory-storage cells of your mind.

Sentence 2: This magic key opens up the memory-storage cells of your mind and enables you to perform amazing feats of memory.

Ad for a Car Loan Plan:

Sentence 1: Now you can get a forty-eight-month car loan.

Sentence 2: Now you can get a forty-eight-month car loan that gives you more months to pay, so you pay less each month.

Ad for a Set of Books:

Sentence 1: The first volume is yours free.

Sentence 2: The first volume is yours free, with no obligation to buy anything.

Ad for a Book on How to Win Friends:

Sentence 1: This book tells you nine ways to influence people.

Sentence 2: This book tells you nine ways to influence people without giving offense or arousing resentment.

*   *   *

When a manufacturer gives you an assignment to write an ad, your first step should be to obtain from him a list of product features. The manufacturer calls these "product specifications."

You could put together an ad by simply mentioning these specifications. But that would not be the most effective ad. It is up to you, the copywriter, to use your imagination and transform the manufacturer's specifications into sentences that *sell*.

HOW ABOUT SHORT SENTENCES?

An alternative method of writing ad copy is to use short, punchy sentences that pile up benefits in telegraphic style. This puts speed and excitement into your ad.

Here is a punchy paragraph from a mail order ad selling a digital watch. Notice how the copy is speeded up by omitting verbs from some of the sentences.

DIGITAL WATCH SALE . . . $39.95

Each watch includes one-year battery. Extra batteries are available at any jewelry store. Slim executive-type styling. Solid state. No humming, ticking or vibration. Completely shock-resistant. Finest quality watchband. Has no gears, hands or moving parts to go wrong. No oiling, cleaning. Simple and quick to reset. Water resistant. Each instrument is thoroughly checked out at factory. One minute per year accuracy. One-year manufacturer's warranty. Single button control. Exact same watch is selling elsewhere at much higher prices.

Both the short-sentence technique and the long-sentence technique have been used successfully in direct marketing advertising. The best technique is to combine the two methods. Use long sentences for explanation. Use short sentences for action-getting. This avoids monotony, and gives the reader a change of pace.

YOU, YOURS, YOU'LL

As mentioned previously, the most frequently-used word is *you*—or derivatives such as *yours* and *you'll*.

Below is a passage from a Book-of-the-Month Club ad in which *you* or its derivatives have been used eleven times in a single paragraph. I have capitalized the words *you, yours,* etc., so that you can pick them out at a glance.

Notice how the "you" technique personalizes the copy and makes it seem like a friendly letter from the writer to the reader.

Once YOU start shopping in America's Bookstore— YOU'LL be enjoying the most dependable reading reminder system in the world. YOU'LL be kept regularly informed of important new books, and given ample opportunity to choose the ones YOU want. YOU'LL soon come to depend on the Book-of-the-Month Club's thrifty shop-at-home service. Without leaving YOUR home, YOU can window-shop, browse and buy—and have the books YOU want delivered straight to YOUR door. And by continuing YOUR membership past the trial period, YOU'LL be eligible for our unique Book-Dividend plan.

A ONE-SENTENCE PARAGRAPH

If you have an important sentence that you want to emphasize, you can make that sentence stand out by letting it occupy an entire paragraph between two longer paragraphs.

An example of how this technique was used in a successful ad for a correspondence course in business training is shown below. The ad had a coupon, and the copy described the course not as a set of books, but as an imaginary trip to industrial centers.

Here are the three opening paragraphs of the ad. Note that the second paragraph consists of only a single sentence that is given emphasis by isolating it.

Headline:

A WONDERFUL TWO YEARS' TRIP AT FULL PAY
BUT ONLY MEN WITH IMAGINATION CAN TAKE IT

Copy: About one man in ten will be appealed to by this page. The other nine will be hard workers, earnest, ambitious in their way, but to them a coupon is a coupon; a book is a book; a course is a course. The one man in ten has imagination.

And imagination rules the world.

Let us put it this way. An automobile is at your door. You are invited to pack your bag and step in. You will travel to New York, etc., etc.

The important sentence, "And imagination rules the world," would have lost much of its effectiveness if it had been buried at the end of the first paragraph. Instead, it was given great force by setting it apart in a paragraph by itself.

A LESSON FROM FAMOUS AUTHORS

Famous authors such as Shakespeare and Robert Burns have strengthened some of their sentences by repeating important words. Here are instances of this technique. The important words are capitalized so that you can identify them at a glance. These words were not capitalized in the original versions.

For example, here is an often quoted remark by Shakespeare's character, Hamlet: "Oh, that this TOO, TOO solid flesh would melt."

In another play, Shakespeare described in the following lines the sentiments of a group of refugees who had fled to the wilderness to escape persecution:

BLOW, BLOW thou winter wind,
Thou art not so unkind,
As man's ingratitude.

FREEZE, FREEZE thou bitter sky,
Thou dost not bite so nigh,
As benefits forgot.

Robert Burns, in a poem dedicated to his beloved, wrote:

My love is like a RED, RED rose
That's newly sprung in June.

MODERN EXAMPLES

Today's ad writers and salesmen have also used the word-repetition technique.

The circus barker tries to induce customers to come into his tent by shouting: "HURRY, HURRY, HURRY . . ."

The Auctioneer tries to get bids from the crowd by calling out the words: "GOING, GOING, GOING . . ."

A toothpaste commercial emphasized its exclusive ingredient by saying: "What is it that's MISSING, MISSING, MISSING from every other toothpaste?"

An advertisement for *Reader's Digest* listed some article titles in an issue and then added the line "and MUCH, MUCH more."

A book club ad selling books with fine bindings used the headline: "BEAUTIFUL, BEAUTIFUL Books"

A singing commercial for clothing said: "The values go UP, UP, UP . . . and the prices go DOWN, DOWN, DOWN."

*   *   *

The benefit of repetition was told in Lewis Carroll's book, *Alice in Wonderland.* One of the characters in the book said, "What I tell you three times is true."

OPENING AND CLOSING SENTENCES

The most important sentences in an advertisement are at the beginning and at the end.

The opening sentences cause the reader to either continue reading or to turn the page.

The closing sentences cause the reader to act or fail to act.

Opening Sentences

A Mail-Order Course in Writing:

For years and years a relatively few people have had a corner on one of the most profitable authors' markets ever known.

New Mexico Real Estate:

Do you know people who wake up to sunshine 355 days a year . . . people who don't know what it is to be oppressed by humid heat in the summer or by the cold clutch of winter damp?

Car Cleaning Cloth:

Now, in ANY weather, your car can be so spotlessly clean and show-room shiny that your neighbors will ask how you do it.

Kiplinger Washington Letter:

Will you be ready for the new KIND of boom ahead?

Forbes Magazine:

A prominent industrialist once told an editor of *Forbes* that a single sentence in *Forbes* saved him a quarter of a million dollars.

Closing Sentences

Rare Coin Collection:

It may be necessary to close the subscription rolls before *(date)*—so enter your application promptly.

Diet Book:

Be the first in your area to enjoy the benefits of the Astronauts' Diet.

Repair Kit:

Equip yourself with this amazingly complete outfit . . . and you're ready for just about any repair job that comes along.

The Lazy Man's Way to Riches:

Just try it. If I'm wrong, all you've lost is a couple of minutes and a postage stamp. But what if I'm right?

How to Turn Box-Tops into Dollars:

I understand that if I don't collect at least $500 as promised in your book, I may return the book and get my money back.

*   *   *

A while back, we compared the writing of famous authors of the past—Shakespeare and Robert Burns—with modern advertising copy.

To the lover of literature, this may seem presumptuous—like going from the sublime to the ridiculous. But the fact is that when the history of the present era is written, it may be recorded that the authors of today's advertising copy were among the best writers of the Twentieth Century. Certainly, no writers have surpassed them in force and clarity.

IN CONCLUSION

In 1918, William Strunk, a professor of English at Cornell, published a book that contained a set of rules for effective writing. The book is titled *The Elements of Style*. It became a guidebook for many writers. Years later, it was republished in paperback.

In the book, Professor Strunk included a definition of good writing that has become famous. It is included in the latest edition of *Bartlett's Familiar Quotations*. Here it is:

> Vigorous writing is concise. A sentence should contain no unnecessary words, a paragraph no unnecessary sentences, for the same reason that a drawing should have no unnecessary lines and a machine no unnecessary parts. This requires not that the writer make all his sentences short, or that he avoid all detail and treat his subjects only in outline, but that every word tell.

A Successful Headline Formula

The longest lived mail-order ad ever written was Max Sackheim's ad for a correspondence course in correct English. Headline: "Do You Make These Mistakes In English?" The ad ran for forty years. Why so long? Because in all that time, nobody could write one as successful, although many skilled writers tried. This ad uses the same formula. Don't hesitate to copy other people's ideas. Just be sure to copy *successful* ideas.

You'll never drive a dirty car again!

Now You Can Keep your car so gleaming clean—all the time, rain or shine—that neighbors will ask how you do it!

New The secret is this NEW WAY to use KozaK*—the specially treated, thick, soft, deep-nap cloth that has been keeping fine cars showroom-clean and shiny for proud owners, for 50 years.

Now, with this remarkable KozaK Dry-wash* Cloth, you can also have KozaK's **NEW SUPER HELPER***, used like a chamois. It brings glowing beauty back to your car, even if the weather is bad and your car dripping wet.

We Wash Your Car By Mail

Thousands of delighted car owners call KozaK "the car wash that comes by mail". In just minutes on a nice day, a few easy swipes with the time-tested KozaK Auto Drywash* Cloth **(good for at least 50 times)** gently cleans your car of dust and grime—no hose, no pail, nothing to cause rust, squeaks, chapped hands or wet feet.

It's so gentle, so thorough, so safe, thousands of careful car owners entrust the precious finish of even Rolls Royces, Cadillacs, Continentals and other costly cars to KozaK care—and have for years.

Then, on wet days, the new Kozak's Super Helper—just as quick and easy to use—wipes off your car in only minutes. Paint dries to a gleaming shine in seconds. Glass and chrome really sparkle!

If Not Delighted After 30 Days Use—Your Money Back, You Keep the Cloths!

That's our out-and-out Guarantee. Can you imagine us being able to afford it, if many users wanted refunds? They don't because KozaKs do exactly what we say. And this new way, with the KozaK's Super Helper, works even better than ever before.

Check coupon below: get Super KozaK for dry car, Super Helper for wet car—or both, at $1.00 saving, for all-weather car protection and beauty. If, after 30 days use, either or both don't do every last thing we promise—simply tell us, you keep the order, we'll refund every cent to you. Could anything be fairer?

Never drive a dirty car again. Let KozaK keep your car clean, proud looking; protect its finish, prolong its beauty, boost its trade-in value. To let $9 save you at least $50 in ordinary car washes, mail coupon below with your remittance NOW to . . . *®

- - - - - - - - - - - - - -

KozaK, 977 S. Lyon Street,
Batavia, N. Y. 14020
Established — 1926

On your 30 day no-return but full-refund Guarantee, please send me at once:

☐ Super KozaK (For Dry Car) $5.00 Postpaid
☐ Super Helper (For Wet Car) $5.00 Postpaid

☐ **BOTH for only $9.00, Postpaid**

☐ Check   ☐ MO

N.Y. State Residents Must Add Sales Tax.

Print
Name ....

Street ....

City .... State .... Zip ....
Lady KozaK—(for furniture only) ☐ $2.50

This Ad Was Repeated Many Times

When you see a mail-order ad repeated again and again, you should study that ad and learn its secrets of success. This ad has a dramatic headline, uses long copy, plenty of subheads, and a hard-to-resist guarantee "money back if not delighted—and you keep the cloth."

7

Sales Appeals That Last Forever

Advertisers should use every possible means to keep a finger on the public pulse—to learn about people's problems and desires, and to discover the basic sales appeals that never seem to go out of date.

One way to do this is to observe the titles of articles printed each month on the paper cover stickers attached to newsstand copies of *Reader's Digest.*

For example, in a twelve-month period, the following titles were displayed in big print on the cover stickers of four different issues of the *Reader's Digest:*

7 Ways to Break the Overweight Habit

The Fat-Controlled Diet

You and Your Diet

A Diet that Will Last a Lifetime

The emphasis on diet is evidence of a continuing problem of millions of Americans. They are looking for ways to reduce fat. If you have a product or a service that will solve this problem, your fortune is made.

Each month, three or four titles are featured on *Reader's Digest* cover stickers. Some of these titles are of no importance to advertisers. For example, the title "UFO's—the Evidence Mounts" is of no importance because nobody is selling UFO's. On the other hand, many of the titles displayed are important because they show what is on people's minds that can be related to the product or service you want to sell.

The titles printed on *Reader's Digest* cover stickers are not ordinary titles picked at the whim of a single editor. These titles represent the judgment of many editors throughout the U.S., plus the judgment of *Reader's Digest* editors.

For example, every month, hundreds of magazine editors read thousands of manuscripts, in order to select the best ones to print in their publications. After that, the editors of *Reader's Digest* review these publications and select the cream of the crop.

But that is not the final selection. The business department of *Reader's Digest* then picks, from the thirty or more articles in an issue, the three or four titles that will sell the most copies of the magazine. Over the years, these titles have been featured in newspaper ads, radio commercials and printed on cover stickers. These selected titles have helped to sell millions of copies of the magazine.

SCIENTIFIC SELECTION

How does the business department select the outstanding titles? This is done by carefully controlled tests, not by opinion or guesswork. The selection method can be best explained by recounting a bit of history.

One day at a luncheon meeting, the circulation manager of *Reader's Digest* asked me: "How can we find out which articles in our magazine have the greatest sales appeal to readers? We want to run radio commercials to increase newsstand sales. We want to mention in the commercials the articles that will sell the most copies. As you know, every issue of *Reader's Digest* has a long list of titles. We wouldn't have enough time in a sixty-second commercial to mention all of the titles. How can we select the three or four titles that will get the most people to buy the magazine?"

In trying to find an answer to this question, I conidered several alternatives. How about doing an opinion test? We could show a list of article titles to a hundred people, and ask them which articles they would most like to read.

Another method would be to study the letters that readers send to the editors every month commenting on various articles. Perhaps the remarks of the readers would furnish a clue regarding which articles are most popular.

I was not satisfied with either of these methods. I had previously done opinion tests by mail and interviews. I found that these tests do not always agree with sales tests.

For example, a sex-appeal ad or a fat-reducing ad will often be the winner in a sales test. But in an opinion test, the average person is too embarrassed to point to a sex-appeal ad or to a fat-reducing ad and say to the interviewer: "That ad is my favorite."

While turning this problem over in my mind, I recalled the experience of a publisher who sold thousands of inexpensively printed booklets at the amazingly low price of twenty for a dollar.

These booklets were called *Little Blue Books* and they were sold via mail-order ads in newspapers and magazines. Each ad contained a list of about 350 booklet titles and an order form. The reader was invited to send a dollar and to indicate on the order form which twenty booklets he wanted. Previous page 101 shows a condensed version of one of the ads.

Regarding the preceding advertisement, I thought "This is a true test of peoples' preferences. The reader selects the titles he really wants. He is not influenced by the presence of an interviewer. So, why not use the same method to test the relative popularity of *Reader's Digest* article titles?" On page 103 is an abbreviated version of an ad I prepared.

This ad was published in a daily newspaper. When the results were tabulated, it was found that there were wide differences in interest among various articles.

For example an article entitled "The Facts About IQ Tests" pulled three times as many requests as an article entitled "What Makes It Rain?"

An article entitled "It Pays to Increase Your Word Power" drew eleven times as many requests as an article about how baseball is played in Japan.

And an article entitled "How to Stop Worrying" pulled the astounding total of seventeen times as many requests as an article titled "College Athletics—Education or Show Business."

This method of discovering the most popular article titles was extremely valuable to the Circulation Department of *Reader's Digest*. By publishing a title-testing ad every month, it became possible to pinpoint just which articles to feature in radio commercials, in newspaper ads and on *Reader's Digest* cover stickers, in order to sell the most copies of the magazine.

Now, what can you and I learn by observing the sales-tested titles that are featured on *Reader's Digest* cover stickers every month? We can learn a lot. We can learn to read the minds of the people we are trying to reach when we write ads. We can learn what people are concerned with—their problems, hopes, worries and ambitions.

Headline:

FREE . . . ADVANCE COPIES
OF READER'S DIGEST ARTICLES

Here's how to get them: To acquaint you with the interesting articles in *Reader's Digest,* we make this special offer:

From the descriptions below of some of the articles to appear in the May issue of *Reader's Digest,* pick the three articles you'd most like to read. Circle in pencil the numbers of these three articles on the coupon below. Then mail the coupon to us with your name and address. We'll send you free copies of the three articles you choose.

This offer is good for only a few days, so send us the coupon TODAY.

1. Article Title	11. Article Title	21. Article Title
2. " "	12. " "	22. " "
3. " "	13. " "	23. " "
4. " "	14. " "	24. " "
5. " "	15. " "	25. " "
6. " "	16. " "	26. " "
7. " "	17. " "	27. " "
8. " "	18. " "	28. " "
9. " "	19. " "	29. " "
10. " "	20. " "	30. " "

To: Dept. "A", Reader's Digest Association, Pleasantville, New York

Gentlemen: Please send me FREE the 3 articles I have circled below by number.

1 2 3 4 5	Name_____
6 7 8 9 10	
11 12 13 14 15	Address_____
16 17 18 19 20	
21 22 23 24 25	City_____State_____
26 27 28 29 30	

(May)

In order to get a better picture of these things, I reviewed the cover stickers that appeared on newsstand copies of *Reader's Digest* over a period of ten years. Here are my findings:

A TEN-YEAR ANALYSIS

Below are *Reader's Digest* article titles grouped by subject matter and listed in order of popularity. Let's begin with the subject that turned out to be the most popular of all.

Health Care

In ten years, the cover stickers on newsstand copies of *Reader's Digest* featured health care twenty-nine times. Here are a few examples:

How to prevent—relieve—an aching back

Flu—how to protect yourself

How to build a better body

How to feel fit at any age

Can middle age be postponed?

Seven steps to fitness

How to beat tension without pills

Obviously, Americans are vitally concerned about their health. If you have or if you can invent a product or service that will relieve an aching back, protect against flu or build a better body, you can appeal to a large audience.

Advertising copywriters can learn an additional lesson from *Reader's Digest* titles; namely, how to write effective headlines. Note the economical wording of *Reader's Digest* titles. Few adjectives. Few superlatives. No words such as finest, smoothest, best or greatest. No attempts at cleverness—just the simple facts, plainly stated.

In my ten-year study, I found that sometimes the actual title of an article was reworded for greater sales punch before it was printed on the cover sticker. For example, one article title in the magazine was "Hot Tips on Heating Your Home." But on the cover sticker, this title was given more popular appeal by changing it to "How to Cut Fuel Bills."

Money

The second most popular subject was money. In ten years, nineteen money article captions were displayed. Let's take a look at some of these titles and see what we can learn.

How to save money buying a car

How to keep your debts under control

How to stretch your inflated money

Ten ways to beat the high cost of living

Shopper's guide to bargains

Six ways to avoid income tax troubles

How to get the most interest on your savings

Note that these titles, if used as ad headlines, or as catch lines in sales letters, would get high readership.

Self-Improvement

The third most popular subject was self-improvement. In ten years, twelve cover stickers featured self-improvement titles. *Examples:*

Science finds a new way to self-confidence

How to cope with criticism

What concentration can do for you

Seven steps to greater personal freedom

The secret of self-renewal

How to improve your voice

How to make habits work for you

Marriage

The next most popular subject was marriage—how a successful relationship between a man and a woman can be achieved. Here are some titles:

How to live with a woman

What makes the perfect husband?

Why husbands and wives remain strangers

How wives can communicate

What makes a woman lovable?

How to support your husband's ego

Why men don't talk to their wives

Note the appeal to both sexes in some of these titles. For example: "Why men don't talk to their wives." Wives will read this to find out why their husbands aren't talking. Husbands will read it to find out why other husbands are not communicating.

There are advertising ideas in many of these titles. For example, the appeal "What makes a woman lovable" could be used to sell a variety of products.

Get Ahead

Here are some titles on another popular subject—"How to get ahead":

Seven steps to the job you want

Should you see a career doctor?

Are you a self-starter?

How to get more work done

What it takes to be a leader

Other subjects of popular appeal follow.

Pursuit of Happiness

> One sure way to happiness
> Time out for happiness
> How to be a happier person
> Seven ways to get more out of life
> The secret of having fun

Child Care

> Your child may be more gifted than you think
> Why good parents have problem children
> How to say no to your children
> You can raise your child's IQ
> Guide to being a better parent
> How to make your child feel loved

Popularity

> How to start a conversation
> The essence of charm
> The secret of reaching others
> The right way to win friends

Another lesson that can be learned from *Reader's Digest* titles is the skillful use of *key* words with which to begin an advertising headline. *Examples:*

> How to . . .
> Seven steps to . . .
> Ten ways to . . .
> Science finds . . .
> The secret of . . .
> Why . . .

What makes . . .

Should you . . .

Are you . . .

What it takes to . . .

One sure way to . . .

Guide to . . .

Reader's Digest sells over 31 million copies a month, in 17 languages. It is the most popular magazine in the world. And since it is read from cover to cover, it is also one of the world's most effective advertising mediums. A famous advertising slogan comes to mind. "Such popularity must be deserved." So the next time you are searching for a way to get people to act, don't forget the tested appeals you can find in the titles of *Reader's Digest* articles.

OTHER EXAMPLES OF LASTING APPEALS

Premiums

As I write this, I have before me a book published years ago, entitled *Advertising for Immediate Sales.*

One chapter in the book is entitled "Using Premiums to Increase Sales." Here are some premium offers that were advertised at that time.

Company	Premium	Requirement
General Mills	Teaspoon	Mail coupon from sack of Gold Medal Flour
Quaker Oats	Chromium bowl	Mail 2 Quaker trademarks and $.10
Ovaltine	Shake-up mug	Mail Ovaltine seal and $.10

| Procter Gamble | Gotham silk stockings | Mail $.50 and 3 box tops from Ivory Flakes |
| General Mills | Cut-glass dish | Mail $.25 and sales slip showing purchase of two boxes of Wheaties |

Is the premium appeal still in use today? It certainly is—bigger than ever. Not long ago, a Premium Show at the New York Coliseum exhibited thousands of premiums and attracted thousands of visitors.

An ad for a New York Savings Bank showed pictures of seventy-two free gifts you can get if you open a savings account.

Contests and Sweepstakes

Another sales promotion device that was used years ago and is still in use today, is the money give-away.

For example, Camel cigarettes once offered "$50,000 reward for the best answer to this question: What significant change has recently been made in the Camel package?"

Recently, a *Reader's Digest* direct-mail piece announced their annual $400,000 Sweepstakes. The sweepstakes technique has two advantages over contests. The prizes are bigger and the contestants don't have to do any work. They simply send in their names and addresses. But the basic appeal is the same—big money for small effort.

Editorial-Style Ads

Another long-lasting technique is the use of ads that don't look like ads—in other words, ads that look like editorial material.

For example, the makers of Flit mosquito killer once used cartoons signed by famous cartoonists. This same technique is used today.

At one time, the makers of Lifebuoy soap used ads in newspapers that looked like news items. One such ad had the headline "Tip-Less Days Ended for Pretty Waitress." Subhead: "Friend's hint solves problem." The copy told how the waitress regained her popularity when she started using Lifebuoy.

Editorial-style ads are still going strong today. A split-run test in *Reader's Digest* showed that the pulling power of a mailorder ad set in ad style was increased by 80 percent when the identical copy was set in editorial style.

Headline Formulas

Here are some headline appeals that have come down through the years:

Old—Free to brides . . . $2 to anyone else
Today—Free to executives . . . $2 to others

Old—Limited time only . . . $.75 Noxzema $.49
Today—Last chance to get this bargain

Old—Sears Sale . . . Housewares
Today—Macy's . . . Housewares Show and Sale

Old—Do you make these mistakes in English?
Today—Do you make these travel mistakes?

Old—Buy no desk until you've seen the sensation of
    the business show.
Today—Don't buy Florida land until you read this
    message.

Techniques change, but basic sales appeals go on forever. Therefore, when you are searching for an idea to sell your product or service, don't forget to review the ideas that have been successful in the past.

HOW TO USE THE BARGAIN APPEAL
TO GET INCREASED SALES

"I've advertised my house for sale for several months, but I've had no buyers," said a friend. "Can you help me write an ad that will get a buyer?"

My friend showed me a small display ad he had been running in a local newspaper. The ad contained a photo of his home and the headline: "House for Sale."

"How much do you want for your house?" I said.

"Eighty thousand dollars," he replied.

"What is the highest valuation ever put on it?"

"One hundred and fifty thousand dollars," he answered.

"I think you should put a different headline on your ad. Try this headline: Was $150,000—Now $80,000."

A few weeks later, my friend came to see me with a big smile on his face.

"I got a lot of inquiries from that ad," he said. "Yet I only ran it twice—once in the daily paper and once on Sunday."

"Did you sell the house?"

"Yes."

"How much did you get?"

"Eighty thousand dollars."

PEOPLE GO FOR BARGAINS

The bargain appeal is as old as the hills and as new as today's newspaper. Advertisers who can trace the sales results from their ads use it all the time.

Classified advertisers use it. Mail-order advertisers thrive on it. Department stores would perish without it. When a woman buys a dress for $49 that was formerly marked $75, she is as happy as a lark. And the store is happy too. They move out slow selling inventory and make room for new merchandise.

I was introduced to the bargain appeal on my first day as a copywriter. My assignment was to write a mail-order ad for a book on personality development by Edmund Shaftesbury. My boss, the copy chief, handed me a bunch of proofs of ads for the book.

"These ads were successful," he said. "Study them and try to figure out what qualities made them successful. Then put those success qualities into your ad."

In reading the ads, I found the bargain appeal. The copy said:

> Edmund Shaftesbury at one time received fees as high as $500 for personal resident instruction. But there were many people who could not attend in person. And so Shaftesbury was prevailed upon to put his methods into book form. Prices up to $100 were paid for a single book.
>
> But now, through the efforts of a group of his students, Shaftesbury's teachings are within the reach of everyone. As a special introductory offer, this important work is now offered to you at the amazingly low price of only $3.

That copy ran fifty years ago. Similar copy is getting results today. For example, here is an offer by the Book-of-the-Month Club that is appearing in current magazines.

Headline:

THE MOST COMPLETE AND MOST SCHOLARLY
DICTIONARY OF THE ENGLISH LANGUAGE

Subhead: $17.50 . . . Publishers list price: $90
Copy: The *Oxford English Dictionary* is generally regarded as the final arbiter of the English language. Until recently, it had been available only as a 13-volume set, currently priced at $350. Now, through the combination of micrographic reproduction and a fine Bausch & Lomb optical lens, every single one of its 16,569 pages, fifty million words and close to two million illustrative quotations appears, in easily readable form, in *The Compact Edition.*

The bargain appeal is a favorite among book publishers. They don't often offer such drastic price cuts as the above examples—from $500 down to $3—from $350 down to $17.50. But lesser bargains are effective and are advertised all the time. Here is a recent example:

The Webster's Dictionary Company featured a bargain right in the headline of a full-page mail-order ad that has been repeated many times.

Headline:

THE COLOSSAL WEBSTER'S
8-POUND, 1,454-PAGE
158,000-DEFINITION,
$39.95 DICTIONARY
NOW ONLY $19.95

The first paragraph ties in with current conditions, as follows:

Because of the depressed economy, some book companies are in financial trouble. The Webster's Dictionary Company is no exception. And just as major auto companies have taken drastic steps to improve sales, we hereby announce an incredible price slash. . . .

Note that this paragraph gives a logical reason for the bargain. This is important. It makes the bargain believable.

Merchandise Bargains

Here are some merchandise bargains that were featured in an eight-page Spiegel direct response ad in *TV Guide:*

CAR STEREO PLUS SPEAKERS. STEREO WAS $29.99. SPEAKERS WERE $14.99. YOURS FOR THE PRICE OF STEREO. SAVE $15.

SOFT-SIDE LUGGAGE—3-PC. SET $49.88.
WAS $59.88. SAVE $10.

MINI CALCULATOR $48.77 WAS $89.98.
SAVE $41.21.

Some typical mail-order bargains appeared in an issue of *Family Circle:*

LOG CARRIER BASKET $19.97
REGULAR STORE RETAIL $27.97

NAVAJO TURQUOISE RING ONLY $17
AVERAGE RETAIL $30

54-PIECE FLATWARE SET
NOT $39.95 . . . NOT $29.95 . . . ONLY $17.76

Miscellaneous Bargains

Headline:

THAT FANTASTIC RING
. . . IT CHANGES COLOR WITH YOUR MOODS

Subhead: Now a fantastic bargain at only $2.95

Illustration: Picture of Ring

First paragraph: A touch of space-age science made it possible. Thousands rushed to be first to own them at prices up to $40.

*   *   *

Headline:

A MILLIONAIRE'S COLLECTION OF
PRICELESS ANCIENT-DYNASTY PANELS

Illustration: Reproductions of four art prints

Subhead: Decorator-Quality Lithographs in Breathtaking Color—Publishers List Price $20.00—Yours for only $3—complete set of four

*   *   *

Headline:

NOW . . . SLIM DOWN IN
JUST MINUTES A DAY

Illustration: Picture of Exer-toner exercise machine

Subhead: Nationally advertised for $7.95 & $9.95 . . . NOW ONLY $2.77

Here is an ad from Crown-Castle Tableware that illustrates, step by step, the effective use of the bargain appeal:

Headline:

50 PIECE SET . . . PISTOL-HANDLED FLATWARE OF 1776

Illustration: Photo showing all fifty pieces

Subhead: Authentic replicas in satin finish stainless
Not $44.95 . . . Not $34.95 . . . ONLY $22.95

Reason for bargain: "Through a special purchase, we can offer you, etc."

Reason to act at once: "Due to the rising cost of quality stainless steel, the price of this set will be increased in the very near future."

In most bargain ads, the advertiser features odd-numbered prices such as $19.97, not $20.00 . . . $49.88, not $50.00. Why? People have come to believe that odd-numbered prices are reduced prices. $50 sounds like a lot of money. $49.88 sounds like a bargain.

A surprising experience was told to me by the circulation manager of a nationally known publication. He tested, by direct-mail split-run, two different prices for a trial subscription; namely, $2.50 versus $2.67. He said: "Believe it or not, the higher price of $2.67 was the winner. It sounded more like a bargain than $2.50"

Not only mail-order advertisers, but general advertisers are making use of the bargain appeal today. Here are typical headlines from *Time Magazine:*

INSURE YOURSELF FIRST,
THEN SIGN UP THE FAMILY
AT A BARGAIN RATE

NEW YORK LIFE

NATIONAL'S DEFLATED RATES.
LOW, LOWER, LOWEST.

NATIONAL CAR RENTAL

TESTS SAY A LOT OF DRIVERS COULD SAVE NEARLY 3 MONTHS'
WORTH OF GASOLINE ANNUALLY

SHELL

EUROPE 50% OFF

CUNARD

The bargain appeal dates back to time immemorial. It worked yesterday. It works today. It will work tomorrow. It is the most frequently used of all sales appeals. After years of inflation and constantly rising prices, the bargain appeal is especially appropriate right now!

SUMMING UP

At a recent Direct Marketing Day convention at the New York Hilton Hotel, I made a speech entitled "Is the Market Changing . . . Or isn't It?"

I submitted two conclusions, as follows:

1. The methods for conveying sales messages to prospects are constantly changing and improving.

2. The basic sales appeals that have motivated people for centuries have not changed, nor are they likely to change in the foreseeable future.

For example, consider the money appeal. It is modern and it is also ancient. When Dr. Samuel Johnson auctioned off the contents of a London brewery, he said: "We are not here to sell boilers and vats, but the potentiality of growing rich beyond the dreams of avarice."

Regarding methods for conveying sales messages: In the 1920s the direct marketing advertisers had only three tools to work with:

1. Newspapers
2. Magazines
3. Direct Mail

Since the 1920s, new inventions have added many new tools. Here are some:

1. Radio
2. Television
3. Business Reply Mail
4. Postcard inserts in magazines
5. Free-standing inserts in newspapers
6. Credit cards
7. The 800 number for ordering by phone
8. Zip-coded mailing lists
9. Split-run copy testing
10. Computers

Regarding sales appeals: Many age-old sales appeals continue to win new customers year after year. Here is a list of successful appeals.

26 TESTED ADVERTISING APPEALS

Protect health
Reduce fat
Improve appearance
Get ahead in business
Make money
Save money
Win money
Cash in on bargains
Gain social advancement
Win friends
Influence people
Win praise from others
Gain prestige

Be a leader
Have a happy marriage
Care for children
Improve education
Be creative
Avoid worry
Avoid drudgery
Avoid embarrassment
Avoid discomfort
Avoid boredom
Enjoy comfort
Enjoy leisure
Attain security in old age

Eleven Benefits in a Single Ad

Benefits . . . benefits . . . benefits. That is what makes people
read your copy and buy your product. Here is a summary of the
benefits in this ad: A headline that offers quick results. A subhead that says: "My husband went wild about it." Plus pictures
(in color) of three delicious-looking pies, three testimonials, each
featuring a benefit, and three recipes with complete cooking
instructions.

Why an O-Cedar Angler gets the dirt other brooms miss.

More tips
Angler's special angle cut keeps more bristle tips on the floor while you're sweeping.

Closer tips
Angler tips are closer together. Each Angler bristle has about 100 tiny tips.

More durable, too
O-Cedar bristles don't fall out and break like straw bristles.

O-Cedar makes your life easier.
© 1978, The Drackett Products Company

Selling Via Demonstration

One of the most effective forms of salesmanship is to show the customer how the product works. When Claude Hopkins was a young man, he sold silver polish from door to door. He said: "When I could get inside the house and polish a piece of silver, I almost always made a sale." The above ad sells via demonstration. The big picture shows how the O-Cedar broom is superior to ordinary brooms. The small pictures demonstrate additional features.

Who else wants a *whiter* wash — *with no hard work* ?

H OW would you like to see your wash come out of a simple soaking—whiter than hours of scrubbing could make it!

Millions of women do it every week. They've given up washboards for good. They've freed themselves *forever* from the hard work and reddened hands of washday.

Now they just soak—rinse—and hang out to dry! In half the time, without a bit of hard rubbing, the wash is on the line—*whiter than ever!*

Dirt floats off—stains go

The secret is simply Rinso—a mild, granulated soap that gives rich, lasting suds even in the hardest water.

Just soak the clothes in the creamy Rinso suds —and the dirt and stains float off. Rinse—and the wash is spotless.

Even the most soiled parts need only a gentle rub between the fingers to make them snowy. Thus clothes last longer, for there's no hard rubbing against a board.

Safe for clothes, easy on hands

No laundry soap is easier on clothes or on hands than Rinso. Contains no acids, harsh chemicals or bleaches—nothing to injure white clothes or fast colors.

Rinso is all you need on washday. No bar soaps, chips or powders. Get Rinso for small cost from your grocer. Follow easy directions on package.

Use in washing machines

Rinso is wonderful in washers. Recommended by 23 leading washing machine makers for safety, and for a whiter, cleaner wash.

Guaranteed by the makers of Lux
Lever Bros. Co.

"Rinso suds soak e[...] thing clean, so I hav[...] more boiling to do [...] hard rubbing on a w[...] board. Little wonder [...] my clothes last a lot [...] er. And Rinso isn't [...] on my hands, either [...] have used all kind[...] laundry soaps—bar s[...] and chip soaps—fo[...] good many years, [...] nothing but Rinso for [...] now. It makes my w[...] day so easy and my clo[...] so white and bright. R[...] deserves to be the Bo[...] woman's very own l[...] dry soap."

MRS. GEO. N. T.
13 Haviland St.
Boston, Ma.

Millions use Rinso. Those
write us letters like this

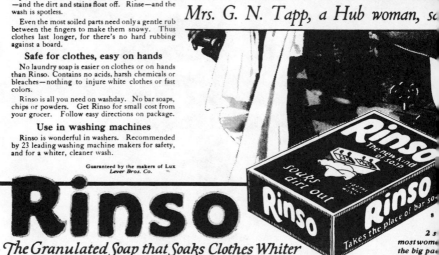

Mrs. G. N. Tapp, a Hub woman, s[...]

Rinso

The Granulated Soap that Soaks Clothes Whiter

SOAKS dirt out

Rinso
The new kind of soap

Takes the place of bar so[...]

2 s[...]
most wome[...]
the big pa[...]

The Power of Localized Testimonials

Printing plates of this ad were sent to a list of newspapers. The space for a testimonial (upper right corner) was left blank. The newspapers were told that they could publish the ad if they would insert a testimonial from a local woman. The above ad ran in Boston. This campaign was so successful in selling soap powder that it ran for years. Rinso sales multiplied over 10 times. Then came the invention of detergents and Rinso was dropped. But the lesson this campaign taught is still valid—the sales power of localized testimonials.

This Ad Worried the Advertiser

This ad was the first time an advertiser had the courage to use the theme, "Double your money back if you don't say this product is the best." The advertiser was afraid that thousands of women would ask for double their money back. The ad was tested by running it in a Chicago newspaper. The ad was very successful in selling soup and only twelve women asked for double their money back. In the years that followed, many packaged goods advertisers used the same theme. *Warning:* Don't use this theme in advertising an expensive product such as an automobile!

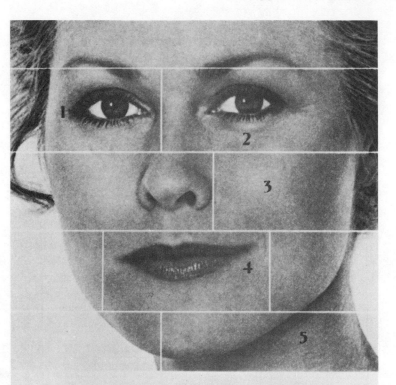

Is dry skin making you look older than you should? Touch these 5 spots and find out.

1. Corner of your eye. Does it feel tight and drawn? Chances are, you're drying your skin with soap. And that can make it look older.

2. Under the eye. Does this area feel smooth and soft? If it feels dry, stop using soap. Soap strips away much of your skin's natural moisture.

3. Your cheek. Does it feel dry, almost chapped here? Remember, all soaps are drying. But Dove® is not soap, and it can't dry your skin like soap.

4. Corner of the mouth. If it feels tight and pinched, your skin needs moisture. And only Dove is one-quarter moisturizing cream.

5. Your throat. The key sign here is a rough, dry feel. But with Dove you can start having smoother, younger looking skin in just 7 days.

Well, how did you do? Need a little help? Then stop drying your skin with soap. Start moisturizing it with Dove. For younger looking skin.

Dove. For younger looking skin.

How to Get Attention

A picture of a face looking straight at you is a good attention-getter. If you can add something to the face such as an eyepatch or the design shown above, the attention value is increased. Regarding the headline phrase: "Touch these 5 spots," this is a successful headline formula. Other examples: "Five familiar skin troubles—which do you want to overcome?" . . . "Can you spot these 7 common decorating sins?"

8

How to Write Headlines That Make Money

My interest in advertising headlines dates back to the time when I was a cub copywriter and was not allowed to write headlines.

Ev Grady, the copy chief, would hand me a layout with the headline already lettered in. Below the headline was a blank space.

"Write copy to fill the space," he would say.

Evidently I was not considered good enough to write headlines. I don't know how you can impress a young man more forcibly than to imply that there is a task to which he is not equal. From that time on, I was determined that some day I would write headlines.

Not long after that, I was assigned to write an ad for the U.S. School of Music correspondence course in piano playing. This time no layout was handed to me. I was to do the entire job. So I wrote the headline and copy for the ad, "They laughed when I sat down at the piano."

The ad was approved and published. It produced a large number of sales and was rerun many times. After that, I was able to join the ranks of those experienced copywriters who were allowed to write both headlines and copy.

Over the years, and to this day, I am thrilled when I see a new and exciting headline. I feel as pleased as a gardener when he sees a new rose, or an astronomer when he sights a new star. For example, one day while walking by a bank window, I saw a poster with an exciting headline. It said:

"BE $2,278 RICHER"

The copy told how a $10,000 deposit would produce $2,278 in interest in a short time. How much more effective this headline is, than the familiar repetition of interest figures that banks have been featuring for years. "Be $2,278 Richer." These three words instantly dramatize the reward you get for saving.

THE IMPORTANCE OF HEADLINES

If you have a good headline, you have a good ad. Any competent writer can write the copy. If you have a poor headline, you are licked before you start. Your copy will not be read.

A headline is the label on the package, the sign on the door, the frosting on the cake. It is the deciding factor regarding whether or not the reader will open the package, or enter the door or eat the cake. The same thing applies to the teaser lines printed on direct-mail envelopes, and to the opening sentences of direct-mail letters. If you don't stop your direct-mail prospect in the first five seconds, he will never get to your order form.

Advice to copywriters: When you are assigned to write an ad, write a lot of headlines first. Spend hours writing head-lines—or days if necessary. If you happen to think of a headline while walking along the street or while riding in a bus, take out pencil and paper and write it down.

After you have written a number of headlines, select the headline that seems best and write the copy. The discarded headlines are not all wasted. Some of them may be used as sub-heads or as lines in the copy.

TEN HEADLINES THAT MADE MONEY

1. Get Rid of Money Worries for Good

This headline for a life insurance ad induced thousands of men to write for a free booklet offered in the coupon. The coupon leads were followed up by the sales team. The copy in the ad told about the peace of mind a man feels when he has acquired enough life insurance to take care of the future needs of his family and himself—enough to clear his home of debt, to protect himself against disability and to send his child to college.

In the past, too many life insurance ads have started off on the wrong foot. The ads began by saying in effect "You ought to buy life insurance."

The average man does not welcome the idea of buying life insurance. It is an expense. The ad reminds him that he will die someday, a distasteful subject. He quickly turns the page.

To stop a reader, it is necessary to offer him a reward at the beginning. Promise him benefits. After you have made the reader want the benefits, you can tell him what he must do to get them. For example, in the case of life insurance, after you have told the reader that there is a way to end money worries, you can tell him the way is through life insurance.

2. To Men Who Want to Be Independent in the Next 10 Years

This headline for a correspondence course in business training was extremely successful. It implied a benefit without making a specific claim that could not be substantiated. The figure "ten years" was well chosen. Five years would have been unbelievable, and twenty years would have seemed too long.

3. Any Four for Only $1 (*Illustration:* Pictures of books)

This line is more than a headline. It is a basic selling idea that has been making money for mail-order advertisers for years. Here are current examples:

Take these 3 all-new Disney books for only $1.95

Get a lavish $12 beauty kit for only $1

Your choice! Records or tapes. Any 8 for 99¢

The theme of all these ads is the same: (1) an irresistible offer, followed by (2) a commitment to buy a stated number of future offerings.

4. How to Get Rid of an Inferiority Complex

Copy Plot: He was good at his job. No one denied that. But he lacked the all-around education of college men. So he read *The Harvard Classics*. After that he began to forge ahead.

This ad sold thousands of sets of *The Harvard Classics*—the famous five-foot shelf of books put together by Dr. Charles W. Eliot, former president of Harvard.

5. "No Time for Yale—Took College Home"

Although this headline talks about Yale, it was the caption of another winning ad for *The Harvard Classics*. In just seven words, the headline captured the attention of prime prospects; namely, the men and women who, for one reason or another, missed out on a college education. The copy told the story of a well-known person who "took college home" by reading the classics recommended by Dr. Eliot.

6. Order Christmas Gifts Now . . . Pay After January 1

This headline was used in November and December. It sold thousands of gift subscriptions to a popular magazine. The appeal to "buy now—pay later" sells millions of dollars worth of merchandise every year.

7. Free to High School Teachers—$6 to Others

This headline was printed on the envelope of a successful direct-mail package that was sent to high school teachers. The purpose of the package was to sell teachers the idea of using educational film strips for classroom instruction. Before embarking on a large-scale campaign, ten headlines were tested. Each headline was printed on 2,000 envelopes, making a total mailing of 20,000 direct mail packages. The copy in each package was the same. The offer was a free filmstrip worth $6. Various headlines were tested such as "Free gift certificate enclosed" . . . "Free teaching guide" . . . "9 Aids for Guidance Counselors." The direct-mail package with the headline "Free to high school teachers . . . $6 to others" was the winner by more than 70 percent.

8. How I Improved My Memory in One Evening

Many persons have poor memories and feel handicapped in this respect. This headline selects the right audience and offers them quick results. And it is a true headline. With proper instruction, the average person can improve his memory in one evening.

9. How $20 Spent may Save You $2000

This is the headline of an ad that was effective in selling subscriptions to a business publication. The secret of the head-line's success is that the potential benefit (save $2,000) is so large that the price ($20 spent) seems small by comparison. This headline also has the advantage that it lets the reader know in advance the price he will have to pay. There is no unpleasant surprise when the reader reaches the order form containing the price.

10. How a Man of 40 Can Retire in 15 Years

This headline for retirement annuities was used for years, and brought a large number of qualified leads for life insurance salesmen. The headline is a combination of two previously suc cessful headlines as follows:

a. An ad with the caption, "Retire in 15 years," had been successful in selling an investment plan. Evidently the mention of the specific number of 15 years was an appealing idea.
b. An ad with the caption, "To a man who is 35 and dissatisfied," had successfully sold correspondence courses in business training. Apparently, the mention of a specific age was effective.

These two successful ideas were combined in a single head-line that became a super success.

As previously mentioned, the best headlines are selling ideas expressed in the simplest possible words. No frills. No adjectives. No attempts at cleverness.

The best headlines appeal to basic human desires such as the desire for self-improvement, for good value, for peace of mind, and for security in old age. These appeals have worked successfully for years, and can be expected to work successfully in the future.

A QUIZ FOR HEADLINE WRITERS

Listed below are twenty headlines of ads that were tested by direct response. Ten of the ads were successful in getting replies. Ten were failures.

The headlines are arranged in pairs. Each pair contains a success and a failure. Read the first pair of headlines and decide which headline you think is the caption of the successful ad. Then proceed to the next pair of headlines and decide which one you think was the caption of the winning ad.

Follow the same procedure with the remaining pairs of headlines. In each case, decide which headline you think was the winner. After you have read all the headlines and picked one from each pair, read the list of actual winners at the end of this quiz.

You may say: "Isn't it necessary to read the copy in an ad before judging its pulling power?" The answer is that the copy story in each pair of ads was essentially the same. Furthermore, experienced mail-order men have agreed that 75 percent to 80 percent of the pulling power of an ad depends on the headline.

If you guess five out of the ten headlines correctly, your score is 50 percent. If you guess seven headlines correctly, your score is 70 percent. If you guess more than seven headlines correctly, you should ask your boss for a raise.

1. ☐ **If you are a careful driver you can save money on car insurance**

   ☐ **How to turn your careful driving into money**

These captions were printed atop ads that presented a car insurance plan that enables careful drivers to avoid paying for the accidents of reckless drivers. The ad coupons offered a free booklet entitled: "How you can save money on your automobile insurance." One ad pulled 50 percent more sales leads than the other.

2. ☐ **How to make your food taste better**

☐ **How to get your cooking bragged about**

The purpose of these two ads was to sell housewives the idea of using a popular brand of food seasoning. The ads were identical except for the headlines. Each ad invited the reader to write for a free sample of the food seasoning. One ad brought 42 percent more sample requests than the other.

3. ☐ **How to build an attic room**

☐ **How to build your own darkroom**

These ads were addressed to men who are handy with tools. The ads appeared in *Popular Science* and in other magazines. The copy told how you can use a well-known brand of wallboard to build attic rooms, game rooms, dens, etc. The coupons offered a free booklet. One ad brought in three times as many coupons as the other.

4. ☐ **How to do your Christmas shopping in 5 minutes**

☐ **The gift that comes 12 times a year**

These ads ran in the pre-Christmas season and sold the idea of giving friends a one-year subscription to a popular monthly magazine. Each ad contained an order form which the reader could use to order Christmas gifts. One ad brought 90 percent more sales than the other.

5. ☐ **How to get a loan of $500**

☐ **When should a family get a loan?**

Each of these ads for a well-known finance company contained a panel of copy that invited the reader to telephone for information on how to get a loan. One of the ads pulled more than twice as many phone calls as the other.

6. ☐ **To every woman who would like a career in Interior Design**

☐ **Can you spot these 7 common decorating sins?**

These are headlines of ads selling a correspondence course in Interior Decorating. The coupons in the ads offered further information regarding the course. One ad brought 250 percent more coupons than the other.

7. ☐ **Announcing an important revision of the Bible**

☐ **Most important Bible news in 340 years**

The mail-order ads with these headlines described the Revised Standard Version of the Bible. The ads were split-run tested in the New York *Daily News*. One sold 71 percent more Bibles than the other.

8. ☐ **How to make chocolate pudding in 6 minutes**

  Illustration: Picture of pudding being mixed in a bowl

☐ **Tonight serve this ready-mixed chocolate pudding**

  Illustration: Picture of a smiling woman eating pudding

These two ads were split-run tested in a daily newspaper. The last paragraph of each ad said: "Tear out this ad and send it with your name and address for a sample package of chocolate pudding mix." One ad pulled 66 percent more requests than the other.

9. ☐ **Good news for men who want attractive, well-groomed hair**

Illustration: Picture of man being admired by attractive woman

☐ **Will your scalp stand the "Fingernail Test"?**

Illustration: Picture of a man scratching his head and looking at his fingernails.

These two ads were split-run tested in *The New York Daily News.* Each ad offered a sample bottle of hair tonic for $.25. One ad brought 56 percent more requests than the other.

10. ☐ **Girls . . . Want Quick Curls?**

Illustration: Picture of a girl looking in a mirror, setting her hair.

☐ **Does he still say . . . "You're lovely"?**
Illustration: Picture of a girl being admired by a man.

These two ads had identical copy. The last paragraph of each ad offered a sample bottle of Hairset. The ads were split-run tested in small size in the New York *Daily News.* One ad brought 104 requests. The other ad brought 341 requests.

THE WINNING HEADLINES

Listed below are the ten winning headlines, together with comments regarding the effectiveness of the headlines.

1. If You Are a Careful Driver You Can Save Money on Car Insurance

This headline is a clear and simple statement of an attractive proposition. The other headline "How to turn your careful driving into money" makes a simple proposition complicated. It might be an offer of jobs for careful drivers.

2. How to Get Your Cooking Bragged About

This headline has two advantages: (a) it implies that you can improve the flavor of the food you serve, and (b) it offers the housewife the reward of praise. She gets her cooking bragged about. The other headline "How to make your food taste better" offers only a single benefit.

3. How to Build an Attic Room

The fact that this headline was the winner simply shows that there are more men who want to build attic rooms than there are photographers who want to build darkrooms.

4. How to Do Your Christmas Shopping in 5 Minutes

This headline offers a quick, easy way to do a time-consuming task. The other headline, "The gift that comes 12 times a year," stresses only the benefits to the receivers of the gifts.

5. How to Get a Loan of $500

This headline offers the reader a benefit in plain, simple language. The other headline "When should a family get a loan?" does not offer a benefit. It employs a philosophical approach to the subject of borrowing money. When a man is hard pressed financially, he does not want philosophy. He wants cash.

6. Can You Spot These 7 Common Decorating Sins?

This headline involves the reader, arouses curiosity and offers a free lesson in interior decorating. It appeals to a large audience. The other headline "To every woman who would like a career in Interior Design" appeals to a limited audience.

7. Most Important Bible News in 340 Years

This headline has a momentous sound. The specific figure "340 years," carries conviction and implies news of great consequence. The other headline, "Announcing an important revision of the Bible," is a perfectly good news headline, but it does not sound as important or as far-reaching as the other one.

8. Tonight Serve This Ready-Mixed Chocolate Pudding

This headline offers the reader a pudding that is ready-made. This saves time and work. The illustration shows the fun of eating the pudding. The headline, "How to make chocolate pudding in 6 minutes," gives the reader the job of making the pudding. The illustration shows the work of making the pudding.

9. Will Your Scalp Stand the "Fingernail Test"?

This ad has shock value. It offers a remedy to a common problem—dandruff. The "Fingernail Test" sold millions of bottles of Wildroot Hair Tonic. The other ad, showing a man being admired by an attractive woman, is less convincing. Can a man become popular by putting hair tonic on his head?

10. Girls . . . Want Quick Curls?

This headline has three success qualities. The word *girls* selects prime prospects. The prospects are offered a benefit; namely, curls. The headline promises quick results. The other headline "Does he still say . . .

'you're lovely'?" lacks these success qualities. It merely raises a question.

The hairset copy test was run more than twenty-five years ago. Twenty-five years later, a copy test was run for a home permanent. Here are the headlines:

1.   New Home Permanent
                 Conditions Hair as It Curls

2.   Girls . . . Want a
                 Fast Permanent?

The ad with headline Number 2 pulled nearly three times as many replies as the other ad. This result is evidence of the long-lasting durability of tested sales appeals. World conditions may change, but human nature remains the same.

In conclusion: Do not be discouraged if you guessed wrong on some of these headlines. Experienced agency men and clients considered that all twenty of the headlines, including both winners and losers, were sufficiently promising to warrant spending money to test the headlines.

HOW TO MAKE A GOOD HEADLINE BETTER

Here is the headline of an ad for a gasoline additive: "Save one gallon of gas in every ten." The ad pulled a large number of requests for a sample of the product.

It was then decided to try a more selective approach. The words *Car Owners* were inserted at the beginning of the headline as follows:

"Car owners! Save one gallon of gas in every ten"

There was no other change. The copy in both ads remained the same. The two versions of the ad were split-run tested in a daily newspaper. The second version, beginning with the words *Car Owners,* pulled 20 percent more sample requests than the first version.

This test is just one of many experiments that have been tried over the years involving changes in headlines. In a number of cases, these changes have resulted in appreciable improvements in results. Examples:

Headline: **"Hay Fever"**

A maker of a hay fever remedy got good response from a sample offer contained in a small ad headlined "Hay Fever." This advertiser then tested other ads containing the same copy, but with different headlines. One of the new headlines was "Dry Up Hay Fever."

Here are the results of a newspaper split-run test: The ad with the headline "Hay Fever" pulled 297 sample requests. The ad with the headline "Dry Up Hay Fever" pulled 380 sample requests. This is a 27 percent increase—obtained by merely adding two words. These two words, *Dry Up*, added a promise of a benefit to the purely selective headline "Hay Fever."

Headline: **"How to Have a Cool, Quiet Bedroom"**

A manufacturer of portable air conditioners ran ads with the headline "How to Have a Cool, Quiet Bedroom." The ads contained a telephone number and offered further information. The telephone replies were switched to salesmen who invited prospects to come to the manufacturer's showroom. Later on, four words were added to the headline of the ad as follows: "How to Have a Cool, Quiet Bedroom—Even on Hot Nights." This change made the headline more dramatic and strengthened the promise of a benefit. Replies and sales increased.

Headline: **"How to Repair Cars—Quickly, Easily, Right"**

A speaker at an advertising convention gave this case history. An ad with the headline "How to Repair Cars—quickly, easily, right" was successful in getting orders. Then the word *Repair* was changed to *Fix*. The new headline was: "How to Fix Cars—quickly, easily, right." Orders increased 18 percent.

OTHER EXAMPLES

At a Direct Marketing Day meeting at the New York Hilton Hotel, Jim Howard of Wunderman, Ricotta & Kline said: "We published an investment book ad with the headline, 'Why some people always make money in the stock market.' At the request of one newspaper, we changed it to 'Why some people *almost* always make money in the stock market.' This increased results."

Some years ago a book publisher was planning to bring out a book on country home ownership entitled *Five Acres*. The publisher tested two titles as follows:

1. *Five Acres*
2. *Five Acres and Independence*

The latter title, *Five Acres and Independence* was the winner by a wide margin. The book was published and it sold well.

Here are two more book titles that were tested a number of years ago:

1. *How I Raised Myself to Success in Selling*
2. *How I Raised Myself from Failure to Success in Selling*

The latter title, containing the words *from Failure,* was the winner. This book became a best seller.

A LESSON FROM THE *READER'S DIGEST*

In Chapter 7, we discussed how to find basic sales appeals by observing the article titles printed on the cover stickers attached to newsstand copies of the *Reader's Digest*. Another lesson you can learn from these cover stickers is how to improve the wording of titles.

The next time you buy a magazine that has a paper sticker attached to the front cover, read the article titles printed on the sticker and then open the magazine and read the actual article titles. Sometimes the wording is different. For example:

"How to Beat Insomnia Without Sleeping Pills" was the title of a recent magazine article.
"How to Sleep Without Pills" was the shorter and simpler title printed on the front cover sticker.

It is the job of the circulation department to sell as many copies as possible, and so they sometimes simplify, modify or reconstruct the titles of articles in order to give them more sales punch. In doing this, the ad men in the circulation department are, in effect, working with headlines. They try to make a good headline better. Sometimes they do this by shortening an article title, as in the above example. Sometimes they do it by lengthening a title. Sometimes they reconstruct the entire title.

MAKING THE HEADLINE SHORTER

Here are some magazine article titles that were given more impact by being shortened.

Original title:	Hot Tips on Heating Your Home
Revised title on cover sticker:	How to Cut Fuel Bills
Original title:	A Smart Shopper's Guide to Bargains
Revised title:	Shopper's Guide to Bargains
Original title:	Three Ways to Mothproof a Marriage
Revised title:	3 Ways to Save a Marriage
Original title:	How to Understand the Perplexing Teen-Ager
Revised title:	How to Understand Your Teen-Ager
Original title:	Which Diet Tips Pay Off?
Revised title:	Diet Tips that Pay Off

MAKING THE HEADLINE LONGER

Here are some article titles that were given more sales appeal by being lengthened:

Original title:	When Your Husband's Affection Cools
Revised title:	When Your Husband's Affection Cools—and What to Do About It
Original title:	Birth Control for Men
Revised title:	Now—Safe, Simple Birth Control for Men
Original title:	You Can Read Faster
Revised title:	Read Faster—a 20-Day Plan
Original title:	Key to Fitness at Any Age
Revised title:	Key to Fitness at Any Age for Men and Women

RECASTING THE HEADLINE

Here are some article titles that were given greater interest by reconstructing:

Original title:	The Smugglers of Misery
Revised title:	Where All the Drugs Come From
Original title:	Building on the Positives in Marriage
Revised title:	4 Ways to Keep Your Marriage Young
Original title:	High Blood Pressure—New Light on a Hidden Killer
Revised title:	New Protection Against Heart Attack
Original title:	Backyard Gardens Are Back in Style
Revised title:	How to Start a Backyard Garden
Original title:	What You Can Do to Combat Inflation
Revised title:	10 Ways to Beat the High Cost of Living

The next time you write a headline, don't be satisfied with your first draft. Put it aside overnight, and then read it again. See if you can make it better by shortening it, lengthening it or reconstructing it.

106 HEADLINES THAT MADE MONEY

1. They laughed when I sat down at the piano—but when I started to play!

As previously mentioned, one of my earliest assignments was to write an ad for a correspondence course in piano playing. I wrote an ad with the above headline. The ad was successful.

2. They grinned when the waiter spoke to me in French—but their laughter changed to amazement at my reply

A year after writing the piano ad, I was assigned to write an ad for a correspondence course in French. I wrote an ad with the above headline. The ad was successful.

This experience taught me a lesson. One successful headline may give you an idea for another successful headline.

Here are examples of how various copywriters have used this same method in order to write successful headlines for other products:

3. Do you make these mistakes in English?
4. Do you make these travel mistakes?
5. How a "fool stunt" made me a star salesman

This was the headline of a successful ad for a course in salesmanship.

6. How a strange accident saved me from baldness

A headline for a successful ad about a hair growing treatment.

7. Who else wants a screen star figure?
8. Who else wants a lighter cake
   —in half the mixing time?
9. Free to brides—$2 to others
10. Free to high school teachers—$6 to others

One successful headline can lead to another. This is not intended to cripple your imagination; you should continue to invent new ideas. But there are times when every copywriter is stuck for an idea. That is when this list of successful headlines can help you.

11. Announcing the new Ford cars for *(year)*
12. Are you ashamed
    of smells in your home?
13. Buy no desk until you've seen
    this sensation of the business show
14. Can you talk about books
    with the rest of them?
15. Car insurance at low cost
    —if you are a careful driver
16. Car owners . . . save one gallon
    of gas in every ten
17. Double your money back
    if this isn't the best onion soup
    you ever tasted
18. Free book tells you 12 secrets
    of better lawn care
19. Get rid of money worries
    for good
20. Girls . . . Want quick curls?
21. Greatest Bible news
    in 341 years
22. Great new discovery
    kills kitchen odors quick!
    —makes indoor air "country fresh"

23. Hand woven by the
    mountain people of New Mexico

24. Have you any of these five skin troubles?

25. Have you these symptoms
    of nerve exhaustion?

26. Here's how to have a long and healthy life.

27. Here's a quick way to break up a cold

28. How a man of 40
    can retire in 15 years

29. How I became popular overnight

30. How I improved my memory
    in one evening

31. How I made a fortune
    with a "fool" idea

32. How investors can save 75%
    on broker commissions this year

33. How I raised myself
    from failure to success
    in selling

34. How I retired on a
    guaranteed income for life

35. How I started a new life with $7

36. How $7 started me on the road
    to $35,000 a year

37. How the next 90 days
    can change your life

38. How to beat tension
    without pills

39. How to collect from
    Social Security at any age

40. How to do your Christmas shopping
    in 5 minutes

41. How to feel fit
    at any age

42. How to get rid of an
    inferiority complex

43. How to get your cooking
    bragged about

44. How to have a cool, quiet bedroom
    —even on hot nights

45. How to make money
    writing short paragraphs

46. How to stop worrying

47. How to stretch your inflated money

48. How to win friends
    and influence people

49. How $20 spent may
    save you $2,000

50. How you can get a loan of $500

51. If you are a careful driver
    you can save money on car insurance

52. I gambled a postage stamp
    and won $35,840 in 2 years

53. I lost that ugly bulge
    in 2 minutes

54. Imagine me . . . holding an audience
    spellbound for 30 minutes!

55. It cleans your breath
    while it cleans your teeth

56. I've tried 'em all, but this is
    the polish I use on my own car
    . . . Frank Mills, Essex Garage

57. I was tired of living on low pay
    —so I started reading the *Wall Street Journal*
    By a Subscriber

58. Lose ugly fat
    —an average of 7 pounds a month

59. Men who "know it all"
    are not invited to read this page

60. Money-saving bargains from
    America's oldest diamond discount house

61. New . . . a cream deodorant
    which safely stops perspiration

62. New house paint made by Du Pont
    keeps your white house whiter

63. No time for Yale.
    —took college home

64. Now! Own Florida land this easy way
    . . . $20 down and $20 a month

65. 161 new ways to a gourmet's heart
    —in this fascinating book for cooks

66. One place-setting free
    for every three you buy

67. Order Christmas gifts now
    —pay after January 20

68. Owners save 20% to 50% on fuel
    with the G.E. Oil Furnace

69. Play guitar in 7 days or money back

70. Quick relief for tired eyes

71. *Reader's Digest* tells why
    filtered cigarette smoke
    is better for your health

72. 7 ways to break
    the overweight habit

73. 10 ways to beat
    the high cost of living

74. The deaf now hear whispers

75. The lazy man's way to riches

76. The most amazing Shakespeare
    bargain ever offered

77. The most comfortable shoes you've
    ever worn or your money back

78. The most complete and most scholarly
    dictionary in the English language
    $17.50 . . . Publisher's list price: $90

79. The secret of making people like you

80. The tastiest ocean treat from Gloucester
    —plump, tender, juicy salt mackerel fillet

81. They thought I was crazy to ship
    live Main lobsters
    as far as 1,800 miles from the ocean

82. Thousands have this priceless gift
    —but never discover it

83. Thousands now play
    who never thought they could

84. To a $15,000 man who
    would like to be making $30,000

85. To a man who is 35 and dissatisfied

86. To a mother whose child
    is three years old

87. To men who want to be
    independent in the next 10 years

88. To men who want to
    quit work some day

89. Tonight serve this ready-mixed
    chocolate pudding

90. To people who want to write
    —but can't get started

91. Wanted—safe men for dangerous times

92. Wanted—your services as a
    high-paid real estate specialist

93. What makes a woman lovable?

94. What's new in summer sandwiches?

95. What's wrong in this picture?

96. When doctors "feel rotten"
    this is what they do

97. Which of these five skin troubles
    would you like to end?

98. Who else wants a whiter wash
    —with no hard work?

99. Why G.E. bulbs give
    more light this year

100. Will you give me 7 days to prove
     I can make you a new man?

101. Will your scalp
     stand the fingernail test?

102. You don't have to be rich
     to retire on a guaranteed income for life

103. You're never too old to hear better

104. Linen napkin luxury at a
     paper napkin price

105. Throw your wax can in the trash can—
     the new no-wax floor is here

106. Can you spot these 7 common decorating sins?

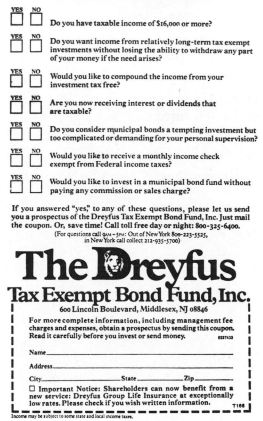

A Quiz for Investors

The headline of this ad asks a question that many people have been asking themselves regarding tax exempt bonds. So they read the copy to find the answer. The copy, which is set in the form of an interesting quiz, asks additional questions of importance to investors. The last paragraph says, "If you answered 'yes' to any of these questions, please let us send you a prospectus." Since the questions are likely to bring many "yes" answers, the reader feels a strong urge to send the coupon for the prospectus.

"I know I should be drinking a decaffeinated coffee because caffein makes me nervous, but I love real coffee too much to make a change."

"Carol, when you drink SANKA® Brand you *are* drinking real coffee. It's 100% real coffee, and tastes it."

SANKA. THE 100% REAL COFFEE
BRAND DECAFFEINATED COFFEE
THAT LETS YOU BE YOUR BEST.

"Mmmm. This is a real cup of coffee!"

If you want to be at your best, and still have the full-bodied aroma and taste of 100% real coffee, try SANKA® Brand Decaffeinated Coffee.

SANKA® Brand gives you all the great taste that makes coffee drinking such a satisfying experience, yet it's 97% caffein-free.

Join the millions of caffein-concerned Americans who have discovered delicious SANKA® Brand: the 100% real coffee that lets you be your best.

©General Foods Corporation 1979

Why Many Ads Feature Older Models

There was a time when advertisers concentrated on the 18-to-45 age group because they live longer and will be customers longer. But now the U.S. population is changing. People 45 and up are living longer. *And they have money to spend.* They buy all kinds of things, from decaffeinated coffee to expensive vacations.

The Picture Tells the Story

Here is another case where the picture tells the story quicker and better than words. The plastic cover over the car explains the product in an instant. The long, hard-sell copy tells the details and lists additional uses for the plastic cover. I have seen this ad repeated for years.

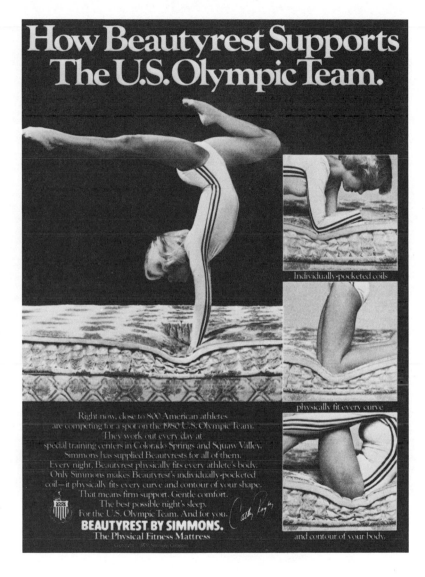

Dramatizing the Product

There is a saying that "a good picture is worth a thousand words." However, the picture must relate to the product. It must not be just an unrelated attention-getter. This ad works two ways. The copy tells the story in print. The illustration tells the story in a dramatic manner that gets instant attention.

9

How to
Use Stories
to Sell
Products
and Services

Two kinds of advertising copy in frequent use are:

1. Reason-why copy
2. Story copy

Reason-why copy appeals to the reader's intellect. It presents logical arguments for buying a product or service.

Story copy entertains as it sells. It goes deep into the reader's subconscious mind. It sells ideas and promotes action.

Telling stories is one of the oldest methods of conveying a message or promoting an idea. In the year 600 B.C., Aesop, the Greek writer of fables, promoted the idea of thrift with his tale about the ant and the grasshopper—the ant who labored all summer long, storing away food for the coming winter, while the grasshopper idled away his time and perished when winter came.

In the Bible are many stories that promote ideas. Here is a famous example from Luke 10: 30-37.

> A certain man went down from Jerusalem to Jericho, and fell among thieves, who stripped him of his raiment, and wounded him, and departed, leaving him half dead.
>
> And by chance, there came a certain priest that way—and when he saw him, he passed by on the other side.
>
> And likewise a Levite, when he was at that place, came and looked at him, and passed by on the other side.
>
> But a certain Samaritan came where he was, and when he saw him, he had compassion on him. He bound up his wounds and set him upon his own beast, and brought him to an inn and took care of him.
>
> And on the morrow when he departed, he took out two pence and gave them to the host and said—Take care of him. And whatsoever thou spendest more, when I come again, I will repay thee.

This story has promoted the idea of compassion for nearly 2,000 years. It is as appropriate today as it was when it was first written.

In more recent times, many writers, including advertising copywriters, have used stories to convey messages and promote ideas. One of the first of these was famed ad man, Frank Irving Fletcher, the highest-paid copywriter of his time. A typical example of his work is a story he wrote for his client Técla, a manufacturer of synthetic pearls. Fletcher was a master of brevity. In only thirty-two words, he created the following classic ad.

A $10,000
Mistake

A client for whom we had copied a necklace of Oriental Pearls, seeing both necklaces before her, said: "Well, the resemblance is remarkable, but this is mine!"

Then she picked up ours!

T É C L A
398 Fifth Avenue, New York
10 Rue de la Paix, Paris

Fletcher increased his earnings by syndicating his copy— that is, he sold the same copy again and again to various stores throughout the United States.

SELLING SELF-IMPROVEMENT

Here is another classic. It pulled so many coupons for a Correspondence Course in business training that it was run for 22 years.

Illustration: Picture of smiling man handing money to his wife.
Headline:

"HERE'S AN EXTRA $100 GRACE—I'M MAKING REAL MONEY NOW!"

Copy: "Yes, I've been keeping it a secret until pay day came. I've been promoted with an increase of $100 a month. And the first extra money is yours. Just a little reward for urging me to study at home. The boss says my spare time training has made me a valuable man to the firm and there's more money coming soon. We're starting up easy street, Grace, thanks to you and that training."

Today more than ever before, money is what counts. The cost of living is mounting month by month. You can't get along on what you have been making. Somehow, you've simply got to increase your earnings.

*   *   *

Note the easy transition from story copy to sales copy with the paragraph beginning "Today more than ever before, money is what counts." The text contained four more paragraphs of sales copy, followed by a coupon.

This ad is as timely today as the day it was written.

MR. ADDISON SIMS OF SEATTLE

This famous story ad ran successfully for years. It was written by Wilbur Ruthrauff, co-founder of the mail-order ad agency of Ruthrauff & Ryan.

The ad told the story of David M. Roth, and how he perfected the Roth Memory Course—a series of seven lessons sold in a single package by mail. Here is the first part of the text. There was no illustration—just a headline, subhead, three columns of type and a free examination coupon.

Headline:

HOW I IMPROVED MY MEMORY
IN ONE EVENING

Subhead: The Amazing Experience of Victor Jones

Copy: "Of course I place you. Mr. Addison Sims of Seattle."

"If I remember correctly—and I do remember correctly—Mr. Burroughs, the lumberman, introduced me to you at the luncheon of the Seattle Rotary Club three years ago in May. This is a pleasure indeed! I haven't laid eyes on you since that day. How is the grain business? How did that merger work out?"

The assurance of this speaker—in the crowded corridor of the Hotel St. Regis—compelled me to look at him, though it is not my habit to "listen in," even in a hotel lobby.

"He is David M. Roth, the most famous memory expert in the United States," said my friend Kennedy, answering my question before I could get it out. "He will show you a lot more wonderful things than that, before the evening is over."

And he did.

As we went into the banquet room, the toastmaster was introducing a long line of the guests to Mr. Roth. I got in line and when it came my turn, Mr. Roth asked, "What are your initials, Mr. Jones, and your business connection and your telephone number?" Why he asked this, I learned later, when he picked out from the crowd 60 men he had met two hours before and called each by name without a mistake. What is more, he named each man's business and telephone number.

I won't tell you all the other amazing things this man did except to tell how he called back, without a minute's hesitation, long lists of numbers, bank clearings, prices, parcel post rates and anything else the guests gave him in rapid order.

*   *   *

These opening paragraphs were followed by twenty-three more paragraphs of story copy. Then came a subhead, "Send No Money," and three paragraphs of sales copy and a coupon.

This ad was written more than fifty years ago. The name Addison Sims became well-known throughout the United States. Men laughingly greeted each other by saying: "Of course I place you. Mr. Addison Sims of Seattle."

AGAIN SHE ORDERS—
"A CHICKEN SALAD, PLEASE"

This line was the heading of a renowned mail-order ad for *The Book of Etiquette.*

The illustration in the ad showed an embarrassed young woman sitting at a table with a menu in her hand. Here is the copy:

> For him she is wearing her new frock. For him she is trying to look her prettiest. If only she can impress him—make him like her—just a little.
>
> Across the table he smiles at her, proud of her prettiness, glad to notice that others admire. And she smiles back, a bit timidly, a bit self-consciously.
>
> What wonderful poise he has! What complete self-possession! If only *she* could be so thoroughly at ease.
>
> She pats the folds of her new frock nervously, hoping that he will not notice how embarrassed she is, how uncomfortable. He doesn't—until the waiter comes to their table and stands, with pencil poised, to take the order.
>
> "A chicken salad, please," She hears herself give the order as in a daze. She hears him repeat the order to the waiter, in a rather surprised tone. Why had she ordered that again! This was the third time she had ordered chicken salad while dining with him.
>
> He would think she didn't know how to order a dinner. Well, did she? No. She didn't know how to pronounce those French words on the menu. And she didn't know how to use the table appointments gracefully. She found that she couldn't create conversation—and was actually tongue-tied, was conscious of little crudities which she just knew he must be noticing. She wasn't sure of herself, she didn't *know*. And she discovered, as we all do, that there is only one way to have complete poise and ease of manner, and that is to know definitely what to do and say on every occasion.

*   *   *

This story was followed by twelve paragraphs of sales talk, interspersed with these subheads:

ARE YOU CONSCIOUS OF YOUR CRUDITIES?
DO YOU MAKE FRIENDS EASILY?
IF A DINNER FOLLOWS THE WEDDING . . .
BOOK OF ETIQUETTE GIVES LIFELONG ADVICE

The "Chicken Salad" ad was part of a campaign that sold two million copies of *The Book of Etiquette.*

EVER HEAR THE ONE ABOUT
THE FARMER'S DAUGHTER?

This headline, accompanied by a photo of an automobile, preceded a story selling Buick cars. Here is the story:

Copy: It seems that one day a traveling salesman in a smart new Buick pulled up at the gate where the girl was standing.

"Nice day," said he, lifting his hat. "Wonderful!" she agreed.

"Nice sort of day to take a nice long automobile ride," he suggested. "Wonderful!" said the farmer's daughter.

"Got a pretty snappy car here," said the traveling salesman. "Just about the handsomest thing to be seen anywhere!" Again the girl agreed—"It's wonderful!"

"It's got a swell engine," said the salesman. "Gets more good out of every drop of gasoline. You ought to see it travel!"

"Wonderful!" said the farmer's daughter.

"Darned comfortable car too. Those springs certainly do make the rough roads behave. Never driven a car that travels smoother."

Said the farmer's daughter: "Just wonderful!"

"And look! Big windows. You can see the country. Why there's 413 more square inches of safety glass in this sedan. It's a treat to travel in a car like this!"

"Wonderful!" agreed the girl.

"Well," said the salesman, "how about taking a little ride with me?"

"Listen, mister!" said the farmer's daughter. "Where

you been? We've two Buicks in the garage. Want to race to town?"

AN AD THAT BROUGHT
A SURPRISE

I once wrote a series of story ads that got good results for a business publication. Let us call it *The Business World*. The theme of the campaign was "get ahead in business." The ads were based on true experiences of subscribers. For example:

Headline:

"HOW A BELLHOP'S BONER HELPED ME GET AHEAD"

Subhead: "By a *Business World* subscriber"

Copy: "One time on a business trip I got to the hotel late at night. The only room I could get was an expensive suite. Next morning a bellhop handed me a copy of *The Business World* by mistake. Some rich guy must have had this room, I said to myself.

"Well, I looked at *The Business World*. For the first time in my life I began to understand why some men get ahead while others stay behind."

*   *   *

The copy continued with a sales talk for *The Business World* and an urge to the reader to send for a trial subscription. This ad brought a large number of subscriptions and it also brought a surprise. The editor of *The Business World* received a letter of complaint from the Bellman's Association in Washington. The letter said: "The word 'Bellhop' is derogatory. Our proper title is 'Bellman.' We deliver a lot of copies of your publication. We believe that we should be treated with more respect."

In subsequent appearances of the ad the word "bellhop" was changed to "bellman."

SELLING MEN'S-WEAR WITH STORIES

Famed copywriter Leslie Pearl has written more than a thousand ads for Wallach's chain of men's-wear stores in and around New York City. The ads are set in editorial style. They appear in daily newspapers. The aim of the series is to make friends for Wallach's. Pearl said, "The ads that get the most comment are those that are based on incidents that happen in the stores. These stories are contributed by Wallach's salesmen. They sound true because they are true."

Here is one of the ads:

SEA STORY

We probably shouldn't be telling this story because it isn't very dignified. But it's true and we can't resist it.

A man came into our Murray Street store some time back and asked to see a suit in a rather old-fashioned pattern that was no longer in stock. We suggested that he might like to see some of the newer patterns and he was more than agreeable. He said, in fact, that he would take *any* Hart, Schaffner & Marx suit in the store. When the fitting was completed, the Wallach's salesman asked him why he had shown so little interest in the model and so much concern with the label.

"Well, it's like this," he answered. "My ship docked down the street. Just got in. We sailors are not always what you might call careful with our money. Sometimes we're flush. Sometimes we're flat and need cash. It's a well-known fact that there is only one suit of clothes that you can hock in any port in the world and that's a Hart, Schaffner & Marx."

That's what the man said. We trust you will never have reason to prove the truth of his statement.

THE LISTERINE EXPERIENCE

How do you use stories in selling a mouth wash? The Lambert Pharmaceutical Company (now Warner-Lambert) did it with some of the most famous story ads ever written. Here is one:

Headline:

OFTEN A BRIDESMAID BUT NEVER A BRIDE

Copy: Edna's case was really a pathetic one. Like every woman, her primary ambition was to marry. Most of the girls of her set were married—or about to be. Yet not one possessed more grace or charm or loveliness than she.

And as her birthdays crept gradually toward that tragic thirty-mark, marriage seemed farther from her life than ever.

She was often a bridesmaid but never a bride.

That's the insidious thing about halitosis (unpleasant breath). You, yourself, rarely know when you have it. And even your closest friends won't tell you.

*   *   *

The copy continued with three paragraphs of sales talk. This ad, plus other story ads in the series, made the word "halitosis" famous and sold millions of dollars' worth of Listerine.

ONE OF THE BEST-READ STORY ADS OF ALL TIME

How do you use a story in selling life insurance? The Travelers Insurance Company did it this way:

Headline:

THE GREATEST REASON IN THE WORLD

Illustration: Picture of a young man and a young woman in earnest conversation in a railway station.

Copy: "Why did you buy life insurance?" I asked him.

"Well," he said, "it was because once I met a young person coming up the stairs of an apartment house with her arms full of packages, one of them dangling from a slender string. I didn't think she'd mind, so I offered to help her. At the door of her apartment, I saw that she was quite pretty. She still is.

"Because late one night, while she and I were waiting at a dimly lighted railway station for the Owl to take me home, I said, 'We could live on the money I'm spending for railroad fares! What do you say we try it?' We did, and it worked.

"Because one day I was offered a job by another company, and when I told my boss, he promised me ten dollars more a week if I'd stay. When I told *her* of the boss's generosity, she said, 'What do you mean, generous? If he knew you were worth that much to him he should have paid it to you before he had to.' So I quit and took the new job.

"Because one night she woke me up and said, 'I think I'd better go.' We went, and the last I saw of her that night, she was being trundled down a long corridor in a wheelchair, in spite of her protests that she could walk. When I saw her the next morning, she was lying very still and white and with the sweetish smell of ether on her breath. A nurse came in and asked, 'Wouldn't you like to see him?' But I wasn't interested in babies just then—not even our own."

THE STORY OF AUNT MEG

Said a Greek playwright to an aspiring writer: "If you want me to laugh, you must laugh first. If you want me to weep, you must weep first." That is why the best writing often comes out of a writer's own experience. In order to transmit an experience, the writer must feel the experience.

I first read the Aunt Meg ad many years ago. Its purpose was to sell Barre Granite grave stones. This is not an easy task. I have read the ad several times over the years, and each time it moved me. Each time I felt what the writer felt.

Here is the first part of the ad:

Headline:

AUNT MEG . . . WHO NEVER MARRIED

Copy: I remember the night Jim Foster went off to war . . . that last brave flutter of the handkerchief . . . and the sigh of the whistle as the train crossed the bridge over Matthews' Falls.

Aunt Meg never talked about Jim Foster. She lived with us till we grew up, moving through all the golden memories of childhood . . . the sound of her voice reading in the dim room the time Jane and I had measles . . . her hands arranging roses in a silver bowl on summer mornings . . . the far-away songs she used to sing.

Aunt Meg never married. And the hopes that echoed in her smile departed with the flutter of the handkerchief, the train whistle sliding into silence behind the mountains.

Aunt Meg died ten years ago, gone to her memories, and leaving happy memories behind. And when we think of her we remember the beauty of all that made her life . . . the scent of roses, distant music, summer light and shadow . . .

When someone we loved has passed away, we face the problem of a suitable memorial—a memorial in keeping with the depth of our affection and the character of the person we wish to honor.

SUMMING UP

Any good writer can write an acceptable reason-why ad. You simply state the sales arguments in proper sequence and in simple language.

It takes an exceptional writer to write story copy. A story comes from the heart, not the head. It goes to the heart, not the head.

Reason-why copy makes the reader nod in agreement with your arguments. Reason-why copy is a necessary ingredient in every good advertisement.

But a good story lights a fire in the reader's subconscious mind. It stirs him to action. In the case of a direct-response ad it makes him reach for a pen and an order form.

If you can skillfully combine reason-why copy with story copy, you can produce an irresistible advertisement.

The Hartford found a cure for hijacking in a cup of coffee.

The trucker was on schedule when he made his usual roadside stop for coffee. That's what the hijackers were counting on. The gang struck the same fleet's trucks again, at a cost of hundreds of thousands of dollars in lost cargo.

Once alerted to the crimes, The Hartford's loss prevention service suggested ways to stop the hijackings. We recommended drivers alternate rest stops so hijackers wouldn't know where to strike. And because it's harder to hijack a truck outside city limits, we suggested drivers make their first rest stop at least 100 miles from the city terminal.

Besides stopping the hijackings, our loss prevention counseling also helped lower the fleet's insurance rate. Proving that when losses go down, rates don't have to go up.

Whatever business you're in, you can always benefit from a loss prevention program. It can help you find better ways to prevent thefts, injuries, accidents, and lawsuits. And that can help you avoid costly business interruptions due to fires or accidents.

The Hartford has over 60 years of experience in designing loss prevention programs for every type of business. Our over 500 loss prevention experts located coast to coast can advise you on chemistry, engineering, product liability, transportation, health care, construction, fire safety, industrial hygiene, and other fields.

It adds up to the kind of preventive help businesses of all sizes need but can't always afford on their own. Which is why more of them are asking for The Hartford's help—and getting results.

To see how loss prevention can make a difference in your business, contact your local independent agent who represents The Hartford.

Get in touch today. After all, wouldn't you rather get help than get hurt?

The best protection is prevention.

THE HARTFORD

The Hartford Insurance Group, Hartford, Connecticut 06115

An Ad That Tells a Story

People like to read stories. An effective way to get people to read your ad is to tell a story. After they start reading your copy, you can lead them into your sales talk. Both the picture and the headline in this ad suggest an interesting story.

This Story Ad Became Famous

This ad tells the story of why a Barre Granite tombstone was chosen. The ad was one of a series that achieved "best read" status in magazines. Sales of Barre Granite Memorials increased about 600 percent. For the complete history of this ad campaign see Julian Watkins book *The 100 Greatest Advertisements* (Dover Publications).

One of a Famous Series

Gerard Lambert of the Lambert Pharmaceutical Company was looking for an idea to increase the sales of Listerine. In an old medical book he found the word *halitosis,* from the Latin *halisus,* meaning exhalation. Ad stories were written about people who became unpopular because of offensive breath. The ads said: "The insidious thing about halitosis is that you, yourself, never know when you have it. And since the subject is so delicate, even your best friend won't tell you."

He came to a land of wooden towns
and left a nation of steel

IN AN ATTIC in Dunfermline, Scotland, he was born on November 25th a hundred years ago—the son of a man and woman who later dared the great adventure of crossing the Atlantic to find opportunity.

They sailed seven weeks in a wooden ship and landed in a country of wooden towns.

From New York to Pittsburgh was another three weeks' journey, by the Erie Canal and the Lake to Cleveland, thence down a canal to Beaver, and up the Ohio River. Andrew was thirteen years old. Before he had reached middle age, steel rails had joined New York and Pittsburgh, and steel Pullmans rolled over them in ten hours. He lived to see automobiles of steel travel from city to city in a day. Now airplanes, powered by gasoline explosions inside cylinders of steel, span the distance in a hundred minutes; and the Atlantic crossing has changed from seven weeks of danger to a hundred hours of comfort in a floating steel hotel.

Great eras are the work of great men. And great men flourish only when they are needed. When a country ceases to need them, it is no longer great. Andrew Carnegie became a master builder because America needed him and welcomed him.

Does our country no longer need great builders? Have we no frontiers left, as some would assert?

Andrew Carnegie, if he were alive, would be the first to deny it. United States Steel, which carries forward the industry he helped to create, protests against any such counsel of despair.

The economic pains we have had are the pains of adolescence—not the pains of old age. America is built, but men are dreaming of building it better.

Those vital arteries of national life, the railroads, are to be rebuilt. New steels—rustless,* stronger, lighter—will lift the burden of dead weight from rolling stock and make transportation more economical and efficient.

Twenty-five million homes are to be rebuilt, and steel will be there to hold comfort and health within the walls—to lift the threat of fires that have wiped out whole communities, from country villages to cities as large as Chicago.

Twenty-five million automobiles are to be replaced with lighter, stronger, safer cars. Already thousands of miles of steel and concrete highways have been laid, and thousands more miles must be added.

Will America ever be finished? Never as long as American ingenuity begets ideas and American ambitions remain unsatisfied.

The nation that Andrew Carnegie helped to build will be rebuilt and *rebuilt* again. Always with more and more steel.

AMERICAN BRIDGE COMPANY · AMERICAN SHEET & TIN PLATE COMPANY · AMERICAN STEEL & WIRE COMPANY
CANADIAN BRIDGE COMPANY, LTD. · CARNEGIE-ILLINOIS STEEL CORPORATION · COLUMBIA STEEL COMPANY
CYCLONE FENCE COMPANY · FEDERAL SHIPBUILDING & DRY DOCK COMPANY · NATIONAL TUBE COMPANY
OIL WELL SUPPLY COMPANY · SCULLY STEEL PRODUCTS COMPANY · TENNESSEE COAL, IRON & RAILROAD COMPANY
U. S. STEEL PRODUCTS COMPANY · UNIVERSAL ATLAS CEMENT COMPANY · *United States Steel Corporation Subsidiaries*

UNITED STATES STEEL

Institutional Advertising at Its Best

The effect of institutional advertising is almost impossible to measure. No coupons. No order forms. No sales figures. Hence this form of advertising has been downgraded in some circles. Nevertheless some magnificent institutional ads have been published. Here is one which ran shortly after U.S. Steel began its first ad campaign. (Copy by BBDO.)

The Lazy Man's Way to Riches

'Most People Are Too Busy Earning a Living to Make Any Money'

I used to work hard. The 18-hour days. The 7-day weeks.

But I didn't start making big money until I did less—a *lot* less.

For example, this ad took about 2 hours to write. With a little luck, it should earn me 50, maybe a hundred thousand dollars.

What's more, I'm going to ask you to send me 10 dollars for something that'll cost me no more than 50 cents. And I'll try to make it so irresistible that you'd be a darned fool not to do it.

After all, why should you care if I make $9.50 profit if I can show you how to make a *lot* more?

What if I'm so sure that you *will* make money my Lazy Man's Way that I'll make you the world's most unusual guarantee?

And here it is: I won't even cash your check or money order for 31 days *after* I've sent you my material.

That'll give you plenty of time to get it, look it over, try it out.

If you don't agree that it's worth *at least a hundred times* what you invested, send it back. Your *uncashed* check or money order will be put in the return mail.

The only reason I won't send it to you and bill you or send it C.O.D. is because both these methods involve more time and money.

And I'm already going to give you the biggest bargain of your life.

Because I'm going to tell you what it took me 11 years to perfect: How to make money the Lazy Man's Way.

O.K.—now I have to brag a little. I don't mind it. And it's necessary—to prove that sending me the 10 dollars... which I'll keep "in escrow" until you're satisfied... is the smartest thing you ever did.

I live in a home that's worth $100,000. I know it is, because I turned down an offer for that much. My mortgage is less than half that, and the only reason I haven't paid it off is because my Tax Accountant says I'll be an idiot.

My "office," about a mile and a half from my home, is right on the beach. My view is so breathtaking that most people comment that they don't see how I get any work done. But I do enough. About 6 hours a day, 8 or 9 months a year.

The rest of the time we spend at our mountain "cabin." I paid $30,000 for it cash.

I have 2 boats and a Cadillac. All paid for.

We have stocks, bonds, investments, cash in the bank. But the most important thing I have is priceless: time with my family.

And I'll show you just how I did it—the Lazy Man's Way—a secret that I've shared with just a few friends 'til now.

It doesn't require "education." I'm a high school graduate.

It doesn't require "capital." When I started out, I was so deep in debt that a lawyer friend advised bankruptcy as the only way out. He was wrong. We paid off our debts and, outside of the mortgage, don't owe a cent to any man.

It doesn't require "luck." I've had

more than my share, but I'm not promising you that you'll make as much money as I have. And you may do better; I personally know one man who used these principles, worked hard, and made 11 million dollars in 8 years. But money isn't everything.

It doesn't require "talent." Just enough brains to know what to look for. And I'll tell you that.

It doesn't require "youth." One woman I worked with is over 70. She's travelled the world over, making all the money she needs, doing only what I taught her.

It doesn't require "experience." A widow in Chicago has been averaging $25,000 a year for the past 5 years, using my methods.

What *does* it require? Belief. Enough to take a chance. Enough to absorb what I'll send you. Enough to put the principles into *action*. If you do just that—nothing more, nothing less—the results *will* be hard to believe. Remember—I guarantee it.

You don't have to give up your job. But you may soon be making so much money that you'll be able to. Once again—I guarantee it.

The wisest man I ever knew told me something I never forgot: "Most people are too busy earning a living to make any money."

Don't take as long as I did to find out he was right.

I'll prove it to you, if you'll send in the coupon now. I'm not asking you to "believe" me. Just try it. If I'm wrong, all you've lost is a couple of minutes and a postage stamp. But what if I'm right?

Sworn Statement:

I have examined this advertisement. On the basis of personal acquaintance with Mr. Joe Karbo for 18 years and my professional relationship as his accountant, I certify that every statement regarding his personal and business status is true. [Accountant's name available upon request.]

Bank Reference:
Citizens Bank of Costa Mesa
2970 Harbor Boulevard
Costa Mesa, California 92626

Joe Karbo
17105 South Pacific, Dept. 437-D
Sunset Beach, California 90742

Joe, you may be full of beans, but what have I got to lose? Send me the Lazy Man's Way to Riches. *But don't deposit my check or money order for 31 days after it's in the mail.*

If I return your material—for *any* reason—within that time, return my *uncashed* check or money order to me. On that basis, here's my ten dollars.

☐ Please send First Class. I'm enclosing an extra dollar.

Name _____

Address _____

City _____

State _____ Zip _____

© 1976 Joe Karbo

How to Work Less and Earn More

"I used to work hard. The 18-hour days. The 7-day weeks. But I didn't start making big money until I did less—a lot less." Those are the words with which Joe Karbo begins this irresistible testimonial-style ad. The ad has many advantages. Long copy—900 words. Short sentences. Short paragraphs. A list of benefits. Proof that his method is easy. A sworn statement. A money back guarantee. This ad has been repeated many times.

"God: Give me the strength to smile..."

The Ad I Didn't Want to Write

Jim Breslov called this, "The ad I didn't want to write." He said: "You see, I, myself, am the man in the picture. This is something that happened to me—and this ad, feeble as it may be, was a first effort to strike back."

How to Get High Readership

For more than 50 years, readership studies have shown that comic strips are among the best read features in publications. Making an ad look like a comic strip can greatly increase readership. This ad tells the Reynolds Wrap story in attractive comic strip form.

Now JAL offers full-fare passengers special privileges before, during and after the flight.

JAL feels that the full-fare passenger deserves better than just a couple of free in-flight gestures. That's why JAL's Executive Service starts working for you the minute you book. Ask your Travel Agent, Corporate Travel Dept. or Japan Air Lines for further details. And find out what it is like to be pampered Japanese style, all the way.

We never forget how important you are.

JAPAN AIR LINES

Bilingual business cards, English on one side, Chinese or Japanese on the other, at a nominal fee.

Special Executive check-in at selected airports.

True Japanese hospitality in the Executive Service section.

Free earphones—for in-flight entertainment.

Free alcoholic beverages—cheers!

1st Class offers the Sky Sleeper Service, a private bed at an additional charge, on all 747 Transpacific flights.

JAL's Executive Hotel Service offers a room at a special rate and allows check-out as late as 6 p.m.

At hotels all over the Orient, JAL's Hospitality Desks give any assistance you may need.

The Executive Service Lounge in the Imperial Hotel, Tokyo, "your office away from the office."

Executive Service

A Sales Talk in Print and Pictures

In the primary grades in school, children read textbooks that have captions printed under the illustrations. Thus the habit of reading captions under pictures is formed early in life. Readership studies show that this habit is continued throughout life. People will often skip the big print in ads and read the picture captions set in small print.

"You are going to have national advertising whether you want it or not!"

Bruce Barton

Bruce Barton is best known as one of the founders of BBDO. He was nominated to the Advertising Hall of Fame in 1969, and served as a U.S. Congressman for five years.

Some years back, Bruce Barton and others from BBDO went to Pittsburgh to present a new advertising campaign to U.S. Steel.

Some startling news awaited them: U.S. Steel had decided to stop its national advertising.

Any comments, Mr. Barton? Yes, indeed!

"Gentlemen, you can can cel your national advertising; that is, if you mean canceling the limited fraction of your advertising you originate and place.

"The part you do not and cannot control will roll on in ever-increasing volume. It is the advertising given you by politicians with axes to grind...by demagogs who may point you out as typical of all that is bad in big business...by newspapers that hope to build circulation by distorting your acts... by labor leaders misrepresenting your profits...by all other operators in the field of public opinion, some unfriendly and many merely misinformed.

"Thus you are going to have national advertising whether you want it or not!"

Mr. Barton went on: "...in the present state of world politics, where the electorate is the court of final appeal in ALL business decisions, can you afford to take the risk of having *all* your advertising emanate from sources beyond your control?"

The advertising was reinstated.

Bruce Barton's point is even more important today when, literally, *everybody* can influence a corporation's life — not just traditional *"thought leaders."* Because, quite frankly, they don't exist anymore. Nowadays, you don't go after thought leaders, but after thoughtful millions.

So today, this is the logic many companies apply to their corporate advertising:

1. The time to make friends is before you need them.

2. You never know where you will need friends tomorrow.

3. So, your corporate advertising should try to make friends everywhere — among millions.

4. You stand the best chance of making friends among reasonable, open-minded people.

5. Especially when you catch them in a friendly mood, prepared to believe what you have to say.

Which has led to this conclusion for some of America's best companies:

Run corporate advertising in Reader's Digest.

For scores of major U.S. companies, it really pays off.

Reader's Digest
The place to make friends for your company.

Quote from Sid Bernstein's column in Ad Age (6/26/78).

The Day U.S. Steel Decided to Stop National Advertising

This ad tells about a dramatic incident in the life of a famous adman. Bruce Barton is best known as one of the founders of BBDO. He was elected to the Advertising Hall of Fame in 1969 and served as a U.S. Congressman for five years.

10

Tips on Copywriting: 12 Ways to Get Started, 11 Ways to Keep Going, 14 Ways to Improve Your Copy

The hardest part of copywriting is getting started. When you sit down to write an ad, your mind is cold. It is like the engine of an airplane that has been parked all night on the runway. It takes extra power to get off the ground. The same is true with writing. It takes extra power to get started.

Listed below are tested ways to warm up your mental motor. These proven methods have helped many copywriters start the flow of words. Not all of the methods will work for you. Select the methods that suit you best.

12 WAYS TO GET STARTED

1. Don't Wait for Inspiration

Start by starting. One writer said: "I sit down and write the word *the* over and over again until other words come into my head."

If you wait for inspiration, you will build up a mental blockade. Nothing you think of will sound good enough to write down. The blank sheet of paper in front of you will remain blank. You will end up writing . . . nothing.

In the beginning it doesn't matter what you write. Write words, phrases, random thoughts—anything. The idea is to get your typewriter going—or to start your pencil moving across the page. Your output will improve as you put on paper every thought that comes into your head.

2. Start with Something Easy

A friend of mine who writes a lot of letters gets started by addressing envelopes first. It takes little mental effort to copy names and addresses from an address book. But the mechanical action of using a pen helps to start the flow of ideas.

3. Write as if Talking to a Companion

Dr. Samuel Johnson said of an acquaintance: "He was brisk as a bee in conversation but the touch of a pen made his hand numb." Many copywriters have had the experience of being able to talk about a product, but unable at times to put anything on paper.

David Ogilvy said: "In writing an ad for an automobile, I imagine that I am sitting beside a woman companion at a dinner party. I simply write down what I would say about the car to my companion."

4. Write a Letter to a Friend

Write your copy as if you were writing to one person— someone you know and like. Forget the millions of readers or viewers. The thought of a vast audience will cramp your writing style. Remember that only one person at a time will read your copy. Write to that one individual. Queen Victoria of England once complained to her prime minister, Benjamin Disraeli: "You speak to me, not as a person, but as if I were Parliament."

Make believe you are writing a letter to your best friend. Put down the words "Dear Joe." Then tell Joe everything you want him to know about a wonderful new product you have just discovered. Get excited. Get worked up. Let your words tumble out in a torrent of enthusiasm. Then turn your letter into an ad.

5. Forget the "Do's" and the "Don'ts"

Forget, for the time being, the technical specifications of the product. They can be put in later. Forget the legal restraints. The lawyers will take care of them. If you write with a string of *do's* and *don'ts* in your mind, you will write cold copy. And cold copy can never be warmed up. Write hot copy. It can be toned down later. It will still retain warmth.

6. Describe the Product

An easy way to start is to describe the product. If it is a small item—a packaged product or a mechanical gadget, put it on your desk and make a list of its qualities such as size, shape, color, etc. Then pick a key word that fits the item. Let's say the word is *small*. Write down the word *small*, and then write down the advantages that the word suggests, such as: portable, compact, light, handy, easy to carry, put it in your pocket, etc.

7. Make a List of Benefits

Write down a list of benefits that the product or service will give to the customer. Include the positives and the negatives. The positives are the advantages the customer will gain by using the product. The negatives are the disadvantages the customer will suffer if he fails to buy the product.

8. Write What Interests You Most

Begin by writing about the particular feature of the product that interests you most and excites you most. That way you will write with enthusiasm. Your enthusiastic style of writing is likely to stay with you when you describe other features of the product. If you want your reader or listener to be enthusiastic about the product, you must be enthusiastic first. Lead the way, and he will follow you.

9. Get Inspiration from Others

If you want to write a retail ad, you can guide your mind into the retail style of copy by reading retail ads in your daily newspaper. If you want to write a classified ad, you should read classified ads and steep yourself in their telegraphic, abbreviated style. The same approach can be applied to corporate image ads, institutional ads, packaged product ads, etc. On the other hand, if you want to write a hard-sell mail-order ad, make a collection of mail-order ads that have been repeated again and again. These are the ads with proven records of sales success. Read them and use their tested methods when you write your own ad.

10. Copy Successful Copy

Put a successful ad on the desk in front of you and start copying it in your own handwriting, word for word, sentence by sentence. This will limber up your writing muscles and unclog your brain. After you have been copying for awhile, you can put the ad aside and start writing your own copy.

11. Start by Writing Headlines

See if you can state a product advantage in headline form. The headline may be four words, or seven words, or ten words, or even fifteen words.

Get these words down on paper. Then do the same with other product advantages. Keep this up until you have portrayed, in concise language, every product benefit you can think of.

Keep paper and pencil handy wherever you are. Keep thinking about the product. Write down every headline that comes to mind. Later on, you can select the headline that seems best—the headline that promises the most important benefit to the prime prospect. Then write your first paragraph by enlarging on that important benefit.

How about the other headlines you have written? Some of these may be used as subheads or as sentences in your copy.

12. Write Fast and Edit Later

A copywriter said: "I hate to write, but I like to edit. So I write fast. I put on paper everything I can think of. I get the creative process over with as quickly as possible. Then I sit back and review what I have written. This part of the job is fun. Sometimes I edit a piece of copy four or five times before I am satisfied with it."

*   *   *

As mentioned above, not all of these methods will work for everybody. Choose the method that works for you.

11 WAYS TO KEEP GOING

The two greatest barriers the copywriter faces are: (1) inability to get started, and (2) inability to keep going. Tested ways to keep words and ideas flowing are discussed below.

If you have trouble sticking to your work, you are not alone. Some famous writers have had the same difficulty. For example:

Ernest Hemingway—"I start with a blank piece of paper and put all I know at the time on blank paper. Most of the time it is tough going."

Stuart Cloete—"I have cycles of writing. I work like hell for three months, and then for a month or more I'm certain that I'll never have another word to say."

William Styron—"I get a fine, warm feeling when I'm doing well . . . but that pleasure is pretty much negated by the pain of getting started each day. When I'm writing steadily, I average two and a half or three pages a day—longhand on yellow sheets. I spend about five hours at it, of which very little is spent actually writing."

Joseph Conrad (in a letter to his editor)—"I sit here religiously every morning. I sit down for eight hours every day—and sitting down is all. In the course of that working day of eight hours, I write three sentences which I erase before leaving the table in despair. At night I sleep. In the morning I get up with the horror of that powerlessness I must face through a day of vain efforts." (Yet Conrad kept going and wrote great novels.)

Bergen Evans—"I usually begin by going over what I wrote yesterday, to get warmed up. It always seems that there is a paragraph or two that can be improved, something I finished in haste the preceding day. I do such paragraphs over and in doing this, I get ideas started and carry on."

Somerset Maugham—"No professional writer can afford to write only when he feels like it. If he waits until he is in the mood, till he has the inspiration, he waits indefinitely. The professional writer creates the mood. He has his inspiration, too, but he controls and subdues it to his bidding by setting himself regular hours of work.''

KEEPING GOING

Listed below are some tested ways that have helped advertising copywriters to keep going:

1. Make an Outline

Some copywriters find that it helps them to outline an ad before starting to write. Some use a written outline. Some make a mental outline. An outline gives your ad a starting point, a middle and an ending. Example:

Headline
First paragraph
Recital of benefits
Proof of claims
Testimonials
Urge to action
Reason to act now

An outline helps you to keep going because you always have something ahead to give you direction—to keep you on the right track.

2. Choose the Writing Tools That Work Best for You

Some copywriters prefer a typewriter. They like to see their copy in neatly typed lines. The sound and the rhythm of the typewriter inspires them and keeps them going. Certain writers have said that they prefer an old-fashioned typewriter that they have used for years. They believe that the ancient machine has brought them good luck on many occasions, and they don't want to change a winning combination.

A few writers speed up their output by dictating their copy to a secretary. How they can do this, I'll never understand. I can dictate letters, but not copy. I find copywriting too difficult to be trusted to the spoken word. When I write a line of copy, I like to see my previous sentence in written form before me.

At times I write several sentences in rapid succession. Other times, I pause for five minutes between sentences. Sometimes, in trying to organize my thoughts, I stare at my desk or at the wall. Or I get up and walk around. Or I turn to my dictionary for a synonym. Under these circumstances, I would be self-conscious in the presence of another person. One copywriter said that he writes his best copy while sitting in a bathtub at home.

My favorite copywriting tools are a yellow pad, a pencil and an eraser. I like to use two pads, one for the immediate writing and the other for writing down unrelated thoughts that stray into my head. For example, while writing the first paragraph of an ad, I may think of an idea that belongs in the middle of the ad. If I don't capture this idea immediately, it may be lost. So I jot it down on the second pad—perhaps just a word or a phrase. I refer to it later. I write small and tightly so that I can easily erase and revise. I leave wide margins for revisions and afterthoughts.

One advantage handwriting has over the typewriter is that paper and pencil are available almost anytime, anywhere. And paper and pencil are silent. I can write at midnight or at 5 a.m., without disturbing anybody.

My favorite time for writing is in the early morning hours at home. I usually postpone my writing until then. But if I am given an imminent closing date, I find that I can write any time, any place—day or night. I avoid interruptions. I keep going until the job is done.

3. Work in Comfortable Surroundings

Write at a desk or a table that is large enough for you to spread out your papers and notes. Sit in a comfortable chair. Be comfortably dressed when you write. Keep your reference books handy. If you write at home, as some do, have a room, or part of a room where you can do your writing and leave your papers where they will be undisturbed when you return to them later.

4. Avoid Noise and Interruptions

Peace and quiet are important. It is true that newspaper reporters can write their copy amid noise and clatter. Of necessity, they have trained their powers of concentration to such a degree that distractions are blanked out. More power to them. But most advertising copywriters find that they can do their best work in quiet solitude—in the office or at home. In the copy department, where I first worked, there was silence most of the time. Each writer had an enclosed cubbyhole where he could shut out the world. No telephones were permitted on the desks of any of the copywriters. If you wanted to make a phone call, you went to a pay phone in another room.

5. Read What You Wrote Yesterday

There are advantages to reading over what you wrote yesterday. You can probably improve it by substituting a better word here and there. You may be able to change a long, rambling sentence into a short sentence that says the same thing and says it better. You may add an idea or two that previously escaped your notice. This editing is easy and fun. And it gets you going. It gets you back into the swing of writing. Before you know it, you are writing new material.

6. Set a Deadline

There is nothing more effective to get you going and keep you going than a deadline or a closing date.

If a deadline is not imposed upon you, it is a good idea to set one of your own. In the advertising business, your closing dates are usually specified by the media or by clients. And this is a good thing.

A closing date overcomes the human tendency to postpone and to procrastinate. If you have two days in which to write a piece of copy, you will probably take two days. But if you have only two hours, you will somehow bat it out in two hours.

Much of the work in advertising agencies is done under the pressure of closing dates. It is rush work. This has gone on for so long, that rush work has become almost a habit—a necessity, in some quarters. This story will illustrate:

A visitor was being shown through the copy department of a large agency. He saw some copywriters working feverishly, while others were idling away their time, reading books or magazines, or having coffee breaks.

The visitor said: "Don't these people have work to do?"

His guide replied: "Yes, they have work to do, but they are waiting until the closing date is near. They can't work on an assignment unless it's rush."

7. Solving Writing Problems

What do you do when you strike a problem? Do you struggle with it? Do you agonize over it without solving it?

One writer said: "I stick at it until I solve it, no matter how long it takes. If I quit at a problem point, I will have difficulty getting started again. I prefer to stop when the going is good, when I know what I'm going to say next. Then it is easy to get going again."

Another writer expressed a different view. He said: "If I am stopped by a problem, I do something else for awhile. I dictate a letter, or do some research, or work on another assignment or take a walk. Sometimes when I least expect it, a solution to the problem pops into my head."

Some writers get warmed up by working first on the easiest portions of an assignment. Once they get going, they are better able to tackle the difficult portions. Other writers say: "I can't write the second paragraph of an ad until I am satisfied with my first paragraph."

8. Avoid Self-Criticism

When you start to write, you may find that your first few sentences do not please you. Never mind. Keep on writing. A bad start is better than no start.

9. Avoid Heavy Meals Before Writing Copy

Food steals the blood from your brain and puts it into your stomach. A well-known copywriter said: "I write my best copy when I'm hungry."

10. Avoid Liquor When You Are Writing

The copy you write after two martinis sounds great while you are writing it, but the next day, it may sound terrible.

11. Advice from a Famous Author

Write regularly. Don't let your writing talent slip from your grasp through lack of use. Discipline yourself. Sinclair Lewis, author of many best-selling novels, said: "The art of writing is the art of applying the seat of the pants to the seat of the chair."

14 WAYS TO IMPROVE YOUR COPY

1. Write More Than One Headline

Your first step toward a good ad is a good headline. In the case of a sales letter, your first step is a good opening sentence.

How many headlines did you write before you selected the headline you are planning to use? Your chances of success will be greatly improved if you write five headlines or even ten headlines before you make your final choice.

2. Choose the Best Headline

How do you make your final choice? Put your headlines aside overnight. Look at them the next day. Which one promises the greatest benefits to your prime prospects? Can you combine the best qualities of two of your headlines into a single headline?

Compare your headline with these ten successful mail-order captions. Does your headline have equal force?

1. How to collect from Social Security at any age
2. The lazy man's way to riches
3. The most comfortable shoes you've ever worn or your money back
4. The secret of making people like you
5. Do you have these symptoms of nerve exhaustion?
6. Play guitar in 7 days or money back
7. How I improved my memory in one evening
8. Own a Rembrandt for only $7.95
9. To men who want to be independent in the next 10 years
10. How to retire on a guaranteed income for life

3. Do an Opinion Test

If you have written several headlines and you don't know which to choose, you can do an opinion test. Type your headlines on a single sheet of paper and make five copies. Give a copy to each of five friends or associates. Ask them to mark the headlines that interest them most. An opinion test is not the most accurate testing method, but it often reveals useful information.

4. Write More Copy Than Required . . . Then Cut

It cannot be emphasized too often that you should write more copy than you need to fill the space. If you have room for 500 words, you should write 1,000 words. Then cut your ad down to the essentials.

5. Omit Introductory Remarks

One way to cut copy is to omit introductory remarks. Suppose you have written ten paragraphs. You may find that your first paragraph is unnecessary. Or you may find that the "sell" in your ad doesn't really begin until your third paragraph.

An old saying among veteran copywriters reveals the attitude of your prospects:

> "Tell me quick and tell me true,
> Or else, my friend, the hell with you."

How to start the selling process at the very outset is illustrated by the opening sentences of successful sales letters.

1. If you could find a way to save *hundreds of dollars* a year on home and car repairs, would you do it?
2. Here's the quick, easy way to write all your business letters, without wasting time and effort.
3. From now on, you should be able to solve any kind of customer complaint—even if it never came up before.
4. Here are 33 good reasons why you should be reading *U.S. News World Report* right now
5. Here's a promise—Six months from today you can have more money in the bank—be on a sounder financial footing—even without an increase in your family income.

6. Omit Unnecessary Wordage

It is good to put your copy aside overnight, just as with headlines.

Here are things to look for when you read your copy the next day:

> Are there any paragraphs that can be omitted or cut to single sentences?
> Are there any long sentences that would be more effective if cut in two?

Are there any sentences that can be shortened? A short sentence saves space and has more punch. Examples:

Long	*Short*
He does not have any money.	He has no money.
He is a man who is very wealthy.	He is very wealthy.
There are a great many people who use this method.	Many people use this method.
It was not long before he attained the popularity he desired.	He soon became popular.

Briefly stated, here is a technique for improving copy:

Cut paragraphs to single sentences. Reduce sentences to punchy phrases. Reduce phrases to single words. Change long words to short words. Omit all unnecessary words. Cut away all the fat in your copy, until there is nothing left but bone and muscle.

7. Ask for Action

How about the ending of your ad? How can you put in extra sales punch at this crucial moment? Here are examples:

48-Piece Stainless Steel Flatware Set

At this special low price, you'll want to order one set for yourself and another as a special gift for a cherished friend. But don't delay. Supplies are truly limited. Mail the coupon today to avoid disappointment.

World of Beauty Club

Join the more than 10,000,000 women who have already discovered the fun, excitement, convenience and savings of World of Beauty. Mail your coupon today.

Viking Boots

Wear them for 2 weeks. Really test them. If you aren't completely satisfied, simply return them to us, postage prepaid, for a full refund.

Book: "How to Turn Box Tops Into Gold"

Send just $5.95. The book (plus 4 Extra Free Reports) will be sent to you immediately by return mail. Quit dropping quarters and dollars into your trash can. Claim your rightful share of the million dollar refunding giveaway now.

Here are the final paragraphs of three successful sales letters:

Fortune Magazine

It's a simple matter to return the invitation card that's enclosed. You'll be in the good company of 475,000 businessmen the world over who know a profitable idea when they see one.

Encyclopedia of Home Repair Hints

Send no money now. Simply fill in and mail the enclosed postpaid card. Book will be rushed to you for ten days absolutely free. After checking out its fantastic money-saving repair shortcuts, send us $7.95 if you'd like to keep the book. If not, just return it without cost or obligation.

Changing Times Magazine

To get your free book "99 New Ideas" and start your *Changing Times* subscription, just check and return the enclosed card. Total cost to you: only $3. That isn't much to risk—is it—to find out if you can live better, buy more and save more, than you ever did before.

8. Use Judgment in Revising Copy

Revision usually improves copy. But don't throw away your first version until you have reread it. Sometimes you will find a word or a phrase that has a freshness and spontaneity that is lacking in your revised version.

9. Read It Aloud

Read your copy aloud. This may reveal flaws that were not apparent previously. Reading aloud is especially important with radio and TV copy.

10. Ask Someone Else to Read It

Ask someone else to read your copy. Better still, ask them to read it aloud while you listen. This may uncover additional flaws.

11. Invite Criticism

If you want a true opinion of your copy, find a real critic, not just a praising friend.

12. Give Your Critic a Choice

You will get a more revealing judgment of your copy if you show your friend two ads, not just one. Ask two questions: (1) Which ad did you like better? (2) Why did you like it better?

13. Aim for the Stars

Set high standards for yourself. Do not let an ad leave your hand when a better word will improve it. You are competing with the best ad writers in the United States.

14. Write Every Day

Write something every day. A machine that is not used regularly gets rusty. Once stopped, it may never start again. I know a copywriter who quit writing for a spell. He was disappointed when he tried to take up writing again. His hand had lost its skill.

I know another writer, now retired, who has retained his writing ability by writing ads and sales letters for local merchants, for charities, for church bazaars, etc. He is doing on a small scale the same kind of work he used to do on a large scale. Sometimes he works for pay, sometimes for free. He says that he is having more fun than he ever had in his life.

The ability to write is a priceless gift. Unlike many other activities, it can stay with you for life *if you practice it regularly.*

SUMMARY OF 37 TIPS ON COPYWRITING

For your convenience, in three specific groups, the 37 tips on copywriting are summarized below:

12 Ways to Get Started

1. Don't wait for inspiration
2. Start with something easy
3. Write as if talking to a companion
4. Write a letter to a friend
5. Forget the "do's" and the "don'ts"
6. Describe the product
7. Make a list of benefits
8. Write what interests you most
9. Get inspiration from others
10. Copy successful copy
11. Start by writing headlines
12. Write fast and edit later

11 Ways to Keep Going

1. Make an outline
2. Choose the writing tools that work best for you
3. Work in comfortable surroundings

4. Avoid noise and interruptions
5. Read what you wrote yesterday
6. Set a deadline
7. Solving writing problems
8. Avoid self-criticism
9. Avoid heavy meals before writing copy
10. Avoid liquor when you are writing
11. Advice from a famous author

14 Ways to Improve Your Copy

1. Write more than one headline
2. Choose the best headline
3. Do an opinion test
4. Write more copy than required . . . then cut
5. Omit introductory remarks
6. Omit unnecessary wordage
7. Ask for action
8. Use judgment in revising copy
9. Read it aloud
10. Ask someone else to read it
11. Invite criticism
12. Give your critic a choice
13. Aim for the stars
14. Write every day

11

How Editorial-Style Ads Can Bring Increased Sales

When Saturday Review Editor Norman Cousins decided to launch a new magazine called *World Review,* he did it with an editorial-style ad.

The ad ran three times in *The New York Times*. Here are the results:

1. A full-page ad in the weekday *Times* . . . costing $8,400 . . . pulled subscriptions worth $34,756.
2. An 850-line unit in the Sunday *Times Week in Review* . . . costing $3,536 . . . pulled orders worth $10,258.
3. A full-page ad in the Sunday *Times Book Review* section . . . costing $3,635 . . . pulled orders worth $9,909.

All told, *New York Times* readers responded with $54,923 worth of subscriptions to advertising costing $15,571.

Harry Hockman, circulation director of *World Review,* commented: "I am glad and astounded . . . We have not changed copy or art and we are selling the product at full price. Still, two-thirds of the subscriptions from *Times* readers are for three years."

Since this ad did so well on sales results, let's look at it carefully and see what made it tick. Maybe we can discover some successful methods we can use on some proposition of our own.

First of all, the Norman Cousins message did not look like an ad. It looked like a letter. It was an all-type job with this headline:

An open letter to
the readers of *The New York Times*
Norman Cousins
Two Dag Hammerskjold Plaza
New York, New York 10017

The phrase *An open letter* says in effect "This is not an ad. This is a letter."

The phrase "to the readers of *The New York Times*" mentions the name of the publication that the reader holds in his hands. This is a sure attention-getter. You can use this device in any newspaper—in any magazine. You can use it in radio or TV by mentioning the call letters of the station or channel to which the prospect is listening.

The name Norman Cousins personalizes the message. Cousins is well known to people who are prospects for an intellectual-type magazine.

The address *Two Dag Hammerskjold Plaza* has an odd sound that arouses curiosity. It does not sound like a business address. It is a United Nations address.

The ad had no illustration. An illustration would have impaired the impression that this message is a letter.

The ad had long copy—more than 800 words—set in three columns of type. You can't induce people to send money if you use short copy. You need a complete sales talk.

At the end of the message was the handwritten signature of Norman Cousins.

Below the signature was a coupon order form addressed to *World Review.*

Now let's read some of the text of the ad. It is informative. It is deeply personal. It is a heart-to-heart talk with the reader. Here is how it starts:

> *Text:* My purpose in writing is to tell you that my colleagues and I have decided to launch a new magazine. The magazine will be published every two weeks. It will be called *World Review.*
>
> Ever since I resigned from the *Saturday Review,* for reasons you may know about, I have been thinking and dreaming about the possibility of starting a magazine that, quite literally, would belong to its readers and editors.
>
> This has never been done before. Usually, new magazines call for a prodigious investment. The reason for this is the traditional way a magazine operates. Magazines and newspapers are the only products sold to the consumer at less than the cost of manufacture. Advertising is expected to

make up the difference. What compounds this problem is that the standard way of building a subscription list is through cut-rate introductory offers.

On a new magazine, the subscription list generally consists almost entirely of cut-rate introductory offers. This is why massive outside investment has usually been necessary to see a magazine through to the point where introductory-offer readers can be graduated to full-rate subscribers. Outside investment frequently means outside control—and this is something we want to avoid if we possibly can.

My hope, therefore, is that we can find enough readers willing to take a chance on us by becoming long-term subscribers from the very outset. This would make it unnecessary to seek outside financing. It would also put the reader where he should rightfully be—in a position of ultimate authority.

We decided to put these hopes to the test. I am delighted to say that the first responses to our testing have been favorable beyond our most extravagant expectations. As a result, we are scheduling our first issue for late in the spring.

At this point, Cousins wrote seven paragraphs that described, in glowing terms, the contents of the magazine.

At the end of his letter, Cousins included the following offer and coupon:

Offer: We ask no money now. That can come later. What we do need right now is an expression of your interest.

As I said above, in inviting you to join us in what we hope will be an exciting adventure in ideas, we realize we are asking you to take a chance on us. We have high hopes of justifying that confidence. The process begins with the Charter Subscription form below.

Sincerely,
Norman Cousins

(Coupon)

WORLD REVIEW
Two Dag Hammerskjold Plaza
New York, N.Y. 10017

Please enter my subscription and bill me later at the Charter rate.

☐ **$25 for three years**   ☐ **$20 for two years**

☐ **$12 for a one year subscription**

Name_____

Address_____

City_____State_____Zip_____

OTHER EXAMPLES

There have been numerous cases where a heart-to-heart talk with the reader, set in editorial style, and signed by the manufacturer, has made advertising history.

Three history-making ads that come to mind have been reproduced in Julian Watkins' book *The 100 Greatest Advertisements*. Here they are, briefly outlined.

The Introduction of the Model A Ford

Headline:

THE NEW FORD CAR

Subhead: An announcement of unusual importance to every automobile owner
by Henry Ford

Illustration: Photo of Henry Ford

First three paragraphs of copy:

Nineteen years ago we made and sold the first Model T Ford car. In announcing it to the public we said:

"We will build a motor car for the great multitude. It will be large enough for the family, but small enough for the individual to run and care for. It will be constructed of the best materials by the best men to be hired, after the simplest designs modern engineering can devise. But it will be so low in price that no man making a good salary will be unable to own one."

If I were starting in business today, or asked to restate my policy, I would not change one sentence or one word of that original announcement. In plain, simple language it gives the reason for the very existence of the Ford Motor Company and explains its growth.

*   *   *

The rest of the text consisted of four columns of copy, in Mr. Ford's own words, describing the new Ford.

Logotype: Signature of Henry Ford

Results: This ad was important news. It was followed by three ads written in a similar vein.

On the first day of the showing of the new Ford, more than ten million people visited Ford showrooms across the United States. Within a few weeks, more than 800,000 orders were received.

The Introduction of the Plymouth Car

Headline:

LOOK AT ALL THREE!

Subhead: . . . but don't buy any low-priced car until you've driven the new Plymouth with floating power.

Illustration: Photo of Walter Chrysler standing beside the new Plymouth.

2nd Subhead: A statement by Walter P. Chrysler

First three paragraphs of copy:

Thousands of people have been waiting expectantly until today before buying a new car. I hope that you are one of them.

Now that the new low-priced cars are here (including the new Plymouth which will be shown on Saturday) I urge you to carefully compare values.

This is the time for you to "shop" and buy wisely. Don't make a deposit on any automobile until you've actually had a demonstration.

*   *   *

This was followed by three columns of copy about the new Plymouth.

Bottom line of this ad: First showing next Saturday, April 2nd, at Dodge and Chrysler dealers.

(*Note:* This ad appeared when Ford and Chevrolet were the sales leaders. Plymouth was unknown.

At that time, no manufacturers mentioned competitors by name as some do today. But the meaning of the ad was clear; namely, "when you shop for a low priced car, look at all three—Ford, Chevrolet *and* the new Plymouth.")

Results: This ad was followed by two others in editorial style. The day the first ad appeared, dealers reported crowds of viewers from early morning until late at night. In a short time, Plymouth became a leader in the low-priced market.

An Ad That Sold 26,000 Neckties From One Magazine Page

This ad was written by James Webb Young, a former vice president of the J. Walter Thompson Advertising Agency. Young wrote several books on advertising including the famous *A Technique for Producing Ideas.* As a sideline, he sold merchandise by mail.

Headline:

HANDWOVEN BY THE MOUNTAIN PEOPLE
OF NEW MEXICO

Subhead: New Christmas patterns in these unique ties. Wearers say an exceptional value. Sold only direct from weavers to you.

Illustration: Color photos of sixteen neckties. Neckties are numbered so the customer can order by number.

Copy: 700 words of copy, set in small type, in two columns. Here are the first two paragraphs:

> For over 200 years, the Spanish people who settled New Mexico have been raising sheep and weaving wool. Their looms and their craft have been handed down from father to son. And the colorful landscape in which these people have lived and worked has made artists of them.
> Today I take the lovely fabrics these people weave and have them made up into such stunning ties as are shown here. These are as true reproductions as the modern color camera can get, made from the ties.

The above copy was followed by two columns of sales copy and this signature: "Webb Young, Trader, 203 Canyon Road, Santa Fe, New Mexico"

There was no order form. Instructions for ordering by mail were contained in the copy.

Results: The 26,000 neckties sold by this single magazine page were the start of a successful mail-order business.

HOW SALES WERE DOUBLED BY ADS
THAT LOOKED LIKE NEWS ITEMS

A well-known newspaper publisher decided to launch an advertising campaign to sell subscriptions to a daily business newspaper. Let us call the publication *The Business Leader*.

The campaign consisted of a series of small, frequently repeated ads in the Business Sections of Sunday newspapers in the 35 largest cities in the United States.

The ads measured seven inches deep by a single column. Each ad was illustrated with a pen and ink sketch followed by a headline, copy and logotype. Example:

Illustration:

> **Pen and ink sketch of a man reading *The Business Leader***

Headline:

HOW TO GET AHEAD
IN BUSINESS

Copy: A description of the contents of the newspaper
Logotype:

*The Business
Leader*

The last paragraph of the advertisements invited the reader to send $5 for a three-months trial subscription to *The Business Leader.*

This campaign ran for a year and was moderately successful in getting subscriptions.

A Change in Ad-Style

At the end of a year, the publisher decided that editorial-style ads might bring increased results. He switched to ads that looked like news items. The ad layouts were revised as follows:

1. The pen and ink sketches were omitted because news items do not contain pen and ink sketches. This gave room for more sales copy.

2. The ad-style type in the headlines was changed to the style of type that newspapers use for their news headlines.

3. The type in the copy was changed to the same type that newspapers use for news stories. The last paragraph contained the same offer that was in the ad-style ads; namely, "Send $5 for a 3-months trial subscription."

4. The logotype *The Business Leader,* which appeared at the bottom of the ads, was omitted because news items never contain logotypes. A logotype is a signal to the reader that "This is an ad."

Briefly stated, the ads were put together as if they had been set in the composing room of a newspaper.

One concern regarding these "news item" ads was the absence of the logotype *The Business Leader.* Most people merely glance at ads. They read only headlines and logotypes. It was feared that without a logotype, no sales message would be conveyed to newspaper glancers who read only the big print.

To compensate for the lack of a logotype, it was decided to put the name *The Business Leader* in the headline or subhead of every ad. In other words, the logotype was lifted from the bottom of the ads to a more prominent position at the top of the ads.

Here is a comparison of the two styles of layouts: Ad-style is on the left, news item-style is on the right.

(Ad-style)   *(News item-style)*

Pen and ink sketch of a man reading a newspaper

How to Get Ahead
In Business

_____
_____
_____
_____

How to Get Ahead
in Business

by reading *The Business Leader*

_____
_____
_____
_____
_____

————————— Copy —————————

The Business
Leader

————————— Copy —————————

Note these advantages of the news-item style:

1. The ad looks like a typical newspaper item.
2. The copy space is more than twice as large as the copy space in the ad on the left. This gives room for more sales talk.
3. The name of the publication, *The Business Leader,* is raised to a highly visible position at the top of the ad; namely, in the headline.
4. Because the headline contains the name of the publication, it conveys a complete sales message to newspaper glancers who read only headlines. The headline says in effect: "You will get ahead in business if you read *The Business Leader.*" Thus, there is no need to print the name, *The Business Leader,* at the bottom of the layout.

In other words, these ads did double duty:

(a) They contained a quick message to glancers that could be read in four seconds.
(b) They contained a sales message of sufficient length to sell subscriptions to interested prospects.

Since these ads looked like news items, there was concern that the newspapers would refuse to publish them. That never happened. Some newspapers printed the word *advertisement* in small type above the ads. This did not seem to hurt the pulling power of the copy.

These editorial-style ads pulled an average of more than twice as many subscriptions as the previous ad-style ads. Some pulled three or four times as many subscriptions.

Here are typical headlines of the ads. Note that each headline promises a benefit and also features the name of the product—*The Business Leader.*

HOW *BUSINESS LEADER* READERS
GET MORE OUT OF LIFE

NEW WAYS TO EARN MONEY
I FOUND IN *THE BUSINESS LEADER*

BY A SUBSCRIBER

WHY *BUSINESS LEADER*
READERS LIVE BETTER

I MADE $1000 ON A
SINGLE ITEM I FOUND IN
THE BUSINESS LEADER

BY A SUBSCRIBER

I WAS TIRED OF LIVING
ON LOW PAY—SO I STARTED
READING *THE BUSINESS LEADER*

BY A SUBSCRIBER

Sales Results

This campaign, supplemented by direct-mail advertising, was so successful that it was continued for eighteen years. During that period, the circulation of *The Business Leader* increased eightfold—from 97,000 copies sold to 840,000 copies sold.

What made this campaign so successful? The circulation director gave four reasons:

1. The ads helped to increase newsstand sales because the headlines conveyed a sales message to glancers who read only the headlines. The long copy augmented this sales effect among those persons who did take time to read the copy.

2. The ads helped *The Business Leader*'s direct-mail advertising to pull better by preselling readers on the value of *The Business Leader.*

3. The ads helped to keep present subscribers sold. When the annual renewal date arrived, the subscribers were more apt to renew their subscriptions because they had seen frequent reminders of the value of *The Business Leader.*

4. Finally, every ad produced direct sales by offering a trial subscription for $5.

The experience of *The Business Leader* is not unique. Some magazines have used this same method successfully for years. At least two of the most popular magazines in America have increased their circulation by means of small, frequently repeated ads that look like news items.

MAIL-ORDER EXAMPLES

A number of mail-order advertisers have found that:

1. Some of their most successful magazine ads have looked like magazine articles or stories.

2. Some of their best newspaper ads have looked like news items.

For example, here is a successful mail-order ad that was set in news item format. This ad has been repeated many times.

Illustration: Small photo of author of a correspondence course in writing and selling short paragraphs.

Headline:

TELLS HOW TO MAKE MONEY
WRITING SHORT PARAGRAPHS

Subhead: Chicago Man Reveals a
Short-Cut to Authorship

Second Subhead: Discloses little-known angle by which be-
ginners often get paid five to ten times more per word than
the rates paid to famous authors. Now anyone who can write
a sentence in plain English can write for money without
spending weary years "learning to write."

* * *

This was a two-column, eight-inch ad. No coupon. No logotype. The photo of the author was small. It gave the ad the
appearance of an editorial item written by a newspaper colum-
nist. This type of illustration is economical regarding space cost.
Yet it has high attention value.

The copy in this ad was so persuasive that, even though I
have no desire to get paid for writing short paragraphs, I felt a
desire to answer the ad. Here is the first paragraph:

For years and years a relatively few people have had a
"corner" on one of the most profitable authors' markets ever
known. They've been going quietly along selling thousands
and thousands of contributions. None of them had to be
trained authors. None have been "big name" writers. Yet, in
hundreds of cases, they have been paid from five to ten
times as much per word as was earned by famous authors.

This first paragraph was followed by five paragraphs of sales
copy about a home-study course put together by Mr. Benson
Barrett of Chicago.

Here are the last two paragraphs of the ad:

If you would like to see your writing in print and get
paid for it—just send your name and address on a postcard
to Mr. Barrett. He will send full information about his plan
of coaching by return mail—postage prepaid. He makes no
charge for this information. And, no salesman will call on
you. You decide, at home, whether you'd like to try his
plan. If the idea of getting paid for writing short paragraphs
appeals to you, write to Mr. Barrett for information about
these private home sessions by mail.

No telling where it might lead. Such a small start may even open opportunities for real authorship. And, since it can't cost you anything more than a postcard, you'll certainly want to get all the facts. Write Benson Barrett, Dept. 282-S, 6216 N. Clark, Chicago, Ill. 60660.

HOW A "NEWS-ITEM" AD
SELLS HEARING AIDS

Here is a small ad that has been repeated many times. Single column by four inches deep. Set in news-item style. No illustration. A dateline—Chicago, Ill.—helps to make the ad look like a typical news item.

YOU'RE NEVER
TOO OLD
TO HEAR BETTER

Chicago, Ill.—A free offer of special interest to those who hear but do not understand words has been announced by Beltone. A non-operating model of the smallest Beltone aid ever made will be given absolutely free to anyone requesting it.

Send for this non-operating model now. Wear it in the privacy of your own home to see how tiny hearing-help can be. It's yours to keep, free. The actual aid weighs less than a third of an ounce, and it's all at ear level, in one unit. No wires lead from body to head.

These models are free, so we suggest you write for yours now. Again, we repeat, there is no cost, and certainly no obligation. Thousands have already been mailed, so write today to Dept. 4861, Beltone Electronics, 4201 W. Victoria Street, Chicago, Ill. 60646.

Note these good points about this successful ad.

1. The headline promises a benefit.
2. The free offer is mentioned in the first line.
3. The word *free* is repeated three times in the copy and

is backed up in the last paragraph with the line "there is no cost and certainly no obligation."

4. The embarrassment people feel regarding a hearing aid is taken care of with the sentence "Wear it in the privacy of your own home to see how tiny hearing-help can be."

5. The entire ad is written in news-item style, and without high pressure language.

SUMMING UP

If you want to write an editorial-style ad, you should first take a look through the pages of the publication in which you are going to advertise. Select an editorial format that you can adapt to your product or service.

If you need long copy, you can use the Norman Cousins letter technique. Or you can write an ad that resembles a story, an article, a science feature, a true confession, a column of beauty hints, a recipe column or a household hint column.

If your copy is short, you can put your message into a cartoon, a comic strip, a testimonial, a quote from a famous person, or a photo with a brief sales message underneath.

A news-item style ad can be used for either long or short copy.

If you use the editorial-style approach, you will have a powerful factor working in your favor. People buy newspapers and magazines to read editorial material—not ads. Readership studies show that the reading of editorial material is five times as great as the reading of advertising.

What We All Need Now is <u>Song</u>!

*. . . sung and played
and magically transformed into
shared fun for everyone.*

WHEN was the last time you lost track of all cares of the day because you were singing so hard or concentrating on playing music? Bet you never felt so relaxed, or warm and friendly towards folks, or just plain exhilarated!

Reader's Digest knows the feeling. We know because all four of the songbooks we have published were run-away best sellers. People just couldn't get enough songs of frolic and faith and fun . . . love songs too . . . yesteryear's oldies everybody loves, as well as the new classics of recent vintage . . . songs of togetherness for all people and all ages.

And not just the words. All four Reader's Digest songbooks have brand-new playing arrangements for all "C" instruments (with guitar diagrams, chord symbols and organ pedal notes) that make playing the songs a breeze.

But don't take our word for the wonderful singing and playing fun in store for you. Choose any one—FAMILY SONGBOOK, TREASURY OF BEST LOVED SONGS, FAMILY SONGBOOK OF FAITH AND JOY, FESTIVAL OF POPULAR SONGS —or bring as many as you want into your home for your own free audition. Then get your gang together for a rousing songfest. See if you can remember having more fun or seeing more smiles.

Only if you like everything about the book or books you've picked, should you keep them. Each Reader's Digest songbook costs a remarkably low $13.95 (plus postage). That works out to about 10¢ to 14¢ a song—when sheet music these days can cost at least *ten times* 10¢. And you may pay for each book in monthly installments. If not delighted, return the book or books after your week's free singalong, owe nothing, and we will even pay you back for the return postage.

Send no money now—but use the attached postpaid card to send us your songbook choice today.

Is This a Magazine Article or an Ad?

This is an ad that ran in *Reader's Digest*. It advertises *Reader's Digest* songbooks. The last paragraph says: "Send no money now—but use the attached postpaid card to send us your songbook choice today." Editorial-style ads like this have been used for years by *Reader's Digest* to sell books and phonograph records. This method gets high readership and sales.

TIP-LESS DAYS ENDED FOR PRETTY WAITRESS

Friend's hint solves problem

WHAT *could* be the matter? Patrons she'd waited on before, tried her best to please, pointedly avoided her table when they came back. Her tips dwindled to almost nothing.

In despair she told her troubles to an old school friend who'd dropped in for lunch. Then . . . but let her friend finish the story.

"When she was waiting on me, I plainly noticed a hint of 'B. O.' I had a magazine with me. There was a Lifebuoy ad in it. I tore it out, left it folded on the table under my tip.

"Next time I went to the tea room, she was all smiles. 'Business is great,' she told me. '*Your* tip has brought me plenty of tips. I don't know how to thank you. I'm using Lifebuoy every day. No more 'B. O.' for me!' "

Thousands of letters show what harm "B. O." can do

They're coming all the time to the makers of Lifebuoy, these real letters from real people. Sometimes they're true confessions from men and women who once were guilty themselves. Sometimes (like the above) they tell of unfortunate friends who offended.

But every letter fairly shouts aloud the warning, "Don't take chances with 'B. O.' *(body odor)!*" Keep pores purified, *deodorized*, by bathing regularly with deep-cleansing Lifebuoy.

Watch your complexion improve, too, as this searching, hygienic lather rids face pores of impurities. Yet it's kind to the most delicate skin. "Patch" tests on the skins of hundreds of women show Lifebuoy is more than 20 per cent milder than many so-called "beauty soaps." Its own clean scent quickly rinses away.

Try Lifebuoy Free

If you never have tried Lifebuoy, send a clipping of this offer with your name and address to Lever Brothers Co., Dept. S-81, Cambridge, Mass. Two full-sized cakes will be sent you without cost.

An Ad That Looks Like a News Item

This newspaper ad illustrates four effective advertising methods. 1. The ad looks like a news item. Readership surveys show that news items are five times better read than ads. 2. The ad tells a human interest story. 3. To get stories, Lever Brothers ran an ad asking people to send in letters telling their true experiences. Prizes: $25 for each accepted letter. 4. The ad contains a buried offer and a key number. This tests the pulling power of the ad.

How Investors Can Save 75% on Commissions This Year
Send for free new Commission Schedule

On May 1, 1975, the Securities and Exchange Commission ruled that brokers were no longer required to charge fixed minimum commission rates as in the past. Brokers may now charge whatever rates they choose.

Many brokers are continuing to charge individual investors the same high rates as before. But the Discount Brokerage Corporation has chosen to save you money by charging rates that are much lower than previous fixed minimum commission rates – 75% lower.

For example: If you buy or sell 300 shares of a stock selling for $40 a share, we charge you $45.95, compared to the old fixed rate of $183.81. This is a saving of $137.86, or $1,654.32 a year, if you do this twelve times a year.

How can we do this? Because we do not pay commissions to salesmen and we do not maintain a costly research department, which you may not want. You pay only a very small commission for the actual transactions we perform – namely, the buying or selling of the stocks you want to buy or sell. Minimum commission: $30.

We are a member firm of the New York Stock Exchange. We are governed by the rules of the Exchange. Our clearing subsidiary, Tweedy Browne Clearing Corporation, is also a member of the New York Stock Exchange and is governed by the same rules.

It costs you nothing to become a customer of Discount Brokerage Corporation. No deposits. No advances. No commitments of any kind.

We welcome all investors, large and small. If you do only three or four transactions a year, you are a desirable customer. You can begin buying or selling at any time. You are invited to try our services with just one transaction. With our modern, computerized procedures, any size customer can be profitable for us.

Mail the coupon below or telephone for our free new Commission Schedule, which enables you to quickly understand our rates and then compare them to any broker's commission rates. You will also receive a Free Brochure which describes our assets, background and experience and tells how you can save 75% on commissions whenever you buy or sell stocks.

Call toll-free: (800) 221-4182. In New York State call collect: (212) 747-1101.

Discount Brokerage Corporation. Member New York Stock Exchange. Member Securities Investor Protection Corporation (SIPC).

. . . .

Discount Brokerage Corporation
Member New York Stock Exchange
67 Wall Street, New York, N.Y. 10005

Without obligation, please send me your free new Commission Schedule and Free Brochure. No salesman will call.

Name_____

Address_____

City_____

State_____Zip Code_____

WSJ-12-7

How to Make an Ad Look Like a News Item

1. Set the headline like a newspaper headline. 2. Set the copy in newspaper type. 3. Do not put a logotype at the bottom of the ad. 4. If a coupon is used, make it small and unobtrusive. 5. Instruct the newspaper that the ad must appear at the top of the page. This ad was repeated many times in newspapers and was very successful.

Brown's Job

Brown is gone, and many men in the trade are wondering who is going to get Brown's job.

There has been considerable speculation about this. Brown's job was reputed to be a good job. Brown's former employers, wise, gray-eyed men, have had to sit still and repress amazement, as they listened to bright, ambitious young men and dignified old ones seriously apply for Brown's job.

Brown had a big chair and a wide, flat-topped desk covered with a sheet of glass. Under the glass was a map of the United States. Brown had a salary of thirty thousand dollars a year. And twice a year Brown made a "trip to the coast" and called on every one of the firm's distributors.

He never tried to sell anything. Brown wasn't exactly in the sales department. He visited with the distributors, called on a few dealers, once in a while made a little talk to a bunch of salesmen. Back at the office he answered most of the important complaints, although Brown's job wasn't to handle complaints.

Brown wasn't in the credit department either, but vital questions of credit usually got to Brown, somehow or other, and Brown would smoke and talk and tell a joke, and untwist his telephone cord and tell the credit manager what to do.

Whenever Mr. Wythe, the impulsive little president, working like a beaver, would pick up a bunch of papers and peer into a particularly troublesome and messy subject, he had a way of saying, "What does Brown say? What does Brown say? What the hell does Brown say? —Well, why don't you do it, then?"

And that was disposed

Or when there was a difficulty that required quick action and lots of it, together with tact and lots of that, Mr. Wythe would say, "Brown, you handle that."

And then one day, the directors met unofficially and decided to fire the superintendent of No. 2 Mill. Brown didn't hear of this until the day after the letter had gone. "What do you think of it, Brown?" asked Mr. Wythe. Brown said, "That's all right. The letter won't be delivered until tomorrow morning, and I'll get him on the wire and have him start East tonight. Then I'll have his stenographer send the letter back here and I'll destroy it before he sees it."

The others agreed, "That's the thing to do."

Brown knew the business he was in. He knew the men he worked with. He had a whole lot of sense, which he apparently used without consciously summoning his judgment to his assistance. He seemed to think good sense.

Brown is gone, and men are now applying for Brown's job. Others are asking who is going to get Brown's job—bright, ambitious young men, dignified older men.

Men who are not the son of Brown's mother, nor the husband of Brown's wife, nor the product of Brown's childhood—men who never suffered Brown's sorrows nor felt his joys, men who never loved the things that Brown loved nor feared the things he feared—are asking for Brown's job.

Don't they know that Brown's chair and his desk, with the map under the glass top, and his pay envelope, are not Brown's job? Don't they know that they might as well apply to the Methodist Church for John Wesley's job?

Brown's former employers know it. Brown's job is where Brown is.

Batten, Barton, Durstine & Osborn
Incorporated
ADVERTISING
383 Madison Avenue, New York

An Ad That Became a Legend

This ad is one of a series of business essays published many years ago. It was written by former BBDO Copy Chief, Robley Feland. The ad was first used as a direct-mail piece and then it ran as a full page in *The New York Times*. The ad was so popular that it became a legend in the ad industry. For more than ten years, BBDO received requests for copies or for permission to reprint.

<u>WANTED</u>: SAFE MEN
for Dangerous Times

BUSINESS today needs, and needs desperately, executives with fresh minds and up-to-date equipment — men who are safe, not in the discarded sense of dodging decisions, but in the modern sense of *making* them and making them *right*.

During the next five very dangerous and exciting years, the new competition will make the fortunes of a lot of such men — and incidentally toss a lot of others on the scrap pile.

We are not in the least exaggerating this demand for trained executives. So badly are they needed that the key men of American business today have gone to extraordinary lengths in helping the Institute to train such executives. They have actually prepared for us a whole new Course, designed to meet the new conditions.

The authors of this new Course are men whose success belongs to the present — not the past. Their own success in the future depends in some degree upon their ability to find and develop capable assistants. That is why they have cooperated so enthusiastically with the Institute. Among them are:

Alfred P. Sloan, Jr., *President*, General Motors Corp.; Joseph P. Day, the real-estate wizard; Hon. Will H. Hays, *President*, Motion Picture Producers and Distributors of America, formerly U. S. Postmaster General; Bruce Barton, Chairman of the Board, Batten, Barton, Durstine & Osborn; John T. Madden, *Dean*, School of Commerce, Accounts and Finance, New York University; Dr. Julius Klein, *The Assistant Secretary*, U. S. Department of Commerce; George Baldwin, *Vice-President*, General Electric Company; Hubert T. Parson, *President*, F. W. Woolworth Company; David Sarnoff, *President*, Radio Corporation

of America; F. Edson White, *President*, Armour & Company; and Dexter S. Kimball, *Dean*, College of Engineering, Cornell University.

In preparing the new Course and Service we have drawn, without regard to cost, on the time and interest of these outstanding business statesmen. It is new, challenging, utterly un-academic, vibrant with the energy of men whose names are magic in the councils of modern business. So new is it that the latter sections are not yet off the presses, although the work of assembling and editing is now complete.

We have prepared a new booklet which describes this new Course and Service. It is entitled "What an Executive Should Know." It is for men of serious purpose only. It will take about an hour to read, and it is free. Frankly, it is difficult for us to understand how any man who intends to make himself independent in the next five years can afford *not* to read it.

You *must* equip yourself to deal with what lies ahead. Send for your copy of this booklet today. It will come to you by mail, without obligation.

ALEXANDER HAMILTON INSTITUTE
000 Astor Place, New York City. (In Canada address Alexander Hamilton Institute, Ltd., C. P. R. Building, Toronto.)

Send me without obligation the new booklet, *"What an Executive Should Know"*

Name_____

Business
Address_____

Business
Position_____

Type of
Business_____

Out of this depression will emerge new fortunes, new leaders . . . *You*?

A Famous Ad of the 1930's

This was one of the most result-getting ads ever published by a business correspondence school. It ran at the depth of the Great Depression of the 1930's. A remarkable feature of this ad is that, with a few minor changes, much of the copy could run today and sound as timely and inspiring as it did fifty years ago.

The PENALTY OF LEADERSHIP

IN every field of human endeavor, he that is first must perpetually live in the white light of publicity. ¶Whether the leadership be vested in a man or in a manufactured product, emulation and envy are ever at work. ¶In art, in literature, in music, in industry, the reward and the punishment are always the same. ¶The reward is widespread recognition; the punishment, fierce denial and detraction. ¶When a man's work becomes a standard for the whole world, it also becomes a target for the shafts of the envious few. ¶If his work be merely mediocre, he will be left severely alone—if he achieve a masterpiece, it will set a million tongues a-wagging. ¶Jealousy does not protrude its forked tongue at the artist who produces a commonplace painting. ¶Whatsoever you write, or paint, or play, or sing, or build, no one will strive to surpass, or to slander you, unless your work be stamped with the seal of genius. ¶Long, long after a great work or a good work has been done, those who are disappointed or envious continue to cry out that it can not be done. ¶Spiteful little voices in the domain of art were raised against our own Whistler as a mountebank, long after the big world had acclaimed him its greatest artistic genius. ¶Multitudes flocked to Bayreuth to worship at the musical shrine of Wagner, while the little group of those whom he had dethroned and displaced argued angrily that he was no musician at all. ¶The little world continued to protest that Fulton could never build a steamboat, while the big world flocked to the river banks to see his boat steam by. ¶The leader is assailed because he is a leader, and the effort to equal him is merely added proof of that leadership. ¶Failing to equal or to excel, the follower seeks to depreciate and to destroy—but only confirms once more the superiority of that which he strives to supplant. ¶There is nothing new in this. ¶It is as old as the world and as old as the human passions—envy, fear, greed, ambition, and the desire to surpass. ¶And it all avails nothing. ¶If the leader truly leads, he remains—the leader. ¶Master-poet, master-painter, master-workman, each in his turn is assailed, and each holds his laurels through the ages. ¶That which is good or great makes itself known, no matter how loud the clamor of denial. ¶That which deserves to live--lives.

Is This the Greatest Institutional Ad?

This ad for Cadillac ran just once, years ago. Yet it was voted the greatest by many admen. For more than thirty years, requests for one or more copies of the ad were received. Millions of copies have been distributed.

12

How to Write Sales Letters That Make Money

If you can catch your prospect's interest at the beginning of your sales letters, you are half-way toward making a sale.

But if your first sentence turns him off, he will never get to your order form. Your direct mail will go direct to his wastebasket.

The first sentence of a sales letter is like the headline of an ad. It decides whether you have won or lost a reader.

Direct response advertisers have tried many methods for capturing the attention of readers at the very outset. Let's take a look at ten of the most successful of these methods.

TEN WAYS TO BEGIN A SALES LETTER

1. Make an Announcement

The following announcements waste no time in arousing the interest of the prime prospect. They offer him something new—something that will benefit him in his personal life or in his business life.

Better Homes & Gardens

Dear Apartment Dweller:
    Announcing a brand new, totally different concept in publishing which singles out and gives special attention to your modern, on-the-move way of life—an exclusive new magazine expressly for you: APARTMENT LIFE

Harper & Row

Dear Friend:
    Now, a new and fully revised edition of the classic *Ink on Paper,* a handbook of the graphic arts, which has served thousands of professionals in the printing and graphic arts fields.

Prentice-Hall, Inc.

Dear Business Letter Writer:
    Here's the quick, new way to write all your business letters, without wasting valuable time and effort. Just mail

the enclosed postpaid card and I'll send you free for 10 days the greatest compilation of model business letters ever published.

2. Tell the Prospect Where His Name Was Obtained

There is flattery in the following openings. The prospect is told that he is a superior individual.

Newsweek

Dear Reader:
   If the list upon which I found your name is any indication, this is not the first—nor will it be the last—subscription letter you receive. Quite frankly, your education and income set you apart from the general population.

Centex Homes

Dear Friend:
   Finding you hasn't been easy . . .
   We screened hundreds of mailing lists to come up with a relatively small number of select people like you, who may be seeking a life-style with more comfort and convenience.

Business Week

   Your name appears on a list of people who, we believe, could profit from reading BUSINESS WEEK.
   If you are at all typical, you probably hold one or two credit cards . . . earn a 5-figure salary . . . and make several business trips a year.
   You probably invest in securities. You probably favor scotch or bourbon.

3. Use Straight Sales Talk

These letters begin with a summary of product advantages.

Harper & Row

Speakers:
Here's everything you need to know to conduct and arrange a program your audience will long remember.

Whether you are preparing for a small gathering or a giant rally, this easy-to-use book will show you exactly what your duties are, plus providing over 2,400 ideas to spark the occasion.

Good Housekeeping Magazine

How many of these 33 articles can help you? They're just a few of hundreds which have appeared in *Good Housekeeping*. You'll find more, every issue, in "The Better Way"—a magazine within a magazine—that *Good Housekeeping* readers are so enthusiastic about.

(list of article titles)

4. Make a Prediction

People are interested in predictions of things to come. Note that the prophesies in the letters below are quickly followed up by advice regarding what to do.

Prentice-Hall Tax Guide

Special Alert!
Stiff new *Emergency Tax Boosts* now slated for early action by Congress turn your current tax planning upside down—change the entire tax picture for every individual and company.

Prompt reservation of your *Federal Tax Course* brings you *free*—immediately upon enactment—an extra-measure Emergency Explanation of this costly new law.

Moneysworth

Extend your life 24 years.
One of the world's most highly respected scientists says it is now possible to add up to 24 years to your life.

Biochemist Linus Pauling, the only man in history to have won the Nobel Prize *twice,* reveals how in an exclusive interview in *Moneysworth,* America's largest newspaper on health and wealth.

Changing Times Magazine

Here's a Promise:
SIX MONTHS FROM TODAY . . .
    You can have more money in the bank
    Be on a sounder financial footing
    . . . even without an increase in your family income.
You can do these things, just as more than 1½ million other families do, by following the sound, simple money management advice presented each month in *CHANGING TIMES,* the Kiplinger Magazine.
To prove my point, I'll gladly send you the next six monthly issues of this remarkable publication at a special introductory subscription rate of only $3. And in addition, I'll send you a free copy of the coveted *CHANGING TIMES* Family Success Book, *99 New Ideas on Your Money, Job & Living.*

5. Tell a Story

Stories that combine human interest and a sales message can be wonderful selling tools. For example:

Fortune Magazine

Dear Sir:
Back in 1953, a Tokyo businessman got the idea that transistorized radios would be a fine product for his struggling new company. They were. Now Sony Corporation does an annual volume of over $100 million.
In 1963, a Montreal textile executive got the idea that the most profitable way to manufacture his product was by building a fully automated plant. Today Super Value is the largest producer in its field in Canada.
Both of these ideas came from *Fortune.*

Forbes Magazine

Dear Reader:

A prominent industrialist, now head of a U.S. government agency, once told an editor of *Forbes* that a single sentence in *Forbes* saved him a quarter of a million dollars!

The president of a well-known corporation revealed that an article in *Forbes* led to negotiations that resulted in one of the most ideal corporate mergers in recent years!

6. Use a Computer Letter

Many computer letters have been sent out in the last few years. Here is a typical example from *Reader's Digest*. The purpose of the letter is to obtain subscription sales. Using a computer makes it possible to *individualize* your letters by including specific facts such as names of neighbors and the name of a city.

Dear Mr. Thompson:

You and your neighbors, A. Columbo and Mrs. C. Fitzgerald, are among the lucky persons in Brewster selected to receive 6 Tickets in our Annual $999,000 Sweepstakes. To qualify for all prizes, use the official envelope and mail back this entire Book of Tickets by Jan. 19.

7. Make a Special Offer

Note that the first letter below can be sent only to a special group; namely, subscribers. The second letter *sounds special,* but in fact can be sent to anyone.

Kiplinger Washington Editors

Dear Mr. Caples:

Because you subscribe to our monthly magazine, *Changing Times,* you may appreciate this invitation to subscribe also to our weekly *Washington Letter* on a special try-out basis. The fee: Only $4 for the next 4 months . . . less than half the regular rate.

TV Guide

Dear Friend:
    You have been selected to enjoy *TV Guide*'s New Personal "Charge Card" Service—and that means you can have the next 34 issues of *TV Guide* delivered right to your door, in advance, every week—and save $2.22 off the regular newsstand price.

8. Use a "Last Chance" Appeal

In his book *Confessions of an Advertising Man,* David Ogilvy lists "Last Chance" as one of the great motivating devices.

Good Housekeeping

If you act at once you can get 24 issues of *Good Housekeeping* for only $5.00, same as the regular one-year price.

McCall's

Dear Subscriber:
    This is the only opportunity you will have for advance renewal of your present *McCall's* subscription—before prices go up.

9. Tell How to Save Money

Among the most frequently used devices are money appeals such as: save money, get discounts, avoid expensive errors, etc.

Consumer Reports

Dear Consumer:
    How much can making the wrong decision cost you?

Consumers Digest

Why pay high list prices . . . when you can save hundreds of dollars on big discounts like these:
    (list of discounts)

Money Magazine

Dear Reader:

Can a magazine help you fight inflation? Can it help you get more out of every dollar you earn, spend, save or invest these days?

MONEY can. That's why it is growing so fast.

RCA Music Service

Dear Friend:

I would like to offer you the opportunity to get the kind of music you like best, at *very dramatic savings.*

10. Include a Free Offer

In his book, *My First Sixty Years in Advertising,* Maxwell Sackheim said, "Sixty years ago, the strongest word for getting attention was FREE. Today the strongest word is still the word FREE."

Sackheim's statement is borne out by the fact that the sales device most frequently used in direct mail today is a free offer. Examples:

Northwestern Mutual Life Insurance Co.

Dear Friend:

We would like you to have, with our compliments, a Johnson & Johnson First Aid Kit.

We are offering you this kit because we believe prudent people like to be prepared for those unexpected little crises—and big ones, too.

(*Note:* Reply card asks for prospect's age and what type of insurance he is interested in. This information is useful to insurance salesmen.)

Texaco

Dear Friend:

This is a free trial offer from Texaco.

Texaco is making available through its Star Value program, that complete set of matched Teflon coated cooking utensils you have been promising yourself for some time.

General Cigar Co.

Dear Sir:

To get you acquainted with our brand new Robt. Burns cigars, we'd like you to try 5 of them at our expense.

Just give the enclosed gift certificate to your cigar retailer. He'll give you five new Robt. Burns cigars absolutely free.

Real Estate Corporation

Dear Friend:

Here's an unusual offer you'll want to take advantage of today. Mail the post-paid card and receive absolutely free an important booklet—now in its fourth printing—published by Prentice-Hall, Inc.

The booklet and its accompanying information explains why land is your key to profit and security and is entitled, "How to Successfully Invest in Real Estate." It's yours without any obligation at all.

Some of the above methods can be used in the body of the letter. For example: If the headline of the letter is an announcement, you could tell in the body of the letter where the prospect's name was obtained.

ENVELOPE HEADLINES

Another method for catching your prospect's interest at the very outset is to print a catchy headline on the front of the envelope. This helps to keep your letter from being discarded without being opened. Here are examples of envelope headlines.

OPENING THIS ENVELOPE CAN
MAKE YOU $100,000 RICHER

FREE TO HIGH SCHOOL TEACHERS
$6 TO OTHERS

TWO SPECIAL INCENTIVES
TO HELP YOU GET STARTED IN WRITING

DISCOUNT INFORMATION ON THE NEW
AMERICAN AUTOMOBILES AND
THOUSANDS OF OTHER PRODUCTS

HOW TO LIVE BETTER FOR LESS

AN INVITATION TO JOIN 2 MILLION
COST-CONSCIOUS FAMILIES IN GETTING
MORE FOR YOUR BUYING DOLLAR

JUST SEND US ONE DIME WITHIN 10 DAYS
AND YOU GET ANY 8 TAPES OR RECORDS FOR ONLY $.99

DO WORKING WOMEN AGE FASTER?

YOU ARE INVITED TO APPLY
FOR THE FIRST 30 DAYS OF
INSURANCE COVERAGE FOR ONLY $.10

IF YOU ARE ELIGIBLE FOR MEDICARE
. . . HERE IS IMPORTANT NEWS

NEW INCOME TAX INFORMATION ENCLOSED

FREE SAMPLE AND
MONEY-SAVING COUPONS INSIDE

A GIFT FOR A FAVOR

INSIDE THIS ENVELOPE YOU WILL FIND
A COLLECTOR'S FOREIGN COIN AND STAMP

AN ALTERNATIVE METHOD

Some advertisers have had success with blank envelopes that contain only the prospect's name and address. No company name is printed on the front of the envelope. Nothing whatever is printed on the back of the envelope. There is no clue regarding what the envelope contains. This may arouse the prospect's curiosity and cause him to open letters which might otherwise have been discarded.

TESTING DIFFERENT BEGINNINGS

A veteran mail-order man said: "Never send out a letter without testing *something*."

So, the next time you send out a sales letter, why not test two different envelope headlines or two different opening paragraphs.

For example, you could print Envelope Headline A on half the letters and Envelope Headline B on the other half. Suppose Headline A pulls 20 percent greater response than Headline B. This would show you the way to 20 percent greater profits on future mailings.

In the same way, two different opening paragraphs could be tested.

Also, in the same way, you could test a perfectly blank envelope versus an envelope containing a sales headline and the name and address of the sender.

A SALES LETTER THAT HAS
MADE MONEY FOR 17 YEARS

One of the most successful sales letters of all time is the famous Kiplinger "Boom or Bust" letter.

Half a *billion* copies of this letter have been mailed out in the last 17 years.

The letter sells subscriptions to the Kiplinger Washington Newsletter. Scores of letters have been tested against it, but the "Boom or Bust" letter always wins.

What makes this letter so successful? A number of mail-order experts have agreed that much of its success is due to the headline printed at the top of the letter; namely:

NEW BOOM AND MORE INFLATION AHEAD
. . . and What YOU Can Do About It

This same headline is also printed on the envelope.

This headline contains a promise, a warning and a benefit, as follows:

    1. PROMISE. The reader is happy to hear that a new boom is coming. He wants to know more about it and how he can cash in on it.

    2. WARNING. More inflation ahead. This worries the reader. How much more inflation? How can he protect himself?

    3. BENEFIT. What *YOU* can do about it. This gives the reader a ray of hope. Maybe the letter will tell him what to do. So he reads on. The headline has accomplished its purpose.

Below is the complete letter. I suggest that you read it all. Then we will discuss its success qualities, paragraph by paragraph. You may be able to use some of these success qualities in your own sales letters.

Note: I have numbered the paragraphs in the letter for easy reference. These numbers do not appear in the actual letter.

THE KIPLINGER WASHINGTON EDITORS, INC.
1729 H Street, Northwest, Washington, D.C. 20006 Telephone: 298-6400

NEW BOOM AND MORE INFLATION AHEAD . . . and What YOU Can Do About It
(1)   Over the next few years, inflation will gallop along at nearly twice the rate of recent years . . . despite all efforts to roll it back. And business will boom again. Downturns will be short range. The long term direction of the economy will be significantly UP.
(2)   This may be hard for you to accept under today's conditions. But the fact remains that those who DO prepare for a new boom ahead will reap big dividends for their foresight . . . and avoid blunders others will make.

(3)   You'll get the information you need for this type of planning in the *Kiplinger Washington Letter* . . . and the enclosed form will bring you the next 26 issues of this helpful service on a try-out basis. The fee: Less than 54¢ per week . . . $14 for the next 6 months.

(4)   During the Great Depression, in 1935, the *Kiplinger Letters* warned of inflation and told what to do about it. Those who heeded their advice reaped rich rewards.

(5)   Again, in January of 1946, the *Letters* renounced the widely held view that a severe post-war depression was inevitable. Instead they predicted shortages, rising wages and prices, a high level of business. And again, those who heeded their advice were able to avoid losses to cash in on the surging economy of the late 40s, early 50s and mid-60s.

(6)   And now, regardless of short range prospects, Kiplinger again foresees boom and inflation ahead. And our weekly *Letters* to clients are pointing out profit opportunities . . . and also dangers.

(7)   *The Kiplinger Letter* not only reports, analyzes and interprets current developments, but gives you advance notice of new government programs . . . political moves and their real meaning . . . money policy . . . foreign affairs . . . investments . . . union plans and tactics . . . employment . . . wages . . . anything that will have an effect on you, your job, your personal finances, your family.

(8)   To try the *Letter* for the next 6 months, just check and return the enclosed form with your payment . . . or ask us to bill you or your company later. Either way, the sooner you do this, the quicker you'll profit from the penetrating forecasts, judgments and advice in each weekly issue.

Sincerely,

(Signature)
Stanley Mayes
Assistant to the President

SBM:knb

Comments

Paragraph 1 continues and amplifies the same thought that is expressed in the headline. This is good. You will never lose a reader by enlarging on the headline theme that sparked his interest in the first place.

Paragraph 2 gives the reader good news. It tells him he can reap big dividends if he will prepare himself. This leads effectively into Paragraph 3, which tells him how to prepare himself.

Paragraphs 4 and 5 add believability by telling how the *Kiplinger Letter* has helped readers reap rich rewards in the past. Believability—proof of claims, should be included in every sales letter you write.

Paragraph 6 repeats the "boom and inflation" theme, and tells what the *Kiplinger Letter* is doing for readers *right now*.

Again and again, this letter uses the "carrot and stick" technique; namely, a reward if you subscribe . . . punishment if you don't.

Religious leaders have used this appeal for thousands of years—"a reward if you subscribe to our teaching—punishment if you don't."

The repetition of a successful appeal is always good practice in a sales letter.

Paragraph 7 broadens and strengthens the appeal by including a list of specific things that the *Kiplinger Letters* will do for the reader.

Paragraph 8 is the action paragraph. It makes it easy for the reader to act and gives him a reason for immediate action. These are vital elements in closing a sale.

Enclosures in The Kiplinger Letter

The envelope in which this letter was mailed contains the following enclosures:

1. A convenient order form with the recipient's name and address typed in. This makes it easy for the

reader to order. The order form contains additional sales talk.

2. A Business Reply envelope.

3. A leaflet with this headline:

FREE—WHEN PAYMENT IS ENCLOSED WITH ORDER:
SPECIAL REPORT ON HOW TO DEAL WITH INFLATION

4. A leaflet with this headline:

FREE FOR ANNUAL SUBSCRIBERS
A SPECIAL EXECUTIVE REPORT
THAT WILL HELP YOU CASH IN
ON THE PROSPEROUS YEARS AHEAD

5. A 2-page letter entitled:

THE KIPLINGER SHOP TALK LETTER
AN IRREGULAR SUPPLEMENT TO THE REGULAR LETTERS
(THIS IS A BONUS SUBSCRIBERS GET.)

This letter with all its enclosures, is an *omnibus* full of money-making devices. Try a letter like this some time. Maybe you can put together an omnibus that will make *you* money for seventeen years.

A GREAT SALES LETTER AND
WHAT MADE IT GREAT

One of the most successful sales letters of all time is the famous "Widow" letter that sells subscriptions to *Barron's,* the financial weekly published by Dow Jones. It was written by my friend and former client, the late Leslie Davis, who was Assistant to the Publisher.

This letter has been used for more than 25 years. During that time it has out-pulled more than a hundred letters tested against it.

What makes this letter so effective? Let's analyze it and see if we can discover the secrets of its success.

Here is how the letter begins:

BARRON'S National Business and Financial Weekly
22 Cortlandt Street, New York, N.Y. 10007

Gilbert K. Good
Circulation Sales Manager

Dear Friend of *Barron's:*

Back in 1925, *Barron's* published an article suggesting how $100,000 might be well invested in securities for a widow with two small children.

The plan was based on a set of ten rules for investors, stated in the article.

The securities (stocks and bonds), all picked in accordance with the first seven of the ten rules, are today worth $482,663.

The stocks are worth $484,025—many times over their original value of $51,000.

Average annual income, for the entire forty-nine years, has exceeded $10,988.

Latest reported income was $22,017.

So here you have to date how a list of securities, compiled in the third year of Calvin Coolidge's presidency, weathered the wild twenties, the woeful thirties, World War II, and the 1969–1971 market plunge—*yet without benefit of the important interim supervision provided for in the last three of the original ten rules.*

Comment

Note the salutation "Dear Friend of *Barron's*." This is different from the usual "Dear Friend." It adds warmth to the letter, whether you are familiar with *Barron's* or not.

The letter starts with six short paragraphs containing only a single sentence each. Suppose these six paragraphs had been combined into one solid block of type. This would have been a hard-to-read stumbling block at the very outset. Short paragraphs, with plenty of white space around them, are inviting to the eye and easy to read. Remember this: If you want to get your copy read, use plenty of short paragraphs.

The first paragraph mentions a widow with two small children. This emphasizes *safety,* the most important consideration of every investor. Who would give a widow anything but the safest advice?

The next four paragraphs emphasize *profit,* the second most important consideration of investors.

Note the big increase in value—from $100,000 to $482,663. This is enough to whet the appetite of any investor.

Note the specific figure $482,663. Specific figures are more believable than rounded figures. Never forget to be specific in writing sales copy.

The letter continues as follows:

> We have now reprinted these ten rules in a little *Barron's* booklet, with interpretative comment on each rule.
>
> As a piece of printed matter, the booklet is slight; takes you but a few minutes to read.
>
> But I believe you will agree, its every word is pure gold.
>
> You'll not only welcome the ten rules for their immediate value. I venture to predict you'll also come back to them repeatedly in the future—for their help on your ever-present problem of safeguarding what you have, and making it grow and produce for you.
>
> But you can't buy this booklet. It's not for sale.
>
> I *would like you to accept* it in return for a little favor I'd like to ask of you—one that I think will interest you.

Comment

Notice the frequent use of the words *you, your* and *you'll.* These words are used eleven times in the above six paragraphs. When *you* write *your* copy, *you* should use these words as often as *you* can.

Note also how the copy builds up the reader's desire for the *Barron's* booklet.

The line "you can't buy this booklet," shocks the reader and creates an even greater desire for the booklet. That is human nature. Have you ever observed how children want something if they are told they can't have it?

The last paragraph comes as a relief to the reader. He discovers that he can get the booklet in exchange for "a little favor."

The reader's curiosity is aroused. He wants to know what the little favor is. So he has to read further. He has to read ten *paragraphs* of hard-sell copy to find the favor.

Here are the ten paragraphs:

> *Barron's,* as you probably know, is a national financial weekly—the only one published by Dow Jones, the world's largest, fastest business news-gathering organization.
>
> By virtue of this close connection—this day-in, day-out working contact with Dow Jones' reporters, analysts, editors—*Barron's* is an amazingly well-informed publication, continually surprising its readers with the intimacy and *vital investment significance* of its summaries and forecasts of industrial changes, corporate and government affairs.
>
> *Barron's* own large staff of experts weighs, sifts, interprets—to bring you each week just the information you need about business and market trends, corporation prospects, the intrinsic values of securities—clear, concise reports based on firsthand, intimate knowledge of what's going on.
>
> So you can readily see why *Barron's* (established 1921) has become the source and authority for many economists, stock-market services, investment consultants, and statisticians.
>
> Yet the information for which you pay high fees is just as basically available to you in *Barron's* weekly pages as it is to them.
>
> I think you'll agree with me we have a honey of a story:
>
> 1. A worthwhile saving on what you must pay for financial information.
>
> 2. Thoroughly reliable data every week—to guide you in the continuous supervision of your investment list—in the decisions you make on investment acquisitions or sales.
>
> 3. Comprehensive weekly trend reports—political, industrial, financial—to help you plan your investment moves with greater understanding and foresight—with fewer worries—with added peace of mind.

But you know how "funny," how unpredictable, people are. You can never be sure of their reactions until after you have spent a great deal of money to find out. That is, unless you test first.

Comment

Notice how the copy uses occasional colloquial phrases such as "a honey of a story" and "you know how 'funny' people are." This gives the reader a welcome change of pace, from serious sales facts to the conversational tone of a letter from a friend. The letter continues:

Which brings me to the favor I want to ask of you.
Before we sink a lot of money into mailing thousands of circular letters to the large key groups of prospective new readers we have in mind, we come to you as a representative prospect.
Will you do this:
Merely *try Barron's*—and judge the information in it for scope, brevity, reader interest, and practical money value.
See what you get on stock-market trends, bonds, mutual funds—"growth" stocks—situations to consider for income—securities to stay out of or sell now, because of serious weakness.
Compare *Barron's* with any other financial-information service, or combination of services, costing from $50 to $150 a year, or more. (*Barron's* costs $23 a year.)
Under this special trial arrangement, you pay ONLY OUR SHORT-TERM INTRODUCTORY PRICE, $5.75 for 13 WEEKLY ISSUES (3 months).

Comment

The above copy uses a device that has been successful in mail-order advertising since time immemorial; namely:
Start with a high price and work down to a low price.
In this case, the price reduction is from $150 to $5.75. This magnifies the bargain appeal.
Notice also that this copy doesn't seem to be selling in the usual manner. Instead it invites the reader to take part in an interesting experiment; namely, to judge the information in

Barron's. The $5.75 which the reader is asked to send seems incidental.

The copy continues in the same vein—the reader is being asked to take part in a test. Also, the reader is given a reason for immediate action. Here is the copy:

> If *Barron's* does not live up to your expectations, will you send us a brief note giving us your frank and honest opinion of it?
>
> Whether you become a *Barron's* enthusiast or not, we shall genuinely appreciate your part in this test.
>
> Of course, you understand, if your participation is to be of value to us in deciding our coming mailings to the key groups, your immediate response is necessary.
>
> Will you, therefore, check the accuracy of your name and address on the enclosed card and return it to us today in the accompanying self-addressed envelope that requires no postage?
>
> Thank you for your help.
>
> Sincerely yours,
>
> *(Signature of Gilbert Good)*

GKG:mk
Encs.

Comment

Observe that money is not mentioned in the concluding part of the letter. The reader is merely asked to check the accuracy of his name and address. That is easy to do. Also, the need for immediate response is again stressed.

Many copywriters would be content with a letter of this great length. It occupies four pages, single spaced. However, this letter adds the following P.S., containing more sales talk.

> P.S. When *Barron's* arrives, be sure to examine "Stock Market at a Glance" in the back. Unique ready reference covering prices, earnings and dividends of ALL stocks

traded on New York and American Stock Exchanges—with conspicuous symbols signalling all new dividend declarations or omissions and all new earnings. Weekly range and other statistics. All quotations on all more active stocks on the major U.S. regional exchanges, the leading Canadian exchanges, and over 1,500 Over-the-Counter quotations—all with earnings, dividends, year's high and low. No other service like it anywhere!

Comment

This mailing piece includes a Business Reply envelope and order card with the following copy:

(Order Card)

Yes, I'd like to try Barron's for the next 13 issues at the short-term introductory rate of $5.75 . . . and understand that I will receive, as a gift, a copy of *10 Rules for Investors*. In addition, I understand that if I prefer not to continue, I may notify you to stop at any time and you'll give me a full refund covering the balance of my subscription.

☐ **Check enclosed**

☐ **Send bill**

☐ **Check this box if you wish a full year's subscription for $23**

METHODS TO REMEMBER

Here is a list of successful methods you can use, based on the *Barron's* letter.

1. Tell a story that illustrates the value of your product or service.

2. Use specific figures.

3. Regarding price: Start with a high price and reduce it to a bargain.

4. Offer a free gift and mention it at or near the beginning of the letter.

5. Offer money back.

6. Give a reason for immediate action.

7. Use a postscript for additional sales talk.

8. Don't be afraid to use long copy. If it is good copy, your prospects will read it all and act on it.

SIX WAYS TO END A SALES LETTER

Veteran salesmen say that the hardest part of making a sale is closing the sale—that is, actually getting the money or persuading the customer to sign on the dotted line.

When groups of trainee salesmen are sent out into the field, they often have with them an experienced salesman who acts as a "closing man." The closing man is called in when the trainee has aroused sufficient interest on the part of the prospect to make a purchase seem likely.

The ability to close sales is so important that books have been written on the subject. A few years ago, Prentice-Hall published a book by veteran life insurance salesman Harry Kuesel entitled, *Kuesel on Closing Sales.* Another book on the subject is *Secrets of Closing Sales* by Charles Roth.

What has this to do with sales letters? Just this. Some letters are strong at the start but weak at the finish. Some letters get your attention and create desire, but contain no final urge to action. Or some letters merely end with the words "See your dealer."

A review of successful sales letters reveals a number of effective methods that have been used again and again to get readers to act. Here are examples:

1. Offer a Free Gift

A Mutual of Omaha Sales letter offered free information about health insurance. The letter ended with this sentence:

"You'll also receive—with our compliments—a beautiful Paper Mate pen. So send your request today."

Reader's Digest published an illustrated guide book entitled *Scenic Wonders of America.* The following copy appeared on the Business Reply Card:

Say "Yes" and we'll send you a FREE GIFT—a 32-page booklet jam-packed with additional travel tips and information. Designed for your glove compartment, this pocket-sized *Pocket Guide* lists scores of national parks. Yours to keep, free, when you say YES.

A letter selling *The Harvard Classics* set of books ended with this offer:

We want to send you by mail a copy of a fascinating *Guide Book* to books, absolutely free. It is the most valuable little book of its kind ever written. It shows how to select a library without waste or worry, what books are worthwhile, what are not. It contains advice on just what and how to read for success. The book was printed to give away. Your copy is wrapped up and ready to mail. No obligation. Merely clip and mail the coupon now.

2. Set a Time Limit

A letter from American Express, postmarked March 5, and selling a subscription to *The 100 Greatest Books of All Time,* ended with this paragraph:

If you wish to become a patron, your application must be entered by March 31. May I suggest that you give it your immediate attention.

A letter from *Gourmet* magazine selling cookbooks ended with this paragraph:

> The enclosed form entitles you and your friends to order as many gourmet books as you want, for only $10 a copy. This offer applies only to orders placed by August 30.

A subscription renewal letter from *McCall's Magazine,* offering renewals at the old low rate, concluded with these words:

> Please hurry! You must send your order before October 1. This is the only notice you will receive. May we hear from you today?

An announcement of the new *Encyclopedia Britannica* gave the reader three choices as follows:

☐ I do not own an encyclopedia, but would like further details . . . under your money-saving Pre-Publication offer. Expires March 1.

☐ I own the encyclopedia indicated below and would like further details on . . . your Exchange Program. Expires March 1.

☐ I own the 24-volume Encyclopedia Britannica and would like further details on your exclusive Exchange Offer for recent Britannica owners. Expires April 30.

3. Sales Talk in Order Form

Some ad writers are persuasive and enthusiastic when they write the main text of a letter, but they are cold and formal in the order form.

Other writers carry their enthusiasm into the order form with such lines as "Sure, I want to save money on my car insurance," or "Yes, I want to turn my spare time into cash." Examples:

   a. A correspondence school order form said: "I want that better future. Send me the information I need to get started."

   b. A GAC Properties coupon included this line: "Show me how easy it is to own my own place at Cape Coral, Florida."

   c. The Jackson & Perkins Company included the following order form copy:

Please rush me absolutely free, my copy of your new Spring Catalog, showing unique new roses, spring bulbs, garden vegetables, flowering trees and much more—all in full color.

   d. *Reader's Digest* used persuasive copy in the order form for a songbook:

Yes. Please send my free-examination copy of the *Reader's Digest Family Songbook.* If I am not satisfied that this is the book to gather the whole gang around for some good old-fashioned singing, I can return it at the end of 7 days.

4. Use a Postscript

Some direct-mail advertisers use a postscript for their final punch line. Examples:

Business Week Magazine, in a subscription letter offering a free portfolio, used the following postscript:

P.S. We will be glad to emboss your name in gold leaf on the attractive PORTFOLIO without charge as a thank-you for your prompt response.

The Dartnell Corporation, in a letter selling a book titled *For Executives Only,* added the postscript below:

P.S. I suggest you send for your copy today, since you may want to order additional copies within the next few weeks. *For Executives Only* is an excellent gift choice for executives in your company, as well as other business friends and associates. And, don't overlook the younger men on the way up in your firm. For them this is an invaluable book.

5. Offer a Free Trial

PRENTICE-HALL: If you are not *totally* satisfied, send the book back and pay nothing, owe nothing—we'll take the loss. So why not give it a try? Fill out the card now, while it's still handy!

TIME-LIFE: Return the postpaid order card and we will send you *Perennials* for 10 days' free reading as your introduction to the *Time-Life Encyclopedia of Gardening,* without any obligation to buy.

6. Use Action Words and Phrases

Simple devices such as action words can help to induce the reader to place an order. Here are examples:

Don't delay

Don't put it off

Supply limited

Delay may be serious

No obligation

No salesman will call

No one will phone you

Act now. Tomorrow you may forget all about it.

Remember this is a limited-time offer

For quick information, write today.

You may save time by phoning toll-free,
day or night, *(telephone number).*

POINTS TO REMEMBER

Don't be afraid to use long copy in your letter and in your closing sales talk. And don't forget the time-tested methods for getting response. Offer a free gift. Set a time limit. Put some sales talk in your coupon. Use a postscript. And when you are trying to get action, use *action words*.

A CHECKLIST FOR WRITING
SALES LETTERS THAT MAKE MONEY

When you write a sales letter, you should review the following summary of sales techniques that have made money for others. Be sure you don't omit any time-tested methods.

1. How to Get Attention

Here are three ways to get the attention of readers:

a. Offer a *benefit* in a headline or in your first paragraph. For example, here is a benefit headline that appeared at the top of a letter selling a tax course.

HOW TO REDUCE TAXES BY DIVIDING
INCOME AMONG THE FAMILY

b. Give *news*. Example: This was used in a letter selling a business service.

ANNOUNCING A NEW SERVICE FOR MEN
WHO WANT TO BE INDEPENDENT
IN THE NEXT TEN YEARS

c. Arouse *curiosity*. Here is the curiosity-arousing first paragraph of a letter selling a book on memory training.

This simple trick gives you a lightning-quick memory in just TWO HOURS! A memory so powerful that you can recall anything you want in the blink of an eye!

2. How to Hold Attention

You can hold your reader's attention by continuing and enlarging on the same thought that caught his attention in the first place.

For example, here is the tax course headline mentioned above, followed by the two opening paragraphs of the letter. Notice how these paragraphs continue and enlarge on the headline.

HOW TO REDUCE TAXES BY DIVIDING
INCOME AMONG THE FAMILY

One of the simplest ways for a man with a substantial income to save taxes is to divide his income among the members of his family.

This saves a lot of taxes because it shifts the income from his own high tax bracket to the lower tax brackets of others.

3. How to Write a Sales Talk

Your sales talk is the main body of your letter. In your sales talk you should tell your reader all the good things he will gain from your product or service.

Don't be afraid to use long copy in your sales talk—a page, or two pages or more. Your prospect will continue to read your sales copy as long as you continue to tell him the benefits he will get by accepting your offer.

You can strengthen your sales message by including a paragraph telling your prospect what he will lose if he doesn't buy your product or service.

4. How to Prove Your Claims

After your prospect has read your sales talk, his reaction will be: "That sounds good, but how do I know it's true?"

At this point you should tell your reader everything you can think of that will add believability. For example:

a. Tell how long you have been in business.

b. Tell what your customers say about your product or service. Quote testimonials.

c. Has your product won any awards or gold medals or honorable mentions? Has it passed any government supervised tests or has it been given, for example, the Good Housekeeping Seal of Approval?

d. Is your product made of high class materials such as those manufactured by DuPont or General Electric? If so, say so.

e. If you are a small concern, it helps to include bank references or credit ratings.

f. Include a money-back guarantee.

5. How to Prove It's a Bargain

Thus far you have caught your prospect's attention. You have held his attention. You have made him want your product and you have proved that your claims are true. What's next?

At this point, your reader may begin to wonder if your price is too high. You must demonstrate the value of your product. Prove it's a bargain.

Here is how *Fortune* magazine handled the bargain appeal in a letter selling introductory subscriptions:

> *Fortune* is not the least expensive magazine. It's $1.50 at the newsstand; $1 a copy at the regular one-year subscription price. To you, under our introductory terms, it's $12.50 for 15 issues—just about 83¢ a copy. And you get *What Managers Should Know About Automation* with our compliments.

6. How to Offer a Free Gift

A free gift offer increases response. Before you write your gift offer, you should study the wording of the previously mentioned *Fortune* offer, the *Kiplinger* offer and the *Barron's* offer.

The copy from *Fortune* contains the offer of a free gift.

The Kiplinger letter offers free a "Special Report on How to Deal with Inflation."

The *Barron's* letter offers free "10 Rules for Investors."

Often there are no strings attached to free gift offers. The reader is told that he may keep the gift regardless of whether or not he makes a purchase.

For example, here is the wording of an offer that has been successful in selling subscriptions to magazines.

> Send no money. We will send you the first issue along with a bill. If you are not delighted, just tear up the bill and keep the first issue.

7. How to Make It Easy to Act

Here are methods that have been successful in getting action:

a. Enclose a Business Reply Postcard with spaces provided for the prospect's name and address.

b. Some advertisers send reply cards with the prospect's name and address already filled in.

c. Some advertisers require only the prospect's initials on the order form. They use this line. Initial here . . .

d. Sometimes an adhesive stamp or token with the word *Yes* printed on it is enclosed. All the prospect has to do is to paste the token on the reply card.

e. If you want the prospect to send a check, enclose a Business Reply Envelope, which requires no stamp.

8. How to Get Immediate Action

People tend to delay action—to take time to "think it over." Thus many sales are lost.

Here are methods that help to get people to act quickly.

a. If the price is going up, say so.

b. If the supply is limited, say so.

c. Set a time limit.

d. Use action words such as *Act now* or *Don't delay*

e. Repeat the greatest benefit the prospect will get by buying your product.

How Direct Response Can Help General Advertisers Make Money

The most scientific advertisers in the world are the direct response advertisers.

Chief among these are the mail-order concerns. They test the efficiency of every element of their ad campaigns by actual sales or some form of direct response such as coupon returns or telephone calls.

General advertisers can also use direct response to make their ads produce more sales. Among those who have used this method are Du Pont, General Electric, General Mills, U.S. Steel, Lever Bros., Hormel, Armstrong and many others.

A FAMOUS ADMAN'S EXPERIENCE

David Ogilvy said: Whenever I look at an advertisement, I can tell at a glance whether the writer has had any direct response experience. If he writes short copy, or funny copy, it is obvious that he has never had the discipline of writing direct response.

The key to success in advertising (maximum sales per dollar) lies in perpetual testing of all the variables.

The average manufacturer who sells through a complex system of distribution is unable to do this. He cannot isolate the results of individual advertisements from the other factors in his marketing mix. He is forced to fly blind.

Experience has convinced me that the factors that work in direct-response advertising work equally well in all advertising. But the vast majority of people who work in ad agencies, and almost all of their clients, never heard of these factors. That is why they skid helplessly about on the greasy surface of irrelevant brilliance. They waste millions on bad advertising, when good advertising could be selling many times as much.

MAXIMUM SALES PER DOLLAR

The principal variables that are tested by direct response are *copy, media, position in media* and *seasonal variation.*

Direct response advertisers test copy by running a number of different ads and tabulating the results. In this way, they discover which ads and which sales appeals produce the maximum sales per dollar spent in advertising.

They test media—newspapers, broadcast, magazines and direct mail, by running ads in all of these. It is not uncommon for certain media to produce three or four times as good results as other media.

They test position in media by trying various positions. For example, where will a newspaper ad pull best—the Woman's page, the Sports page, the Financial page or the main News section?

They test seasonal variation in response by running the same ad in various seasons and counting the sales.

How can general advertisers profit from the experience of direct response advertisers? Two ways:

1. Watch what direct response advertisers are doing and learn from it.

2. Use direct response methods to test the various elements that go into a campaign; namely, copy, media, position in media and season.

For example, here is how a drug manufacturer tested sales appeals for various products.

TESTING SALES APPEALS FOR DRUGSTORE PRODUCTS BY DIRECT RESPONSE ADS

Here are the headlines of two ads for shaving cream. Which ad will induce the most readers to send for a sample of the product:

Headline 1:

PUSH-BUTTON SHAVE CREAM

Headline 2:

MOISTURIZED SHAVE CREAM

The answer to this question, and the answers to similar questions, were found by split-run testing small direct-response ads in newspapers.

The ads were set like news items. They measured 50 lines by two columns. Each ad contained about 200 words of almost identical copy, and a free offer in the last paragraph. There was no featuring of the offer. There were no pictures. Hence the pulling power of each ad depended almost entirely on its headline.

Seven pairs of ads for seven different products were tested in the same manner. In some cases the difference in pulling power between the two ads was small. In other cases the difference was large.

Can You Guess the Winners?

As you read these headlines you can check mentally which headline in each pair you believe to be the winner. A list of the winners follows.

Test 1—Shave Cream

☐ Push-Button Shave Cream

☐ Moisturized Shave Cream

Offer: A FREE AEROSOL CAN OF SHAVE CREAM

Medium: Split-run test in *Atlanta Journal* (Each ad ran in half the circulation. Same day. Same page. Same position on page. The only variable was the headline of the ad.)

Test 2—Aspirin

☐ Tension Headache?

☐ When Doctors Have Headaches,
    What Do They Do?

Offer: A free bottle of aspirin tablets
Medium: Split-run test in *Chicago Sun Times*

Test 3—Buffered Aspirin

☐ What Is Buffered Aspirin?

☐ How to Stop a Headache Without Upsetting Your Stomach

Offer:　A free bottle of buffered aspirin tablets
Medium: Split-run test in the *Portland Oregonian*

Test 4—Permanent Wave Outfit

☐ New Home Permanent
Conditions Hair as It Curls

☐ Girls . . . Want a Fast Permanent?

Offer:　A free home permanent outfit
Medium: Split-run test in the *Portland Oregonian*

Test 5—Muscular Pain Remedy

☐ At Last! A Pain Remedy That Goes Through the Skin. Relief Begins in Minutes

☐ Kill Muscle Pain Dead or Your Money Back

Offer:　A free bottle of pain remedy
Medium: Split-run test in the *Richmond News-Leader*

Test 6—Vitamin Tablets

☐ Now Try This Vitamin

☐ Now Try the Vitamin of Champions

Offer:　A free bottle of vitamin tablets
Medium: Split-run test in the *Chicago Sun Times*

Note: The purpose of this test was to find out if the phrase "Vitamin of Champions" would increase or decrease the pulling power of the headline.

Test 7—Hair Spray

☐ Tired of Sticky Hair Sprays?

☐ How to Keep Your Hairdo Prettier Longer

Offer: A free can of hair spray
Medium: Split-run test in the *Washington Post*

The Winners

The answers are given in percentage figures. For the purpose of comparison, the losing ad is given an arbitrary 100 percent and the winning ad is given a higher percentage figure.

1. Shave Cream

(a) Moisturized Shave Cream . . . 100%

(b) Push-Button Shave Cream . . . 182%

Comment: Apparently the convenience of push-button shave cream outweighed the appeal of moisturized shave cream.

2. Aspirin

(a) Tension Headache . . . 100%

(b) When Doctors Have Headaches
    What Do They Do? . . . 171%

Comment: Both headlines attract the right audience by including the word *Headache.* However the winning headline includes the word *Doctors,* which helps to build confidence. The phrase "What Do They Do?" arouses curiosity. This headline is based on the headline of a successful mail-order ad for a book entitled *The Secret of Keeping Fit.* The headline of the mail order ad was "When Doctors 'Feel Rotten'—This Is What They Do."

3. Buffered Aspirin

(a) How to Stop a Headache
    Without Upsetting Your Stomach . . . 100%

(b) What Is Buffered Aspirin? . . . 142%

Comment: Apparently there is curiosity about buffered aspirin. The winning headline offers free information on that subject. Also, the winning headline contains only four words. Therefore it was set in larger type than the other headline, which contains nine words.

4. Permanent Wave Outfit

(a) New Home Permanent
    Conditions Hair as It Curls . . . 100%

(b) Girls . . . Want a Fast Permanent? . . . 245%

Comment: Note the big difference in the pulling power of these two headlines. The headline "Girls . . . Want a Fast Permanent?" pulled 145 percent more replies than the other headline. Why? Let's analyze it. The word *Girls* at the beginning of the headline stops the right audience. The four words "Want a Fast Permanent?" express an important product benefit in the shortest possible space. The 200 words of copy were identical in both of these all-type ads. There was no featuring of the free offer. It was buried under 150 words of copy. So all the difference in pulling power was due to the headline.

Here is an interesting bit of history. Twenty-five years previous to this test, eight headlines for a similar product called Hairset were tested in the same manner, by a free offer of a sample of the product. The best pulling headline of the eight ads that were tested was "Girls . . . Want Quick Curls?" Note the similarity to "Girls . . . Want a Fast Permanent?"

This shows the durability of a successful headline formula. The pulling power of headlines depends on human nature, and human nature does not change. It is true that advertising *techniques* have changed—from stone tablets to handbills to publications to broadcast advertising. On the other hand, if you can find a sales appeal that is rooted in human nature, you can use it again and again.

5. Muscular Pain Remedy

(a) At Last! A Pain Remedy That Goes Through the Skin. Relief Begins in Minutes . . . 100%

(b) Kill Muscle Pain Dead
   or Your Money Back . . . 191%

Comment: The results of this test indicate that a powerful new appeal is contained in the four words "Kill Muscle Pain Dead." However, a legal complication arose. It was pointed out by legal counsel that a pain that is killed dead never returns. But the fact is that a pain which is stopped by a pain remedy may eventually return. Therefore the pain was not killed dead. The headline was changed to "Kill Muscle Pain Fast."

An interesting sidelight on this test was found in the handwriting of the people who sent for the free bottle of pain remedy. The handwriting was often shaky and old-fashioned looking. This indicated that a responsive market for a muscular pain remedy is elderly people. This finding led to a campaign directed to the geriatric set. If you are running a test of this kind, it is a good idea to spot check some of the actual replies yourself. Don't merely depend on the tabulated number of replies.

6. Vitamins

(a) Now Try This Vitamin . . . 100%

(b) Now Try the Vitamin of Champions . . . 117%

Comment: This test did not show a large difference in pulling power between the two headlines. However, it did indicate that the phrase "Vitamin of Champions" has a certain value.

7. Hair Spray

> (a) How to Keep Your Hairdo
>   Prettier Longer . . . 100%
>
> (b) Tired of Sticky Hair Sprays? . . . 179%

Comment: A good way to find an effective sales appeal is to find out what the prospect's problem is. Both of the above headlines deal with problems. The test simply revealed that "Sticky Hair Sprays" are a more common problem than the problem expressed in the other headline.

Direct response testing of this kind offers general advertisers a copy testing method which closely resembles an actual sales test. The direct response ads perform all the functions of an advertisement, as follows:

1. Get attention
2. Create interest
3. Arouse desire
4. Get action

The winning sales appeals that are discovered in a direct response test are then featured in an ad campaign in print or in broadcast, or both.

Media, position in media and seasonal variation are also tested by direct response, to find out which brings the maximum sales per dollar.

Eventually, the advertiser is able to run the best ads in the best positions, in the best media and in the best seasons. This combination of tested factors can make one dollar spent in advertising do the work of five or ten dollars.

OTHER EXAMPLES

Here are some other examples of how the effectiveness of various sales appeals were tested by direct response.

My-T-Fine Packaged Desserts

Ad Number 1

Headline:

HOW TO MAKE
CHOCOLATE PUDDING
IN 6 MINUTES

Illustration: **Three small pictures as follows:**

1. Woman's hand mixing dessert in a mixing bowl.

2. Woman heating pudding in a saucepan.

3. Woman pouring pudding into a mold.

Copy: **A description of how to make pudding in six minutes. The last paragraph of the copy contained an offer of a free sample of My-T-Fine dessert. The offer was not featured in any way. It was printed in the same size type as the regular text.**

Ad Number 2

Headline:

TONIGHT SERVE THIS
READY-MIXED
CHOCOLATE PUDDING

Subhead: **6 minutes to prepare**

Illustration: **Picture of smiling woman eating pudding.**

Copy: **A description of how to make the pudding. The last paragraph contained the same free offer as in Ad Number 1.**

Results of Test

These two ads were run in newspapers. Ad No. 2, with the headline "Tonight Serve This Ready-Mixed Chocolate Pudding" produced 66 percent more sample requests than Ad No. 1 with the headline "How to Make Chocolate Pudding In 6 Minutes."

A successful advertising campaign was built on the winning appeal. In fact, this appeal was so effective that other food advertisers copied it and ran ads with headlines beginning with the words *Tonight Serve This . . .*

Accent Food Seasoning

Here are two ads that were tested by two different methods:

(a) By an opinion test

(b) By direct response

Ad Number 1

Headline:

HOW TO MAKE YOUR FOOD
TASTE BETTER

Illustration: None

Copy: Now—enjoy more meat flavor in meat . . . more chicken flavor in chicken . . . more good natural flavor in all kinds of foods. Now, discover the dramatic difference that a touch of Accent makes.

(This was followed by two more paragraphs of copy.)

Ad Number 2

> **Headline:**
> ## HOW TO GET YOUR COOKING
> ## BRAGGED ABOUT
> **Illustration:** None
> **Copy:** Same as Ad Number 1

These ads were first tested by an opinion test. Rough layouts of the ads were shown to a group of women. They were asked: "Which ad appeals to you most?"

The ad that got the most votes had the headline:

> HOW TO MAKE YOUR FOOD
> TASTE BETTER

The ads were then set in type and run in newspapers. The following offer was included in each ad:

> For a sample package of Accent, write to Dept (Key No.) Amino Products, 20 North Wacker Drive, Chicago. Enclose a postage stamp to cover mailing costs.

A Surprise

The newspaper test reversed the results of the opinion test. The winning ad had the headline: "How to get your cooking bragged about." This ad drew 42 percent more direct responses than the ad "How to make your food taste better."

Why the reversal?

It was decided that the women were embarrassed to tell an interviewer that their chief desire was to get their cooking bragged about, rather than to make food taste better.

The manufacturer wisely chose the appeal "bragged about" because the newspaper test was, in effect, a sales test. The ads ran under normal circumstances, and the respondents had to expend money (a postage stamp) and effort to get a sample of the product.

A successful sales campaign was built on the winning appeal.

Question: Why did the ad "Tonight serve this ready-mixed chocolate pudding" get the most response? A discussion of the results of the test brought forth these comments:

The copywriter said: "The winning headline gives you the pudding ready-made. The other headline 'How to make chocolate pudding in 6 minutes' gives you the work of making the pudding."

The artist who made the layouts said: "The picture in the winning ad showed a smiling woman enjoying the pudding. The three small pictures in the losing ad showed the work of making the pudding."

This boils down to a simple, basic principle. People want their household chores made easy. Further evidence is shown by the popularity of easy-to-prepare foods such as Minute Rice, Instant Oatmeal, and TV Dinners.

Testing Sales Appeals for Murine Eyedrops

The makers of Murine wanted to find the most effective sales appeal for their product. The appeal being used was "Use these eyedrops for bloodshot eyes." Sales results were poor.

A survey was conducted among eyedrop users to find out why they used eyedrops. One of the reasons mentioned by users was "for tired eyes." This appeal and several others were tested by direct-response ads in newspapers.

Each ad featured a different appeal in the headline, and instructed the reader to send a postage stamp for a pocket-sized sample of eyedrops.

The ad that brought the most requests for samples was one that featured the appeal "for tired eyes." That appeal was adopted, and sales improved.

The above case history illustrates the correct use of surveys in conjunction with direct response copy testing as follows:

1. Use a survey to discover a variety of different sales appeals.

2. Use a direct response copy test to find out which of several sales appeals is most effective in getting action.

3. Do not depend on interviews to tell you the relative effectiveness of various appeals. Because of consumer bias, you may get the wrong answer. On the other hand, when you test ads under normal conditions in publications, consumer bias is eliminated.

Additional copy testing was conducted for eyedrops ads. It was discovered that the most effective way to state the "tired eyes" appeal was in headlines such as:

HOW TO GIVE
QUICK REST
TO TIRED EYES

Copy tests were also used to determine the relative effectiveness of various illustrations. It was found that a photograph of a pair of eyes looking straight at the reader was the most effective illustration.

During the next few years, a campaign consisting of 4-inch single-column ads featuring the words *Tired Eyes* and a picture of a pair of eyes was run in magazines and newspapers. Sales continued to improve, and these eyedrops eventually became the best seller in the United States.

In connection with copy testing for eyedrops, a humorous incident occurred. One of the winning headlines was:

BLESSED RELIEF
FOR TIRED EYES

Ads with this headline were included in the campaign. Soon the manufacturer began to receive letters from ministers saying that it is improper to use the word *blessed* in connection with eyedrops. The word *blessed* was eliminated.

Testing Sales Appeals for Gold Bond Wallboard

The manufacturer of Gold Bond Wallboard tested a number of different sales appeals by direct-response ads. Here are the headlines and opening paragraphs of two of the ads:

1. *Headline:* Build an Extra Attic Room

   1st Paragraph: It's easy to build an extra bedroom, workroom or playroom in your attic. You can do it quickly, and at low cost with Gold Bond Wallboard.

2. *Headline:* Build Your Own Darkroom

   1st Paragraph: Build a darkroom, gameroom, laundry, or any extra room. You can do it easily, quickly, and at low cost with Gold Bond Wallboard.

Each ad carried a coupon, which said: "Gentlemen: Send free copy of new Booklet, *Modernizing Magic,* showing remodeling ideas and methods."

Results: Advertisement 1, "Build an Extra Attic Room" pulled more than twice as many replies as Advertisement 2, "Build Your Own Darkroom."

A successful advertising and sales campaign was based on the winning appeal.

*   *   *

Direct-response copy testing opens up a field whereby mail-order methods of testing can be of help to general advertisers in discovering sales appeals that get action.

If it is impractical to mail a sample of the product (as in the case of wallboard), you can mail a booklet about the product.

In order to make a sale, an ad has to get attention, arouse interest, create desire and get action. A direct-response ad does all of these things.

SUMMING UP

Some of the most successful admen got their start in direct-response or in mail-order advertising. David Ogilvy described direct response as "my first love and secret weapon."

Rosser Reeves, the copy genius who became president of the Ted Bates agency, started in a mail-order agency.

Ray Sullivan, founder of SSC&B, got his start in mail order.

In recent years, a number of the largest general advertising agencies have merged with or acquired mail-order ad agencies as subsidiaries.

Doyle, Dane, Bernbach acquired Rapp & Collins. Young & Rubicam merged with the Wunderman Agency.

At an advertising convention in New York, Ed Ney, president of Young & Rubicam, said: "The purpose of our merger was for each agency to learn from the other. So far, we have learned more from Wunderman than they have learned from us."

Any copywriter can improve his or her writing skill by getting direct-response experience. And he can continue to benefit by observing what direct-response advertisers are doing today.

(a) What sales appeals are they using?

(b) What kind of headlines and copy are they writing?

(c) Which ads are they repeating again and again?

That is the key—the repeated ads. Those are the ads that are making money.

Years ago, Claude Hopkins, the father of modern advertising, said: "All my life I have done a certain amount of mail-order advertising. It is difficult and time-consuming, but it is educational. It fixes one's viewpoint on cost and result. The ad writer learns more from mail-order advertising than from any other form."

44 WAYS TO GET DIRECT RESPONSE

Sometimes it is desirable to get as much direct response as possible from your advertising. For example:

To get sales leads for your salesmen.

To sell your products or services by mail.

To get sales leads for follow-up by mail.

To distribute samples of your product.

To distribute literature about your product.

Below are forty-four tested ways to get direct response. You can use any of these methods that are appropriate for your proposition.

1. Use a headline that promises a benefit. *Example:* New ways to cut your taxes

2. Use a headline that selects prospects. *Example:* Free to home owners

3. Mention your offer immediately—in your headline or in the opening sentence of your commercial or direct-mail letter. *Example:* Yours free—a new booklet that tells how to save on food bills.

4. Mention your offer in your first paragraph.

5. Mention your offer in a subheading.

6. Show a picture of your offer—booklet, sample or merchandise.

7. Offer something of value.

8. Sweeten your offer. *Example:* In addition to this guidebook, you will receive a free map.

9. Test several different offers—in order to discover your best-pulling offer.

10. Test several different ads in order to find your best-pulling ad.

11. Tell your reader how your proposition will benefit him. Make as long a list of benefits as you can fit into your ad. You can use small type. No need for larger type than used in the news items in newspapers or the articles in magazines.

12. Include an attractive description of your offer.

13. Build your ad entirely around your free offer.

14. In newspapers, make your ad look like a news

item—by imitating newspaper type and by omitting the logotype.

15. In magazines, make your ad look like a magazine article.

16. Use an attractive booklet title. *Example:* How to get a better job.

17. Feature the word "Free"—but use discretion. Too much emphasis on the free offer may reduce the quality of your sales leads.

18. Offer confidential information in a plain envelope.

19. Include testimonials. *Example:* "My wash is done in half the time." "I made $2,000 on a single article in *The Wall Street Journal.*"

20. Include awards, honors, seals of approval, etc.

21. Make your ad easy to read—avoid unusual type, reverse printing and fancy decorations.

22. Include a coupon—if space will permit. If not, say, for example: "Tear out this offer and send it with your name and address."

23. Include a fold-over coupon. This is an oblong space in a print ad. The top half looks like a Business Reply Card. The bottom half is a reply coupon. The reader can clip it out, fold it in half, seal it with Scotch tape and mail it with no postage.

24. Include some selling copy in the coupon. *Example:* "Yes, send the booklet. I want to know how to cut costs."

25. Include your telephone number. An (800) toll-free number can further increase response.

26. In direct mail, put a headline on your envelope.

27. In direct mail, try using a plain envelope—with nothing printed on either side. This arouses curiosity and sometimes works better than an envelope which identifies the sender. Test both methods.

28. Include a business reply postcard or envelope that requires no postage stamp.

29. Use media that select the right audience.

30. Test various media in order to find the most effective publications or broadcast stations.

31. Use the best-pulling positions in media. *Example:* A test in newspapers showed that ads at the top of the page pulled 40 percent better than the same ads at the bottom of the page.

32. Use the most effective space size.

33. Try a free standing insert. This can be a card containing your ad. Or it can be your circular, booklet or catalog. It is dropped into newspapers, usually on Sundays.

34. Use the best season. You can test seasonal variation in results by repeating the same ad, in the same position, every month for a year. One such test showed that a January ad pulled twice as many replies as the same ad in August.

35. Reinforce your space ads with broadcast commercials. *Example:* "See our ad in next Sunday's *Times.*"

36. Use best time of day for broadcast advertising. *Example:* Don't try to reach men in the daytime. Sometimes low-cost, late-at-night commercials are best, especially when you can buy two-minute spots that permit long copy and time enough for mailing instructions.

37. Say that no salesman will call.

38. Include a money-back guarantee.

39. Skim the cream from various markets. Replies tend to diminish as you continue to advertise. Switch from one media to another, or from one time of day to another.

40. Urge immediate action. *Example:* "Write today" . . . "Do it now" . . . "Supply limited" . . . "Answer by (date)"

41. Promise quick response. *Example:* "By return mail" or "Booklet will be rushed to you," etc.

42. Emphasize "No obligation."

43. Study the ads of your competitors—especially the frequently repeated ads of mail-order advertisers.

44. Keep records of results. A periodic review of these records may reveal valuable information.

Push-Button Shave Cream

Men! When you shave you want lather that doesn't quit in the middle of your shave. You want lather that sets up your whiskers, lets your razor sweep them off smoothly, effortlessly. Now, try Rexall Redi-Shave aerosol shave cream. Just push the button on the Redi-Shave spray can and you get rich, moisturized lather that lasts until the last whisker is off. Whether your beard is coarse stubble or normal, Redi-Shave helps give you a smooth, comfortable shave every time. Kind to your skin, too. There's not a more convenient way to shave...economical, too. The 11-oz. aerosol can gives you months of shaving pleasure. Your choice of regular or cooling menthol. Get acquainted offer: For an 11 oz. 59¢* can of Redi-Shave absolutely Free, mail this ad to Rexall, Dept. RS7, Box 36222, Los Angeles, Calif. Specify type of shave cream desired by placing check mark in box...☐ Regular...☐ Menthol. Limit: ONE to a family. Offer good for 30 days only.

*Suggested minimum retail price.

Rexall Redi-Shave for Tender Skin

Men! If you have a tender skin, you want a shave cream that sets up your whiskers so your razor can sweep them off smoothly, effortlessly. Now, try Rexall Redi-Shave aerosol shave cream. Just push the button on the Redi-Shave spray can and you get rich, moisturized lather that lasts until the last whisker is off. Whether your beard is coarse stubble or normal, Redi-Shave helps give you a smooth, comfortable shave every time. Kind to your skin, too. There's not a more convenient way to shave...economical, too. The 11-oz. aerosol can gives you months of shaving pleasure. Your choice of regular or cooling menthol. Get acquainted offer: For an 11 oz. 59¢* can of Redi-Shave absolutely Free, mail this ad to Rexall, Dept. RS10, Box 36222, Los Angeles, Calif. Specify type of shave cream desired by placing check-mark in box...☐ Regular... ☐ Menthol. Limit: ONE to a family. Offer good for 30 days only.

*Suggested minimum retail price.

Which Appeal Pulled Better?

The Rexall Drug Company wanted to know which appeal to use in newspaper ads for Rexall Redi-Shave aerosol shave cream. The above ads were split-run tested in a daily newspaper. The copy was identical in both ads. Only the headlines differed. Each ad contained a buried offer of a sample can of the product. The ad "Push-Button Shave Cream" pulled 27 percent more sample requests.

I never bought stocks before —how do I go about it?

Where can I find out about stocks that pay dividends? What do they pay? Where can I get facts?

An 18-page booklet, "Investment Facts about Common Stocks and Cash Dividends," has been prepared to answer such questions. This free booklet gives you facts about common stocks in simple language.

It tells you what you own when you own stock. It tells you what dividends are . . . and how often you may expect to receive them.

Did you know that there is a way to reduce investment risks? That's in this booklet, too. Plus a list of companies whose stocks have paid a cash dividend every year for 20 to 103 years. The booklet includes some stocks that sell for less than $20 a share.

If you are interested in extra income, send for this booklet— whether you have $500 or $5000 to invest. Write for your free copy today. Booklet will be sent by mail. No obligation. Address Box 3, Association of Stock Exchange Firms, 24 Broad Street, New York.

What do I own when I own a share of stock?

What are common stocks? What rights do they give me? How big are stock dividends—and how regular?

An 18-page booklet, "Investment Facts about Common Stocks and Cash Dividends," has been prepared to answer such questions. This free booklet gives you facts about common stocks in simple language.

It tells you what you own when you own stock. It tells you what dividends are . . . and how often you may expect to receive them.

Did you know that there is a way to reduce investment risks? That's in this booklet, too. Plus a list of companies whose stocks have paid a cash dividend every year for 20 to 103 years. The booklet includes some stocks that sell for less than $20 a share.

If you are interested in extra income, send for this booklet— whether you have $500 or $5000 to invest. Write for your free copy today. Booklet will be sent by mail. No obligation. Address Box A, Association of Stock Exchange Firms, 24 Broad Street, New York.

Which Ad Brought the Most Replies?

Each ad offers a free booklet entitled "Investment Facts about Common Stocks and Cash Dividends." Each ad contains identical copy except for the first paragraph. The ad "I never bought stocks before—how do I go about it?" was the winner. It offers practical advice to people who are considering buying stocks. The other headline simply asks a question that apparently did not interest many people.

The Bargain Appeal Is Forever

Advertisers have used the bargain appeal in various ways since time immemorial. One method "Save $50 to $100," is shown in the above ad. Car manufacturers feature cash rebates, that is, "You get a check for $500 from General Motors if you buy this car." Department stores constantly advertise reduced prices. In fact, some stores start with high prices for the sole purpose of marking the prices down later on.

Wanted Girl Scout Leaders

Assistant Leaders Wanted, Too.

Why be a Girl Scout Leader?

Because you care about girls, and girls care about you. You want to share good things with them.

If you are a Leader, what do you do? You work with girls — little girls and big girls. You show them the many things you know. They learn from you, and you learn from them.

You have ideas. The girls have ideas. You make plans, and the girls make plans. The plans turn into action. You work on projects. You go places and see things. You have troop meetings and meetings with other leaders. You make friends. And you receive help whenever you need it.

Thousands of men and women have brightened their lives as well as the lives of others by becoming Girl Scout Leaders. Be a Leader, and make some girls happy. It will make you happy, too.

About the Girl Scout Movement

The Girl Scouts of the U.S.A. is the largest voluntary organization for girls in the world. It is open to all girls 7 through 17 who subscribe to its ideals as expressed in the Girl Scout Promise and Law. Founded in 1912 and incorporated in Washington, D.C., in 1915, it was chartered by the Congress of the United States in 1950. Its Honorary President is Mrs. Richard M. Nixon. Girl Scouts is a growing organization. But in order to continue to grow, it needs Leaders — like YOU.

How You Can Qualify

If you can spare the time, and if you qualify, you can become a Girl Scout Leader or an Assistant Leader. Helpers are also needed.

To find out more, just tear out this ad and send it to the address given below with your name and address. You will receive by mail, and without obligation, a 50-page, illustrated magazine entitled: "Girl Scout Leader." This magazine tells you about adults in Girl Scouting today. Send for it now.

Address: Jane Underwood, Girl Scouts of the U.S.A., 830 Third Avenue, N.Y., N.Y. 10022.

If you want quick information, without obligation, telephone collect (212) 753-0510 Monday through Friday between 9 a.m. and 7 p.m. and ask for Jane Underwood, and say: "Please tell me how I can become a Girl Scout Leader."

Thousands of Women Volunteered

The Girl Scouts, U.S.A. wanted Girl Scout Leaders. A number of ads were tested by direct response. The best-pulling ad had the simple headline "Wanted Girl Scout Leaders." It often happens that the simplest approach is the best approach.

An Attention-Getting Headline Formula

Almost all ads tell you to buy something. Hence an ad that says "Don't Buy" gets attention. This ad has the additional advantage that it gets the attention of prime prospects—people who are considering buying. Various advertisers have used this formula. Examples: Buy no insurance until . . . Invest no money until . . . Take no vacation until you read this free booklet.

ANNOUNCING AN IMPORTANT REVISION OF THE BIBLE

For fourteen years Bible scholars worked at the most exciting job in the world—a new revision of our Bible. The New Testament has now been published.

These men realized that the Word of God is needed by men and women today as never before in history. They have freed it from those confusing, archaic expressions that make the King James Version hard to understand. The result is a New Testament in living language—such a delight to read you'll turn to it twice as often.

Newest Testament Really Our Oldest

In the 300 years since the King James translation, dramatic new discoveries of ancient documents have shed new light on the Scriptures. From them we know that the King James Version—translated in 1611—is at times misleading.

The Revised Standard Version of the New Testament is based on the most authoritative manuscripts —some more ancient than any previously known. Thus, this new version is really our *oldest* New Testament. And it is far more accurate and easier to understand.

Easier to Read

Obscure, old-fashioned phrases are gone. Direct, understandable language quickens each verse to glorious meaning . . . yet the poetic beauty of the King James Version is preserved.

Even the way the type is set is easier to read. Instead of cramped double-column pages, familiar margin-to-margin printing makes this New Testament as legible as any popular modern book. Poetry is printed in verse form—as poetry should be.

Religious Leaders Praise It

"Presents the story of Christ in language people can understand," says Toyohiko Kagawa, famous Japanese religious leader. Prominent churchman Frank C. Laubach calls this New Testament "so crystal clear . . . even more faithful to the original Greek than the King James Version." The Revised Standard Version of the New Testament is authorized by the National Council of the Churches of Christ in the U.S.A. Over 2 million copies of this authorized version have already been sold.

Price $1—10-Day Free Trial

To bring this inspiring book to as many people as possible, we've eliminated extras like gilt-edged pages and costly leather bindings . . . offer this special edition at just $1.00! For this amazing low price, you can own the complete New Testament—553 full-size 5″ x 7″ pages in rich sapphire blue interwoven paper binding. (A similar book printed from the same plates with leather binding costs $5.00.)

Keep it 10 days free! See what a delight it is to read—what help it brings you through a real understanding of God's word. After 10 days, send $1.00 or return the book.

Mail this coupon now!

Thomas Nelson & Sons, Dept. S-14
19 East 47th St., N.Y. 17, N.Y.
Please send me, postpaid, the Revised Standard Version of the New Testament. In 10 days I will send $1.00 in full payment, or return the book with no obligation.

Name_____

Address_____

City_____ State_____

MOST IMPORTANT BIBLE NEWS IN 340 YEARS

Back in 1611, the first official English translation of the Bible—ordered by King James—was published. Outstanding *then*, this version has grown harder and harder for today's readers to understand because word meanings and language have changed so much.

Now a *new* official translation of the Bible—in the language we speak *today*—is nearing completion. The New Testament section has already been published. Bible scholars have freed this authorized version of the New Testament from the confusing, old-fashioned expressions that hide much of the Bible's meaning.

Newest Testament Really Our Oldest

In the 300 years since the King James translation, dramatic new discoveries of ancient documents have shed new light on the Scriptures. From them we know that the King James Version—translated in 1611—is at times misleading.

The Revised Standard Version of the New Testament is based on the most authoritative manuscripts —some more ancient than any previously known. Thus, this new version is really our *oldest* New Testament. And it is far more accurate and easier to understand.

Easier to Read

Obscure, old-fashioned phrases are gone. Direct, understandable language quickens each verse to glorious meaning . . . yet the poetic beauty of the King James Version is preserved.

Even the way the type is set is easier to read. Instead of cramped double-column pages, familiar margin-to-margin printing makes this New Testament as legible as any popular modern book. Poetry is printed in verse form—as poetry should be.

Religious Leaders Praise It

"Presents the story of Christ in language people can understand," says Toyohiko Kagawa, famous Japanese religious leader. Prominent churchman Frank C. Laubach calls this New Testament "so crystal clear . . . even more faithful to the original Greek than the King James Version." The Revised Standard Version of the New Testament is authorized by the National Council of the Churches of Christ in the U.S.A. Over 2 million copies of this authorized version have already been sold.

Price $1—10-Day Free Trial

To bring this inspiring book to as many people as possible, we've eliminated extras like gilt-edged pages and costly leather bindings . . . offer this special edition at just $1.00! For this amazing low price, you can own the complete New Testament—553 full-size 5″ x 7″ pages in rich sapphire blue interwoven paper binding. (A similar book printed from the same plates with leather binding costs $5.00.)

Keep it 10 days free! See what a delight it is to read—what help it brings you through a real understanding of God's word. After 10 days, send $1.00 or return the book.

Mail this coupon now!

Thomas Nelson & Sons, Dept. S-2
19 East 47th St., N. Y. 17, N. Y.
Please send me, postpaid, the Revised Standard Version of the New Testament. In 10 days I will send $1.00 in full payment, or return the book with no obligation.

Name_____

Address_____

City_____

Which Ad Sold the Most Bibles?

When Thomas Nelson & Sons published the Revised Standard Version of the Bible, it was an important publishing event. Above are two of seven sales appeals that were tested. Each ad had a coupon offering a paperback edition of the New Testament for $1.00. The ad "Most Important Bible News in 340 Years" pulled 71 percent more sales than the other ad.

14

How to Write Small Ads That Make Money

Some advertisers use large ads exclusively. Others use only small ads. Some use a combination of large and small ads. Often the users of large ads are not aware of the many practical uses of small ads. Seven of these uses are discussed below.

ADVANTAGES OF SMALL ADS

1. Selling Merchandise

A survey of small ads in current magazines—ads ranging in size from a half column down to one inch—shows that the most frequent use of these diminutive messages is to get orders for mail-order merchandise.

Products sold include clothes, cosmetics, jewelry, clocks, watches, hardware, stationery and various novelties.

Some of these small ads run only once. This is because results were so minimal that the advertiser gave up immediately. On the other hand, a small ad offering 1,000 address labels for $1 has been running for years. This ad has the advantage of *repeat sales*. It doesn't have to make a profit on the first insertion. It brings in customers who buy again and again.

2. Distributing Free Literature

The second most frequent use of small ads is to distribute free literature. The offer of literature may take many forms. For example:

Free booklet	Free instruction
Free brochure	Free kit
Free catalog	Free manual
Free details	Free plan
Free information	Free report

These ads depend on sales from people who send for information. Some advertisers have a product that would require a full page to describe. But a full page is expensive. Therefore, a small ad offering a booklet is an economical method. Other advertisers have a long list of products that would take many pages to describe. In these cases, a catalog is offered.

3. Miscellaneous Offers

Here are examples of miscellaneous offers contained in small ads:

Free sample	Free lesson
Sample for $.25	Free aptitude test
Free kit	Stamps for collectors
Catalog for $1	Telephone for information

4. Getting Leads for Salesmen

For six years, I wrote ads to get sales leads for life insurance salesmen. Each year we tested eight or ten half-page ads in *The New York Times* Sunday *Magazine*. However, in order to get a frequency discount, we ran one-inch rate-holder ads in a number of additional issues. At the end of each year, we figured out the cost per inquiry from all the ads. The one-inch ads always got the lowest cost per inquiry. This did not mean that we decided to put the entire budget into one-inch ads. We wanted corporate image advertising in addition to inquiries. But this was a revealing experience in regard to the inquiry-getting power of small ads.

5. Measuring Seasonal Variation

A national advertiser wanted to know which months of the year were best for getting coupon leads for salesmen.

A twelve-month test was run in which the only variable was the *season*. Here's how it worked. A sixty-line ad offering a free booklet was prepared. The same ad was run every other week in the Sunday Magazine section of *The Chicago Tribune* for a year—a total of twenty-six insertions.

Arrangements were made with the publisher to give the ad the same guaranteed position every time it appeared; namely, the upper right-hand corner of the contents page.

As a result of this plan, there were no variations in copy, no variations in media, no variations in position. The only variable was the time of the year.

At the conclusion of the test, a chart was drawn showing the relative pulling power of every month of the year. For example, the chart showed that January ads pulled twice as many sales leads as August ads. From then on, the company advertised heavily in the good months and lightly in the poor months.

6. Testing Media

Suppose you are running full-page ads in five magazines and getting good results. You want to expand your schedule, so you make a list of ten additional magazines that seem logical for your product. Now you would like to test full-page ads in all ten of these magazines. But this would cost a lot of money. Some of the additional magazines might fail to pay off.

You can test the additional magazines at low cost by running a half-column direct-response ad in all of them. After you have recorded the results of this test, you can then run your full-page ads in the best-pulling magazines.

7. Testing Position in Publications

A publisher of children's books wanted to know which of three sections of Sunday newspapers pulled best; namely:

a. The Main News section
b. The Sunday Book Review
c. The Sunday Magazine section

The same 200-line ad was run in all three sections on the same Sunday. The three ads were identical, except that three different key numbers were used in the coupons. Here are the results:

1. Lowest cost per inquiry: the Sunday Book Review
2. Second lowest cost per inquiry: the Sunday Magazine Section
3. Highest cost per inquiry: the main News Section

A media buyer could have foretold this result without testing. However, the test did not cost much, and it reassured the advertiser that he was right in continuing to run his ads in Sunday Book Review Sections.

HELP WANTED SECTION VERSUS SALES HELP WANTED SECTION

A vacuum cleaner manufacturer ran classified ads to get salesmen. Some newspapers have two classified sections that can be used for this purpose; namely:

1. Help Wanted
2. Sales Help Wanted

Classified ads soliciting phone calls from applicants were run in both sections of four newspapers.

The result was a surprise. The Help Wanted Sections pulled more and better quality leads than the Sales Help Wanted Sections.

TOP OF PAGE VERSUS BOTTOM OF PAGE

A manufacturer of building products ran ads measuring fifty lines by two columns offering a free booklet to home owners. The replies were turned over to salesmen.

After testing the pulling power of several different ads, the advertiser scheduled the winning ad to run once a week for ten weeks in the main News sections of a list of newspapers.

Some of the ads ran at the top of the page, some in the

middle of the page, and some at the bottom of the page. The ads were keyed and the results were tabulated. It was found that the ads at the top of the page averaged 40 percent more replies than the ads at the bottom of the page. Thereafter, the advertiser sought the cooperation of publishers in placing his ads at or near the top of the page.

SMALL ADS VERSUS LARGE ADS

The type of product or service you are advertising will affect your decision regarding whether to use small or large ads.

Book Clubs and Record Clubs need large space to show their wares. On the other hand, many items can be adequately described in small space. A third class of products are those that can be profitably sold in both small ads and in large ads. For example, in running ads for a correspondence course, we discovered that several sizes were profitable, from full-page ads down to one-inch ads.

The writing of small ads is a special art. It is the art of condensation. If you are paying sixty dollars a line for space and getting six words to the line, you must bear in mind that each word you print will cost you ten dollars. So use telegraphic language.

Pictorial illustrations must be kept small or omitted. The amount of space occupied by a picture can often be more profitable if devoted to sales talk.

One way to write a good small ad is to write a long ad first, then boil it down. A mail-order copy chief said: "A piece of copy is like a pot of broth. The more you boil it down, the stronger the flavor gets."

You cannot use small ads effectively if your product or service needs big pictures or long copy.

On the other hand, in the case of many items, you can use small ads to: (1) make a sale, (2) distribute literature, (3) give samples, (4) get sales leads, (5) measure seasonal variation, (6) test media, (7) test position in media.

David slew Goliath with a small pebble. Maybe a small ad will work for *you*.

HOW TO USE SMALL COUPON ADS
TO ATTRACT STORE CUSTOMERS

Here is the story of a sales promotion that produced sales that exceeded all expectations.

Thirty-five merchants published thirty-seven small ads in a tabloid section of the San Diego *Evening Tribune* on February 21 and in the San Diego *Union* on February 22.

This was a Washington's Birthday sale. The ads cost each merchant about $140 for a single ad. Here is a typical small ad.

**Kennedy's Firestone
Complete Car Service**

--------------------------------- COUPON ---------------------------------

**FANTASTIC SERVICE OFFER
$5.88 with this coupon
Expires Feb. 28**

1. Complete Lubrication. 2. Oil Change (up to 5 qts.) 3. New Oil Filter. 4. Rotate Tires. 5. Adjust Brakes. 6. Repack Outer Front Wheel Bearings. 7. Check Wheel Alignment. 8. Complete Safety Inspection.

Please Phone for Appointment

(6 Locations listed)

As stated in the coupon, this was a fantastic offer. And it brought fantastic results. With six locations listed, all were booked solid. One store manager reported thirty-five calls within the first half hour after the newspaper was on the newsstands.

Here is another small ad:

Antoine's Sheik Restaurant
2664 5th Ave.
Ph. 234-5888

Cocktails

------------------------------ COUPON ------------------------------

Offer Good 'Til March 1

$2 OFF ON EACH $6.95
COMBINATION DINNER

8 different varieties of Lebanese food for your pleasure.
No limit on number of persons in your party

Antoine's Sheik Restaurant said they had over 150 coupons returned. About 95 percent were new customers. Antoine was very happy.

A department store published a coupon offering a regular $69.95 ten-speed bike at $48.88 with the coupon. They reported over 200 coupons redeemed, with total sales in excess of $10,000. Not a bad return on a small ad costing only $140.

Here are other offers, together with sales figures. These advertisers permitted the publication of the following results.

- **Sambo's Restaurant:** two chicken dinners for the price of one. Over 750 returns. Sales: approximately $1,300.
- **Checker Auto Parts:** Oil filter $.99. Over 1,000 returns. Sales: over $1000.
- **Robo Car Wash:** One free car wash. Over 2,000 returns. Sales: approximately $4,500.
- **Vaughn's Clothing Store:** 10 percent off on all suits, coats, slacks, shirts, sweaters, pants, etc. Sales: over $1,600.

- **A.N.A. Photo and Appliance Center:** FM/AM Radio $16.95, Reg. $37.95 . . . Minolta Camera $169. Reg. $265. Over seventy returns. Sales: approximately $1,500.
- **Worth's Clothing Store:** Wet Look Coats $13. Reg. $30. Over 100 returns. Sales: over $1,300.
- **Pizza Palace:** $1 off any large pizza. Over 1,200 returns. Sales: over $3,600.
- **Fish Monger—Food to go:** 1 cent Special. Buy one at reg. price and pay 1 cent for the 2nd order (Fish & chips $1.35; Swordfish steak $2.75; Halibut steak $2.45). Over 1,100 returns. Sales: over $2,200.

*   *   *

Almost all of the merchants were extremely satisfied and asked the newspaper for another coupon promotion as soon as possible.

Although these ads ran simultaneously in a newspaper tabloid section, the same kind of ads can be used effectively at any time by individual merchants. Your ad need not be part of a group promotion.

HOW TO MAKE SMALL COUPON ADS EFFECTIVE

Here are some points to notice regarding these coupon promotions:

Many advertisers set time limits. Examples: "Coupon good through February 27" . . . "Offer expires Feb. 28th" . . . "Coupon good 1-day only, Feb. 22" . . . "Offer expires March 31st."

Some stores set restrictions: Examples: "Limit 2 items per coupon" . . . "Limit 1 per customer" . . . "Not valid for take-out orders."

Some stores specified that the customer must bring the coupon. *Examples:* "$5.88 with this coupon" . . .

"This coupon entitles, etc." . . . "Come clip us—with coupon."

Miscellaneous items:

"Please phone for appointment" (Kennedy's lube oil change).

"Supply limited. First come! First served" (A.N.A. Photo).

Pizza Palace offered an extra bonus—"Free Charlie Horse Pony Ride for the Kids."

A big advantage of a coupon ad of this kind is that it becomes a *reminder* to the customer after he has torn it out and put it into his pocket or purse. He can't forget it because it is right there staring at him.

Another advantage is that the customer needs to do little or no talking when he approaches the dealer. The customer merely hands the coupon to the clerk or storekeeper. Many people are not articulate. They don't like to walk up to a proprietor and say, "I understand that you are offering a complete lubrication, oil change, new oil filter, brake adjustment, wheel alignment, etc., all for $5.88." The coupon does the customer's talking for him. He doesn't have to say a word if he doesn't want to.

Briefly stated: How can you use small coupon ads to induce customers to take the first important step; namely, to step into the store? Answer: Make a fantastic offer. Print the offer in a coupon. Put the coupon into the hands of as many prospects as possible, and at the lowest possible cost. You may get fantastic results.

HOW CLASSIFIED ADS CAN GET
RESPONSE AT LOW COST

Would you believe that a small, one-inch classified ad in *The New York Times* could bring the advertiser $10,000 in two days?

That is exactly what happened. Here is the copy that appeared in the ad:

PARTNER WANTED

I have just obtained the exciting MRS. AMERICA FRANCHISE for N.Y. Already showing extraordinary potential income. My partner could not raise his $10,000. Can YOU? Mr. Richard Stockton at Mrs. America Headquarters will handle interviews. Phone NYC (212) MU 2-9160

In commenting on this result, *The Times* said:

> The advertisement for Mrs. America Productions, Inc.—a firm that produces pageants and licenses rights to the Mrs. America name in each state—appeared in the Business Opportunities columns of *The New York Times*.
> Only two days after it ran—even before a contract was signed—the advertiser had the $10,000 he had asked for.
> An example of the fast, fruitful results produced by *The Times* Business Opportunities columns—an unusual marketplace where money, ideas and businesses are sought and offered, and all sorts of business ventures proposed.

OTHER SUCCESS STORIES

Newspapers often publish success stories regarding classified ads that appeared in their pages. Here are typical examples: From the Philadelphia *Bulletin:*

---

75 Calls In One Day . . . Sells Home!

WINCHESTER PARK—WOODED LOT: A delightful home in Parkland setting. 3 large bedrms, and 2 baths. Beautifully panelled recreation room. Call to see today (Tel. No.)

*   *   *

> "We received seventy-five calls and sold the home right away through our Bulletin Classified ad. With results like this and ten more homes to sell, we'd make a fortune." **F.G., Northeast Philadelphia**

From the *Washington* (D.C.) *Post:*

> ### I Sold Everything by Noon
>
> BABY FURN.—Stroller, bassinet, port-o-crib, dressing table, sterilizer, misc., $50 for all (Tel. No.)
>
> *   *   *
>
> "It was just amazing. About fifty calls. I sold everything by noon and only wish I had more to sell." **D.H., Washington, D.C.**

From the *Washington, D.C. Post:*

> ### Our Dog Was Returned
>
> MALTESE DOG—Small, white, shaggy male, Bailey's X-Roads area. "Britches." Reward. (Tel. No.)
>
> *   *   *
>
> The advertiser said: "Success! The return of our dog came on the first call!"

From the *Washington* (D.C.) *Post:*

---

25 Job Applicants Called

SUMMER JOB FOR COLLEGE ENGR. STUDENT—With mechanical contractors. Arlington. Varied duties: office work, drafting, field engr., drive pick-up truck. Good exper. on govt. constr. work. Mechaneer, Inc., (Tel. No.)

*   *   *

The advertiser said: "Excellent results. Twenty-five calls."

From the Buffalo *Courier-Express:*

Carpets Sold First Day

CARPETS (3), in good condition, 12 x 15, 6 x 6 and 9 x 12. (Tel. No.)

*   *   *

This ad brought six calls and sold the carpets. Ad cost $.90.

From the Buffalo *Courier-Express:*

Automatic Washer Sold

WHIRLPOOL automatic washer, seldom used. Call 9 a.m. to 12 noon. (Tel. No.)

*   *   *

This ad brought thirty-five calls in three days and the washer was sold. Cost of the ad: $2.40.

From the Buffalo *Courier-Express:*

Bar Stools Sold

BAR STOOLS (2) Captain's, 30-in. high, perfect condition. (Tel. No.)

*   *   *

This ad cost $.90. The advertiser received ten calls the first day.

From the Burlingame, California *Advance Star:*

Pool Table Sold First Day

POOL TABLE—4½' x 8'
8 Mos. Old. Cost $375. Sell $200 (Tel. No.)

*   *   *

"I sold the pool table on the first day my ad appeared."
Mr. S.M., San Bruno, Calif.

ADVERTISING FOR IMMEDIATE SALES

These classified ad results refute the idea that you have to keep hammering at people with a whole series of ads in order to make them buy. Mail-order advertisers know that if you offer something people want, they will act immediately.

Here is a personal experience. One morning, while in my office, I saw in *The New York Times* a small ad for a popular magazine containing an article about the school I went to. The ad said that the article was illustrated with photographs, contained humorous anecdotes and had the words of some of the old school songs. "Now on newsstands" said the ad.

Immediately I went to a nearby newsstand and bought the magazine. The ad that sold me was just an ordinary ad. The copy was not outstanding. It would not win an award. It simply offered something I wanted, at a price I was glad to pay, and at a convenient newsstand. The result: Instant action.

ONE OF THE OLDEST FORMS OF ADVERTISING

In *The Pennsylvania Evening Post,* dated July 6, 1776, there appeared the first public printing of the *Declaration of Independence,* beginning with the famous words "When, in the course of human events . . ." Immediately following the signature of John Hancock, there were eleven classified ads. Here is the first of these ads:

> To be SOLD, the brigantine Two Friends. She is a prime sailor, but three years old, and carries nine hundred and fifty or a thousand barrels of flour.

*   *   *

> The schooner Mary Ann. She is a prime sailor, but four years old, and carries four hundred and fifty barrels of flour. This schooner is loaded and ready to go, and will be sold with her cargo, or alone. She has an inventory suitable and complete.
>
> The brig may be fitted for sea with a very small expense, and the schooner requires none. Both vessels are very good, but any gentleman inclining to purchase may have them

viewed by proper persons. Inquire for Mr. John Parry, on board the brig, at Vine Street Wharf.

This is evidence that classified advertising is not new.

MAKING CLASSIFIED ADS PAY

Classified advertising differs in an important respect from display advertising. In classified ads, you don't have to stop prospects with a big headline. Your prospects are looking for *you.*

For example, if you are advertising a business opportunity, the people who are looking for your type of proposition will turn to the column headed "Business Opportunities" and read your ad. Your job, as copywriter, is to demonstrate clearly and concisely how your proposition will benefit the reader.

The two words, *clearly* and *concisely,* are your guide to a good classified ad. You should use enough copy to make your proposition clear, but at the same time, you should not waste space with excess words. If, for example, you are advertising a house for sale, it may be best to resist the temptation to run a three-inch classified ad in the Real Estate Section on Sunday. You might do better to run a *one-inch* classified ad on three different Sundays. The person who will buy your property may not see next Sunday's Real Estate Section. But he might see it on the following Sunday or the Sunday after that. You can multiply your circulation by using repeated small ads. And the cost of three small ads is the same as the cost of one large ad.

Here are good words to use in classified ads:

amazing	helpful
approved	lifetime
bargain	limited
big	new
complete	now

easy	profitable
endorsed	quick
exciting	reduced
exclusive	secrets
famous	special
fortune	successful
free	unusual
genuine	wonderful
guaranteed	you

Good phrases to use in classified ads are:

Act now	How to
Dime brings details	No obligation
First lesson, $.25	Now you can
Free selling kit	Send no money
Fun-packed	Trial plan
Get started today	Write TODAY

In order to save space, you should cut your copy to the bone. Use a telegraphic style. Omit all unnecessary verbs and adjectives. Use abbreviations whenever possible. Don't bother to write complete sentences. Just use words that convey your meaning. For example, suppose you are offering a free booklet. You can use four words, *Send for free booklet.* Or two words, *Free booklet.* Or one word, *Booklet.* Or an abbreviation, *Bklt.*

Replies by Telephone

If you are using *local* newspaper advertising, you may find that replies by telephone are more profitable than replies by mail.

I once wrote a series of ads for a small private school in New York. At the beginning of the series, the ads offered to send a free circular by mail. A tabulation of results showed that only one out of five persons who wrote for the circular eventually came to the school.

Later a telephone number was included in the ads. The head of the school answered the phone. He was able to adapt his conversation to the needs of the prospect. For example, he would say:

What subjects do you want to study?

What is your objective in studying?

Do you want private or class instruction?

Do you want day or evening instruction?

We are starting a new class at 8 P.M. next Tuesday.

You are invited to sit in. There will be no charge for the first trial lesson, and no obligation to continue unless you wish to.

What is your address?

Here is how to get to the school.

An analysis of results showed that by this method, one out of two inquirers actually came to the school instead of one out of five. Hence, the offer of a circular was dropped from the ads. Only the telephone number was included.

SUMMING UP

In using small ads, you should aim to increase your ad efficiency two ways: (1) increase results by using good selling words, and (2) decrease your cost by using telegraphic language.

Running a small ad is like buying a ticket in a lottery. It is a gamble. But the price of a small ad is not high. If you lose the gamble, you don't lose much. But if you hit the right audience at the right time with the right ad, you may win big.

Big Profits from Small Ads

Small ads like these are repeated month after month and year after year in newspapers and in magazines. The secret of success is to test various ads until you find a winner. Note the simple headlines, pictures of the product and factual text. Also note, at the right, how restaurants can get customers with a special offer and also measure results by counting coupons.

Small Ads Have Many Uses

You can use small ads to offer catalogs or literature, to sell merchandise direct from your ad, to get telephone calls, to get leads for follow-up by mail, to get leads for salesmen, to test seasonal variation by running the same ad in different seasons and to test media by running the same ad in a list of publications.

How to Learn from the Experience of Others

Go through back issues of magazines and newspapers and do
three things: 1. Clip and save frequently repeated ads. These are
the successful ads. Learn their methods. 2. Make a list of publications that run a lot of small mail-order ads. These are the successful publications. Use them. 3. Study seasonal variation. Run your
ads in the heavily advertised seasons. These are the successful
seasons.

Fat Men!

This new self-massaging belt not only makes you look thinner INSTANTLY — but quickly takes off rolls of excess fat.

DIET is weakening — drugs are dangerous — strenuous reducing exercises are liable to strain your heart. The only safe method of reducing is massage. This method sets up a vigorous circulation that seems to melt away surplus fat. The Weil Reducing Belt, made of special reducing rubber, produces exactly the same results as a skilled masseur, only quicker and cheaper.

Every move you make causes the Weil Belt to gently massage your abdomen. R e s u l t s are rapid because this belt **works for you every second.**

FAT REPLACED BY NORMAL TISSUE

From 4 to 6 inches of flabby fat usually vanishes in a few weeks. O n l y solid, normal tissue remains. The Weil Reducing Belt is endorsed by physicians because it not only takes off fat, but corrects stomach disorders, constipation, backache, shortness of breath, and puts sagging internal organs back into place.

SPECIAL 10-DAY TRIAL OFFER

Send no money. Write for detailed description and testimonials from delighted users. Write at once. Special 10-day trial offer. The Weil Company, 922 Hill Street, New Haven, Conn.

THE WEIL COMPANY,
922 Hill Street, New Haven, Conn.

Gentlemen: Please send me complete description of the Weil Scientific Reducing Belt, and also your Special 10-Day Trial Offer.

Name...

Address ....

City....................... State...............

Short Headlines Can Be Effective
if They Convey a Message

This ad was the winner among many that were tested. It ran for years. For example, one of the other ads tested had the headline, "New reducing belt takes inches off waistline." This is a perfectly good seven-word headline. But the two-word headline, "Fat Men," plus the graphic illustration, convey a faster message.

Classified: The Growing Giant

Classified ads are the fastest growing category in the newspaper field. In a recent year, classified grew 21 percent. The year before, it grew 18 percent. Classified advertising accounts for almost a third of newspaper advertising revenue.

SOLD
Through Courier-Express Want Ads   Phone 852-5550

15 Calls First Day

RUGS, 1 each: 14x12 and 9x12. Reasonable. 000-0000.

Ad Cost 90c

SOLD
Through Courier-Express Want Ads. Phone 852-5550

40 Calls in 3 Days

GAS ON GAS Roper range, good condition, Maytag wringer washer. 00 Krupp, 000-0000.

Ad Cost $3.60

Rented
Through Courier-Express Want Ads. Phone 852-5550

12 Calls in 2 Days

ANDERSON PLACE. 3-bedroom upper. 000-0000.

Ad Cost $1.80

SOLD
Through Courier-Express Want Ads. Phone 852-5550

20 Calls in 3 Days

SEARS heater. 70,000 BTU, $50 or best offer. Call anytime, 000-0000.

Ad Cost $2.40

SOLD
Through Courier-Express Want Ads. Phone 852-5550

22 Calls First Day

FRANCISCAN china, Desert Rose pattern, matching crystal, service for 8. Bargain price. Call 000-0000.

Ad Cost $1.35

Rented
Through Courier-Express Want Ads. Phone 852-5550

40 Calls in 3 Days

PROSPECT-VIRGINIA. 2 or 3 bedrooms, furnished or unfurnished. 000-0000.

Ad Cost $2.40

SOLD
Through Courier-Express Want Ads. Phone 852-5550

5 Calls in 3 Days

LIVING ROOM furniture, range, good conditon, reasonable. 000-0000, after 6.

Ad Cost $2.40

Classified Ads Go on Forever

TV has been getting some of the ad dollars that formerly went to newspapers. But TV can never supplant the pages and pages of classified ads that run daily in newspapers. And Mrs. Housewife can't afford the price of a TV commercial to offer a room for rent. The above results from classified ads were featured in a Buffalo newspaper. Actual phone numbers omitted.

Free Press want ads spark buying action!

LIKE THIS...

FP Ad Investment Of $16.59 Returns $1,000 to Customer

Edwin Michelsen, Ann Arbor, found a buyer for a Farfisa organ and an amplifier by placing an exclusive fast-ACTION Want Ad in the Free Press. His $16.59 ad investment resulted in a sale of $1,000. If you have musical instruments or stereo equipment for sale, you'll find a buyer fast in the responsive Free Press audience.

THIS...

FP Customer From Rogers City Sells 11 Puppies

Mrs. Fred Drury, Rogers City, Michigan, found buyers for Labrador Retriever puppies by placing an exclusive Free Press fast-ACTION Want Ad. "I received more than 40 calls from all over Michigan," she said.

THIS...

Sale of Mini-Bike Prompts Placing of Second FP Want Ad

Carol Miller, Detroit, made a fast sale of a mini-bike by placing an exclusive Free Press fast-ACTION Want Ad. "In fact," said Miss Miller, "I want to place another ad right away." She selected her mini-bike buyer from among 16 readers who responded to her Want Ad.

OR THIS!

One FP Action Ad Sells Five Rooms Of House Furniture

"Terrific, tremendou great," are three of th adjectives Mrs. G. Lin say, Berkley, used to d scribe the response to h exclusive Free Press fas ACTION Want Ad. M Lindsay found buyers f five rooms of furnitu the first day her ad a peared.

For your share of the Action Call an Ad Informant 222-6800

Promoting the Use of Classified Ads

Here is another example of how a newspaper promotes the use of classified advertising—this time the *Detroit Free Press*. Classified ads are an important source of revenue for most newspapers. Besides, media buyers of ad agencies sometimes judge the pulling power of a newspaper by its classified advertising. If the paper carries a lot of classified ads, it proves that the paper gets sales response.

Please . . . .
Stop My Phone
Ringing!

"I sold it the first day and I think the Herald Traveler is wonderful." That's what everyone is saying about the Yankee Trader. Got something To Sell or Swap—send it in today—sell it tomorrow.
All you have to do is call 423-4545

Classified—the People's Advertising Medium

During World War II the U.S. government banned large newspaper display ads in order to conserve paper and other materials. But classified ads were never banned because classified advertising is considered to be a necessary public service. Above is another promotional ad—this time from a Boston newspaper.

15

How to Write Radio Commercials That Get Action

Copywriters who are accustomed to writing print ads for publications have found that they must apply some new rules when they write radio commercials.

First of all, as a radio copywriter, you are usually limited to a minute. That is about 200 to 300 words. On the other hand, in writing printed ads, you can use 1,000 words or more to sell a product or service.

Secondly, in switching to radio, you learn that your prospects are not just sitting still and quietly turning the pages of a magazine or a newspaper. They are doing other things—shaving, dressing, eating breakfast, driving a car, washing dishes, cleaning house, or working in the kitchen. They are listening to your commercial with only half an ear. Hence your sales message must be simpler and clearer than ever before.

Another thing: if your prospect fails to understand one of your sentences, he cannot go back and read it over again. He must understand it the first time. One of the most important requirements of a good radio commercial is *clarity*.

BASIC RULES

The rules for writing a good commercial are not entirely different from the rules that apply to writing print advertising. There are basic rules that apply to all advertising:

1. Get attention
2. Create desire
3. Get action

The first sentence of a commercial serves the same purpose as the headline of an ad. It causes the prospect to decide whether or not to listen. If he doesn't listen, you are licked before you start. The first sentence is vital.

The middle of the commercial is like the middle of a print ad. It must create desire and it must be believable.

The ending of a commercial can be divided into two parts: (1) the call to action, and (2) a mailing address or phone number (or both) that can be remembered long enough for the prospect to write it down. This part of the commercial corresponds to the coupon in a print ad. It is very important.

It may seem like an impossible task to accomplish all these things in 200 words. To simplify the task, let's analyze a successful commercial by breaking it down into three parts:

1. the beginning
2. the middle
3. the ending

A Business Week Magazine Commercial

Below is the full text of a one-minute commercial selling subscriptions to *Business Week* magazine. This mail-order commercial has been repeated many times. This frequent repetition is proof of its sales effectiveness. Mail-order advertisers, whether they use print or radio, do not repeat advertising that doesn't pull.

The Beginning: As you read the beginning of this commercial, notice how the first sentence serves the same purpose as the headline of a good mail-order ad. It selects prime prospects, arouses curiosity and promises a benefit.

> If you're an up-and-coming young business executive whose goal is to make between twenty-five and fifty thousand dollars a year, take this advice from some of the nation's top business executives.

The Middle: The middle section of this commercial is the longest part. It holds the prospect's attention by continuing the thought contained in the beginning. It skillfully leads the listener into a sales talk that creates desire by stating numerous benefits. It builds believability by spelling out specific features of *Business Week,* as follows:

> They'll tell you that getting ahead is more than getting the breaks. You have to stay on top of the news that shapes the business world. And that's why more successful business

executives are reading *Business Week* than any other business news magazine. *Business Week* helps you to get ahead in three important ways. It helps you to broaden your business vision by keeping you up to date on marketing, labor, finance, technology, government and law. It helps you make better decisions by giving you fresh, concise data on dozens of critical business indicators, consumer and market trends and Wall Street activity. And *Business Week*'s unique personal business column shows you how to keep more of the money you make, and how to get more enjoyment from your work. If you're determined to get ahead in today's business world, you should be reading *Business Week* every week. At $21.50 for a one year's subscription, you'll be making a wise investment in your career.

The Ending: Note the following features as you read the ending:

1. An extra bonus is offered.
2. A bargain appeal—$.42 a week—is spelled out.
3. The telephone number is repeated three times.

You can order now by calling the toll-free number (800) 228-2200. As an extra bonus you'll also receive absolutely free, *Business Week*'s one hundred and sixty page special report on major business problems. This valuable reference volume is packed with reports and an analysis of today's most pressing business problems. And that's yours at no charge with your order for a one year's subscription to *Business Week* for twenty-one dollars and fifty cents. It works out to less than forty-two cents a week for the magazine more successful executives are reading. To order your personal subscription to *Business Week,* call (800) 228-2200. That's toll-free (800) 228-2200 . . . (800) 228-2200.

*　　*　　*

A Tax Consulting Commercial

Here is another successful commercial—this time for a correspondence course in tax consulting. I have again divided it into three parts: beginning, middle and ending. As you read these parts, you will see that this commercial follows the same format as the *Business Week* commercial.

> *The Beginning:* If you're looking for a way to make extra money or to start a second career—tax consulting may be your answer.

> *The Middle:* Now don't let that job title put you off, because every day people just like you are discovering the part-time and full-time income opportunities of tax consulting. You see, you don't need any special experience, any accounting or bookkeeping background. National Tax Training School will train you and start you on your way with a short, inexpensive home-study course. And you'll be able to set up your own business or earn extra income by working part time. Fact is, you probably can save enough on your own tax return to pay for the course. You may not be aware of it, but tax consultants are needed year 'round, not just from January to April when most everyone needs tax help. So, get all the facts from National Tax Training. The course is approved for veterans' training and is accredited by the National Home Study Council.

> *The Ending:* Write now for free information. There's no obligation, and no sales person will ever call you. Address a card to TAX, WCBS Radio, New York 10019. That's TAX, WCBS Radio, New York 10019.

> *Announcer's ad lib:* I finished working on mine yesterday and I have a feeling that I could have used some help.

Note: This last remark was put in voluntarily by the announcer to help the commercial pull better. Announcers often do this with direct response commercials where sales results can be measured. The announcer wants to make a good showing so that the advertiser will repeat the commercial.

*   *   *

The similarity in format of the above commercials is not a coincidence. This is the format used by most direct-response advertisers. It grew out of years of copy testing. It is the type of commercial that produces the most sales.

In these commercials, there is a notable absence of attempts to entertain or amuse the listener. No music. No jingles. No sound effects. No humor. Just straight sales talk.

So when you write a radio commercial to sell a product or service, take advantage of the experience of the scores of direct-marketing advertisers who have pioneered the radio route. Use their methods. Write an opening sentence that will grab the attention of prospects. Make the middle part of your commercial a bundle of benefits. At the end, give the listener an urge to act. And make it easy for him to act. Give him simple and easy-to-remember instructions regarding what you want him to do.

HOW TO WRITE DIRECT RESPONSE
RADIO COMMERCIALS

Radio commercials can be divided into several categories, for example:

1. Retail Commercials. These are designed to induce people to go to the store. Here is the opening sentence of a typical retail message: "Today is Bargain Day at Sears."

Here is another: "At Syms, we want you ladies to know about our unique markdown system on all dresses, suits and ensembles."

2. Reminder Commercials. For example, recall the meat product commercials that repeat the brand name "Hansel and Gretel" again and again. And there are the frozen food commercials with the slogan "Better buy Birds Eye."

These messages are designed to implant in the housewife's mind a name she will remember when she is in the store.

3. Direct-Response Commercials. These try to get people to subscribe to a publication, order merchandise, attend a lecture, telephone for information, send for a sample product or write for a booklet.

The most crucial parts of a direct-response commercial are at the beginning, the offer and the ending.

The beginning must rivet the attention of the prospects. It must stop them in mid-air, so to speak. People do not always sit still when they listen to the radio. They do other things while the radio is turned on. If your first sentence doesn't get their attention, your commercial is wasted.

Next time you write a radio commercial, try to write an opening sentence that stops prospects in their tracks. Below are examples. Note how these sentences identify their prospects and offer them a benefit or imply one.

Golfers, would you like a free book of golf tips?

Here's a word of advice before you and your family go on vacation.

It's pretty tough when the ax falls and you find yourself out of a job.

Are you an unpublished author?

If your bills are getting to be too much, hear this.

Do you suffer from headaches?

Here's a quiz for pregnant women.

For the sake of contrast, read the following opening sentences that were recently aired. These sentences do not identify their prospects. They do not offer a benefit.

At the turn of the century, life seemed less hurried.

And now, one of America's biggest success stories.

Some words have more impact than others.

How about the ending of the commercial? This is just as crucial as the beginning. The final paragraph containing the phone number or the address must be simple and easy to remember so that the prospect can recall it and write it down. And it should be repeated several times.

On the other hand, if the final instructions are a complicated hodgepodge of rapidly spoken area codes, phone numbers, street addresses, box numbers and zip codes, the listener will be too confused to remember anything at all.

VARIOUS ENDINGS

Some advertisers simplify the ending by referring listeners to the telephone book. *Examples:*

Telephone for information. The number is in your phone book.

Check the Yellow Pages for the dealer nearest you.

You can find a Culligan Man in the Yellow Pages under *Water.*

Retail advertisers depend on the listener's knowledge of store locations. *Examples:*

Spectacular prices. Go to Sears' appliance spectacular today.

All Syms suburban stores are open till 9:30 on weekdays.

Direct-response advertisers almost always give specific phone numbers or addresses or both. And they boil the instructions down to a bare minimum. *Examples:*

Phone (212) 582-5000
Or write CBS New York, 10019

Address: Great Music, Box 1770,
Grand Central Station, New York

Write to WOR, New York, 10008

Most announcers repeat the address several times. *For example:*

Let me give you that address once more:
487 Park Avenue, New York 10022

Just call Judson 2-2000.
I'll repeat that twice more.
Judson 2-2000. Judson 2-2000

If you are advertising a lecture at a specific location, it is necessary to spell out the address:

The free lecture will be given at the Hotel Warwick at 54th Street and 6th Avenue in New York City at 6 p.m. on Wednesday. The address again . . . Hotel Warwick, 54th Street and 6th Avenue at 6 p.m. on Wednesday.

Most important of all, a direct-response commercial must contain an attractive offer. Reproduced below is the complete text of a successful commercial selling subscriptions to a children's magazine. This commercial has been repeated many times—proof enough of its selling power.

Read this commercial carefully and note the following:

1. The first sentence identifies prospects and promises a benefit.
2. The copy makes an attractive offer.
3. The last paragraph repeats the telephone number three times.

A Cricket Magazine Commercial

The First Sentence: If you're the parent of a seven- to ten-year-old, here's an opportunity to do something very special for your child—something that he or she will appreciate for years to come.

The Offer: Take advantage of this special introductory offer of *Cricket Magazine* and help your child discover the pure enjoyment and pleasure of good reading.

Cricket is full of laughter and knowledge and all the things that excite and challenge young minds. Every month *Cricket* brings a parade of could-have-been or might-be-some-day stories, along with magic tricks, puzzles and dozens of other delicious odds and ends of fact and fancy that seven- to ten-year-olds love.

To encourage you to find out just how good a children's magazine can be, *Cricket* is offering this no-obligation, nine-month subscription for only eight dollars and ninety-seven cents. If the first issue doesn't convince you and your young reader that *Cricket* is the very best children's magazine around, then the first issue is yours to keep free and you'll not owe a penny.

The Telephone Number: To order, call (800) 228-2200 and tell the operator you want to order *Cricket*'s nine-month subscription for eight dollars and ninety-seven cents. That number is (800) 228-2200—toll-free (800) 228-2200.

HOW TO MAKE IT EASY TO ACT

An effective aid to direct response is to make it easy for your prospect to try your proposition for a limited time, without obligation. That is why phrases like the following have been used again and again in direct-response advertising, both in print copy and radio commercials.

Send no money

Yours free

No obligation

No salesman will call

Try it ten days at no cost

We will bill you later

One dollar starts you

Money back if you are not delighted

Below is a successful commercial for a health magazine. It has been repeated many times. As you read it, notice these effective devices:

1. The first sentence ties in with the current interest in high-fiber diets.
2. A forty-two-page report is offered.
3. A year's subscription is offered at a special price.
4. The figure "two million subscribers" is mentioned.
5. The copy says "Send no money."
6. The customer is given an easy way to cancel; e.g., "Just Write 'cancel' on the bill."
7. The customer is allowed to keep the first issue of the magazine and the forty-two page report and owe nothing.

A Prevention Magazine Commercial

You've heard about high-fiber diets, but do you know everything you should know about them?

Do you know which cereal products by brand name contain the most fiber?

But you can't eat cereal all day long. Wouldn't you like to know which other foods are rich in fiber, as well as which high calorie foods you can eat, without adding weight, simply because of their high fiber?

These facts, and many more are in a new 42-page report called *Fabulous Fiber.* Yours free for trying *Prevention,* the world's largest health magazine.

Find out why almost two million health-conscious subscribers depend on *Prevention.* Find out now when you get a special price—twelve monthly issues for only $5.85, plus *Fabulous Fiber* at this guarantee.

If you're not satisfied with the first issue, just write "cancel" on the bill you receive and return it. You'll owe nothing. You'll also keep the free report. Send no money now. Just phone area code (212) 582-2006 for *Prevention* and your free *Fiber* brochure. Call (212) 582-2006. Or write *Prevention.* Care of WCBS, New York 10019.

*　　*　　*

A CHECKLIST

Here is a checklist you can use the next time you write a direct-response commercial.

1. Does your first sentence reach out and grab prospects and offer them a benefit?

2. Does your copy contain an irresistible offer?

3. Do you make it easy for people to sample your product without obligation?

4. Does your copy contain an escape clause such as "just write 'cancel' on the bill"? People like an easy way out. It is the same psychology that affects people when they sit in a theater. They feel more comfortable if they can see a nearby fire exit.

5. Is your address simple enough and repeated often enough so that the prospect can remember it long enough to write it down?

HOW TO USE COPY TESTING TO
INCREASE SALES FROM RADIO ADVERTISING

Can copy testing be used to increase the sales effectiveness of our radio commercials?

This was *question 1* asked me by the Circulation Manager of a national magazine with more than eight million circulation. Let us call it *Popular Monthly*.

The Circulation Manager was using radio to increase his newsstand sales. He wanted to get better results.

"Let's try it and see," I said.

The first problem was to decide which articles to talk about in radio commercials. Each issue of *Popular Monthly* contains upwards of twenty articles. We couldn't mention them all in a one-minute commercial.

"The articles are all good," said the client, "but some of them must have more sales appeal than others. How can we find out which articles will make the largest number of people buy *Popular Monthly* at the newsstand?"

Testing Article Preference

My first thought was to prepare a series of commercials and feature a different article in each commercial. At the end of each commercial would be an offer. But that would be an unwieldy test if it were extended to include twenty articles. Imagine testing twenty commercials to find the one or two that brought the greatest response.

I then thought of the copy tests that were done years ago by Haldeman Julius, the publisher of little paperback booklets he sold by mail at the amazingly low price of five cents per booklet.

Haldeman Julius ran ads in newspapers, and listed several hundred booklet titles in each ad. The titles covered a wide range of subjects from Beauty Hints to Plato's Philosophy. The reader was invited to select twenty titles and mail the coupon with one dollar.

I thought: this method is a test of the popularity of titles. The method is not expensive. It brings quick results. It is possible to test many titles in a single ad. And it is a true test, not an opinion test. The respondents selected the titles of the booklets they want to read.

Testing Via Questionnaire

I decided to try this method of testing in connection with *Popular Monthly* article titles, so I prepared a newspaper ad containing a questionnaire as follows:

Headline:

FREE . . . ADVANCE COPIES OF
POPULAR MONTHLY ARTICLES

Subhead: Here's how to get them: To acquaint you with the interesting articles in *Popular Monthly,* we make this offer:

From the descriptions below of some of the interesting articles in the next issue of *Popular Monthly,* pick the three articles you'd most like to read. Circle the numbers of these three articles on the coupon below. Then mail the coupon to us with your name and address. We'll send you free copies of the three articles you chose.

Copy: The copy consisted of a list of twenty article titles and a brief description of each article. The articles were numbered from one to twenty.

Coupon: The coupon contained a list of twenty numbers, from one to twenty, so that the respondent could circle the numbers of the three articles he or she wanted.

The client approved this ad and it was run in a daily newspaper. Several hundred coupons were received and tabulated.

Surprise! The difference in popularity between articles was greater than we expected. The most popular article received more than twenty times as many requests as the least popular article. This result showed the importance of finding out which articles to talk about in radio commercials, before embarking on a radio campaign. By featuring the most desired articles, the effectiveness of the campaign could be multiplied.

Later on, we discovered a by-product from the newspaper ad offering free reprints of articles. Instead of merely sending article reprints, we sent the entire magazine. This was a happy surprise for the respondent and it was an excellent sampling. We found that we could sell magazine subscriptions to about a third of these respondents.

Testing Other Factors

In addition to his first question about which articles to feature, the client had other questions. Here they are:

Question 2: How many articles should we talk about in a one-minute radio commercial? Should we devote the entire minute to describing the most popular article? Or should we briefly mention the titles of several popular articles?

Question 3: Should we use taped commercials so that we could hire an announcer whose voice and manner of delivery we liked? Or should we send typewritten copy to the radio station and let the regular announcer read it.

Question 4: If we used taped commercials, should we dramatize the copy with sound effects, music and several voices? Or should we use just one voice and omit the sound effects?

Question 5: We would need to make an offer at the end of every commercial so that we could get replies. What offer should we make?

Question 6: The offer would have to be keyed so that we could tell which commercial brought the most response. How could we do this? For example, at the end of Commercial A, should we say: "Write to Dept. A, in care of this station"? At the end of Commercial B, should we say "Write to Dept. B"?
Problem: Would the respondents use the key numbers? This is not a problem in print ads, because the key numbers are printed on the coupons.

Question 7: Where could we test Commercial A

versus Commercial B and get an equal size audience for each commercial? This is easy in print advertising. You simply ask a newspaper to give you a split-run test, whereby Ad A runs in half the circulation and Ad B runs in the other half of the circulation on the same day. But how about radio? Who can tell the size of the audience at any given time? Commercial A might be heard by twice as many people as Commercial B. This would upset the test.

How About Key Numbers in Radio Commercials?

Before proceeding further, I obtained the services of an experienced radio director. His first comment was: "You will never get people to use key numbers in replying to radio commercials. They will simply write to the station and omit the key number."

This was bad news. How could we test copy without key numbers?

I decided to try a key number anyway, just to see what would happen. I wrote a one-minute commercial about a popular article, and told listeners to "Write to Dept. A, in care of this station, for a free copy of the magazine containing this article."

We ran the commercial on a small local station. Result: We got upwards of 200 replies. *Ninety-five percent of the respondents used the key number.* From then on, we always put key numbers in our commercials and they were almost always used by respondents. The experienced radio director was wrong. This illustrates a problem that sometimes occurs when you deal with experienced people. They know too many things that they think can't be done.

Now we were ready to test some of the other things we wanted to check up on. We knew which articles to feature. We had an offer that pulled (the free magazine). And we knew we could use key numbers. Now we needed the right size audience for copy testing.

Finding the Right Size Audience

How could we go about locating a radio station that would give us the same size audience, or approximately the same size audience, for every one of a series of commercials?

I scanned the radio availabilities and found a station which put on a program called "Melody Hour," every night at 9 P.M., five nights a week, Monday through Friday.

I scheduled a one-minute commercial to be aired every night for five nights, just preceding "Melody Hour." And I ran the identical commercial for five nights in succession. Only the key numbers were changed on successive nights.

What was the purpose of this procedure? To find out if the size of the audience at 9 PM was the same every night. If the size of the audience was the same every night, we should get approximately the same number of replies every night. On the other hand, if Tuesday night pulled 50 percent more replies than Monday night, the size of the audience was not the same.

We ran this test of audience size for several weeks, and here is what happened. The number of replies varied by about 10 percent from night to night except on Friday night, when the replies dropped 50 percent. Since this test was run in the summertime, we decided that the Friday-night audience was smaller than other nights. Apparently people went out of town or were engaged in other activities on Friday night. So we decided that we would never test radio spots on Friday night.

However, Monday, Tuesday, Wednesday and Thursday nights were okay for testing. On each of those nights, the size of the audience varied by less than 10 percent.

How Many Articles Should We Feature?

Now we were ready to test copy. We began by testing the pulling power of one article versus two articles. I wrote a commercial that devoted an entire minute to talking about a single article. Call this Commercial One. I wrote another commercial that talked about two articles. Call this Commercial Two.

We ran these commercials for two weeks. We alternated

them as follows: On Monday night we ran Commercial One. On Tuesday, Commercial Two. Wednesday, Commercial One. Thursday, Commercial Two. Thus Commercial One was run four times. Commercial Two was run four times.

Result: Commercial Two, which talked about two articles, pulled approximately 25 percent more replies than Commercial One, which talked about only one article.

During successive weeks, we tested commercials featuring three articles, four articles and five articles. We did not test six articles because there was not enough time in a one-minute commercial to mention six articles.

Result: The more articles we mentioned, the better the response.

This was an important discovery. It meant that we could greatly increase the effectiveness of our radio campaign by mentioning as many articles as possible.

This result seemed logical. For example, suppose a one-minute commercial were entirely devoted to talking about an article on baseball. If a listener was not interested in baseball, the commercial would not sell him. On the other hand, if the announcer mentioned five articles on five different subjects, the announcer would have five chances to sell the listener instead of only a single chance.

Should this finding have been obvious without testing? Perhaps. But when you are spending a client's money, you want to be sure you are right. And you want evidence to prove to the client that you are right.

Other Tests

During successive weeks, we tested other things. Here are some results:

A typewritten commercial that was read aloud by the regular announcer pulled better than a taped commercial by an announcer whose voice was unfamiliar to the audience.

Apparently listeners have more confidence in a familiar voice that regularly tells them the news and the weather. A familiar voice is like the voice of a friend—persuasive and believable. A strange voice carries less conviction.

We tried commercials containing sound effects, music, combinations of several voices and dramatizations of articles. None of these drew as great a response as typewritten commercials that were read by the regular announcer.

Another advantage of typed commercials was that we avoided the extra cost of paying for special announcers, sound effects, etc.

Extending the Campaign

At the conclusion of our testing period, a radio campaign, based on the results of our tests, was extended to other cities.

Every month we ran a newspaper ad to discover the most popular articles in the forthcoming issue of the magazine. And, in every radio commercial, we mentioned the five most popular articles.

We continued to use typewritten copy without sound effects or other embellishments—just straight sales talk read by the local announcer.

We dropped the offer of a free copy of the magazine. Instead we told listeners to buy the magazine at the newsstand.

Results were excellent. The sales of the magazine at newsstands exceeded all expectations.

Conclusion: Copy testing pays off—in radio as well as in space advertising. Radio copy testing is more difficult than space ads testing because you can't use coupons and you don't have exact circulation figures. But it can be done.

An ideal solution is to test various sales appeals by means of a newspaper copy test, in which you can test many different appeals quickly, cheaply and accurately. Then broadcast your most successful sales appeal on the radio, and get all the special advantages that radio offers.

HOW RETAILERS GET IMMEDIATE SALES FROM RADIO COMMERCIALS

Direct response advertisers and retail store advertisers have much in common.

They both want sales that are immediate, sales that are abundant and sales that are profitable.

And both can measure the sales results from their ads more accurately than can general advertisers.

So let's take a look at what retailers are doing in radio today. Perhaps you can get some money-making ideas you can use in your own ads.

In order to learn the success secrets of radio retailers, we can use the same proven approach used in studying other forms of advertising; namely:

1. Study carefully the retail commercials that are designed to produce immediate results.

2. Do not be guided by institutional commercials intended to build the image of the store over a long period of time. Results are difficult to measure.

3. Above all, pay particular attention to the hard-sell radio spots that retailers repeat again and again, day after day and month after month. These are the commercials that are paying off.

Nobody who can measure sales results will repeat ads that don't work. Experienced advertisers keep hammering away with ads that do work. Those are the ads that produce sales that are plentiful and profitable. Those are the ads that can teach us something.

Here is a radio commercial for Caldor Stores. It has been repeated many times:

Caldor Stores

This weekend is a good time to shop at Caldor Stores in the New York, Connecticut or Massachusetts area.

Caldor will be open Sunday from 11 A.M. to 5 P.M., so you may take advantage of terrific savings on items for all your home and outdoor needs.

You'll find reductions on Caldor's already low, low prices on seasonal, ready-to-wear clothing, small appliances, sporting goods, outdoor furniture and hundreds of other exciting items ideal for this time of year.

For example, the deluxe portable twin burner gas grill, complete with gas tank hose, regulator and permanent coals, regularly $240, now only $176. You'll save $64.

Or you can buy the Westinghouse twenty-five pint dehumidifier, regularly $150, now only $124.

Don't forget, today Sunday, 11 A.M. to 5 P.M. The nice Caldor people always welcome VISA, Master Card or Caldor charge card. Caldor is working harder and harder to become your department store. Get on over to the Caldor Store today.

*   *   *

Note these elements contained in this commercial:

1. *Timeliness:* "This weekend is a good time to shop at Caldor Stores . . . open today, Sunday."

2. *Types of items are named:* "Ready-to-wear clothing, small appliances, etc."

3. *Bargain Appeal:* "Regularly $240, now only $176 . . ." "Regularly $150, now only $124."

4. *Act Now:* "Get over to the Caldor Store today."

These elements are typical of successful retail store commercials.

Also notice that this commercial does not attempt to entertain the listener. No jingles. No musical interludes. No sound effects. No humor.

The most successful retail commercials are 100 percent straight sales talk. A retailer said: "Why devote part of our precious minute to entertainment? The radio station furnishes the entertainment free."

Here is another often-repeated retail commercial that contains a bargain appeal, plus another element frequently found in store commercials; namely, a reason why the bargains are offered.

Seidman's Store

Announcing the greatest sale in the history of Seidman's, Long Island.

Several weeks ago Seidman's management decided to close the store during the summer for some needed renovations. But, Seidman says, the buyers never got that word somehow. So they didn't cancel any orders.

Now they have a giant store on Old Country Road, across from Fortunoff's in Westbury, Long Island, loaded with brand new spring and summer men's wear. The painters and the decorators can't work with all that stuff in there, so they're having a sell-out of massive proportions.

Everything is going . . . $125 value Prince Ferrari vested suits, $55. And $175 value Pierre Cardin summer suits are $69.

You'll find $175 value MacGregor genuine leather jackets for $79. Luxurious Orsini dress shirts pre-ticketed for $20, selling for $6.50. And $125 polycotton vested suits, $39. And the $235 value, one-hundred-percent-wool, hand-tailored, midweight vested imports—they're only $99.

Everything in the store is going at sell-out prices. And Seidman's is open daily and Sunday on Old Country Road, opposite Fortunoff's in Westbury, Long Island.

Important: If you have a logical reason for offering bargains, put it in your ad. It will make your copy more believable.

Another device for getting immediate sales is to offer a free gift to people who act quickly. This is a successful device in mail-order advertising. It also works in retail advertising. The following commercial for Trader Horn Stores contains a free offer of a $50 U.S. Savings Bond as a "special bonus for a limited time." This commercial has been repeated many times.

Trader Horn Stores

You can always do business with a Trader Horn TV and Appliance Store, but right now is an especially good time. Because Trader has specially reduced prices on some of General Electric's best major appliances.

And General Electric has a bonus offer for you. Here's how it works: When you buy a G.E. JB500 self-cleaning oven range, 970 or 1070 pot scrubber, built-in dishwasher, a micro-wave cooking center or G.E.'s 21 KV model no-frost refrigerator freezer, you'll get, first of all, Trader Horn's low, low price. But then General Electric will mail you a $50 U.S. Savings Bond as a gift.

Imagine getting a $50 Bond as a gift from G.E. just for buying one of those great appliances at the low, low Trader Horn price. Trader knows that quick nickels are better than slow dollars. And satisfied customers will always be his best sales force. He has ten stores now in the chain in New York and New Jersey. You'll find them in Manhattan, Yonkers, Spring Valley, Peekskill, Union, Linden, Fairfield, Paramus and Hasbrouck Heights.

You can always do business with Trader Horn, but hurry because that special bonus offer is on for only a limited time.

*   *   *

In a Nutshell: A recent survey of retail store commercials showed the following:

1. Almost all used the bargain appeal. For years, this appeal has worked in newspaper advertising. It also works in radio.
2. More than half quoted specific reductions such as "regularly $175, now $79."
3. About half gave reasons for price reductions such as "overstocked," "warehouse sale," etc.
4. The opening sentence of most of the spots named the product in order to catch the attention of prime prospects.
5. Most of the spots mentioned the location of the store more than once.
6. Most of the spots urged immediate action, with phrases such as "limited supply," . . . "while they last," etc.

This point is worth repeating. None of the spots attempted to entertain the listener. No jingles, no humor: just 100 percent persuasion from start to finish. There is a precedent for this. There is not a line of humor in two of the world's most influential volumes—the Bible and the Sears Catalog.

NEW OPPORTUNITIES IN RADIO ADVERTISING

A recent media analysis by the Ted Bates agency shows two important findings.

1. In the past ten years, radio's audience increased more than other media. Radio was up 38 percent, outdoor was up 16 percent, TV was up 13 percent, magazines were up 5 percent, and newspapers were down 2 percent.

2. In the same ten-year period, radio's cost per thousand people reached showed the smallest increase. Radio cost was only 22 percent, magazines were up 31 percent, outdoor was up 67 percent, TV was up 76 percent, and newspapers were up 90 percent.

With the audience up and the cost low, radio is an attractive buy.

OTHER ADVANTAGES OF RADIO

In addition to a big audience and low cost per thousand, radio has other advantages. Here are some:

Selectivity. You can use different types of stations to reach different markets. Example: You can use a rock music station to sell bubble gum or a classical music station to sell cultural items. You can reach businessmen in the morning, housewives during the day and a general audience at night.

Radio in Cars. More than 100 million cars are radio equipped. That exceeds the circulation of all daily newspapers. You can advertise to commuters, car pools, car owners and others at times when media such as TV and print cannot reach these people.

Primary News Source. In the morning and afternoon hours, more adults get the news from radio than from any other source. Your radio commercial adjacent to a news broadcast gets attention.

WHAT COPY APPEALS SHOULD YOU USE IN RADIO COMMERCIALS?

Use the same appeals that have been effective in your space ads or in your direct mail.

If a bargain appeal paid off in newspaper ads, use a bargain appeal in your radio commercials.

If a free gift stimulated action in your direct-mail advertising, use a free gift offer in your radio copy.

If a closing date such as "This offer expires in 10 days" got increased results in print ads, use a closing date in your radio ads.

And don't try to sell via radio those items you were unable to sell in other media. Stick to your popular items.

GETTING MORE FOR YOUR MONEY

Sometimes you can get a more convincing sales talk from a radio announcer if you let him personally sample your merchandise, see the advertised item, visit your store or view the vacation spot you are selling. This can add enthusiasm to his or her delivery.

If this is impractical, you can send a written description of your goods or services. Let the announcer sell in his own chatty style, as if he were having a heart-to-heart talk with a friend.

Regarding time costs: if you send a one-minute taped commercial to a radio station, you will get exactly one minute. But if you send a typewritten commercial, you may get more than one minute—and at no extra cost. Here is an actual case history.

The following 187-word direct-response commercial was sent to several radio stations in New York. Most of the announcers ad-libbed a bit by adding personal comments to the copy. This increased the time allotted by fifteen or twenty seconds without increasing the cost. Announcers seem to try a little harder with direct-response commercials. They know the client will count the number of replies.

Read below the 187-word commercial. Then read the 312-word expanded version as it was actually spoken on the air by one announcer.

187-Word Commercial That Was Sent to the Station

Do you suffer from headaches? The Stresscontrol Center has a method that has helped four out of five people get lasting relief. Come to a free explanatory session conducted by a prominent doctor and find out how you can be helped, how you can rid yourself of headache pain.

No pills. No drugs. Just a pleasant, relaxing method that uses Biofeedback—the space-age technology developed for use by the astronauts. This method is used by leading hospitals and clinics. Once you learn the method, you can use it anywhere—at home, on the job, on the subway, or driving your car.

One woman said: "I got wonderful relief." A businessman said: "I'm rid of headaches for the first time in years."

The free session on headache relief will be given at the Hotel Warwick at 54th Street and 6th Avenue in New York City at 6 P.M. this Wednesday. Your questions will be answered. No obligation. The address again . . . Hotel Warwick, 54th Street and 6th Avenue at 6 P.M. this Wednesday. Or for more information, call The Stresscontrol Center, 486-8950. That number again—486-8950.

312-Word Expanded Commercial as Actually Spoken by the Announcer

I do this job. I love it. You know I love it. I've been doing it for a long time. And if I didn't love it, I wouldn't be here. And yet, loving my job the way I do, and having the fun I do here, there's a certain amount of stress involved, you know. There's a certain amount of stress involved in everything. No matter what you do, there's a certain amount of stress involved. You've heard people say "He's not himself" or "She's a pain in the neck." Or "This job is a headache." You know, when you make mistakes.

Do you suffer from headaches? The Stresscontrol Center has a method that has helped four out of five people get lasting relief. Now you can come to a free explanatory session conducted by a prominent doctor and find out how you can be helped—how you can rid yourself of headache pain.

No pills. No drugs. A pleasant, relaxing method that uses Biofeedback—the space age technology developed for use by the astronauts. And this method is used by leading hospitals and clinics too. And once you learn the method, you can use it anywhere, at home, on the job, on the subway, driving your car.

Now one woman said, and I quote—"I got wonderful relief." A businessman said, and I quote: "I'm rid of headaches for the first time in years."

Now the free session on headache relief will be given at the Hotel Warwick at 54th Street at Sixth Avenue in New York City at 6 P.M. Wednesday . . . 6 P.M. Wednesday could be the start of a new world for you. Your questions will be answered. No obligation whatsoever. The address again is Hotel Warwick, 54th Street and 6th Avenue at 6 P.M. this Wednesday. Or for more information, you can call the Stresscontrol Center—486-8950 . . . 486-8950.

*   *   *

Parts of this commercial sound rambling and repetitious when put into cold type. But that is the information style of this announcer. This commercial, when listened to on the air, sounded warm and conversational—like one friend talking to another.

MAKING A COMMERCIAL
DO DOUBLE DUTY

Some direct-response commercials not only sell on the air, but they also sell the idea of reading the sponsor's newspaper ad. Here is such a commercial as actually spoken on the air.

The Dreyfus Fund

You have probably heard about tax exempt bond funds lately. And perhaps you've wondered—is it right for me?

If your combined family income is more than $16,000 a year, certainly it's something you should consider.

Now the Dreyfus tax exempt bond fund pools your money with that of others to buy tax exempt municipal bonds. Your money earns daily dividends. The dividends from the Dreyfus tax exempt bond fund have been one hundred per cent free of Federal tax. And those dividends can be compounded monthly to produce even more tax exempt income.

The Dreyfus tax exempt bond fund has no sales charge when you invest or redeem. And you can cash in your shares on any business day at the quoted daily price.

For more complete information, including charges and expenses, simply send your name and address to me, John Gambling, in care of Dreyfus, WOR New York 10018.

Or better yet, see the Dreyfus ad in today's Wall Street Journal. Or call this toll-free number—(800) 325-6400. That's (800) 325-6400.

*   *   *

SUMMING UP THE ADVANTAGES OF RADIO ADVERTISING

1. Radio is flexible. You can pick the right time and station for your product.

2. There are 100 million radios in cars.

3. Radio is a primary source for news.

4. You can sell on the air and, at the same time, promote the reading of your print advertising—either your space ads or your direct-mail ads.

5. In the past ten years, the radio audience has increased more than any other media.

6. Radio gives you low cost per thousand listeners.

16

How to Apply
Mail Order Know-How
in Writing
Television Commercials

"How can you tell if a television commercial is funny?"

"If the client laughs, it's funny," said a television commercial writer.

This approach to television commercial writing is about as wrong as you can get.

First of all, you should not try to write humorous commercials. You can entertain a million people and not sell one of them. Famous copywriter, Claude Hopkins, said: "Don't try to be amusing. Money spending is a serious matter."

Secondly, humor is a tricky thing. What sounds funny to you may sound ridiculous to others. Mail-order copywriters avoid humor. You won't find a single line of humor in mail-order ads or in mail-order catalogs. Humor does not sell merchandise.

And finally, you should not depend on the client's judgment of the sales value of an ad. The client knows too much about his product. He is not a typical prospect. "I get suspicious of the value of an ad when the client says he likes it," said the head of a large ad agency.

TIPS FROM MAIL-ORDER EXPERIENCE

Mail-order advertisers can measure the sales results of every advertisement they run, whether it be print or broadcast. They can do this with an exactness that no other advertiser can match. Hence, mail-order advertisers have accumulated a store of proven principles regarding how to make ads pay. These principles can be applied to all forms of advertising—from matchbook covers to television commercials.

For example, I recall an early experience with an offer we made in a TV commercial. The offer was a weather map. It was offered from time to time, on an evening weather report program sponsored by Con Edison in New York.

In the beginning, the weather map offer brought about 2,000 requests every time it was mentioned.

As time went by, the number of replies dropped to 1500, then to 1,000 and finally down to 500. As every mail-order copywriter knows, this is a typical experience. The first time you make an offer, you skim the cream off the market. Later on, the offer doesn't pull as well.

The client wanted to restore the pulling power of the offer. It is a well-known fact in mail order that the more time you devote to talking about an offer, the more replies you will get. So I added two elements to the weatherman's sales talk about the weather map as follows:

1. I suggested that he begin his program by saying: "Get paper and pencil ready. I am going to offer you a free gift at the end of this program."
2. I also suggested that, at the end of the program, he should show the audience the carton in which the weather map was mailed. I told him to point to the address label on the carton and say: "Send me your name and address so I can put it on this label and mail your free gift to you."

As a result of these two additions to the weatherman's pitch, the number of replies rose from 500 to 2,000.

SEVEN MAIL-ORDER PRINCIPLES
THAT CAN BE APPLIED TO TELEVISION COMMERCIALS

1. Attract Prospects

Many television viewers watch for your commercial—not because they want to listen to it, but because they want to take that opportunity to go to the refrigerator or to the bathroom.

Now, you don't care about the non-prospects who skip your message. You care only about prospects who may buy your product. These people will stop and listen to what you have to say if you can catch their attention immediately.

During the first four seconds of your commercial, the prospect decides whether or not to pay attention. Therefore, your opening line is like the headline of a mail-order ad. You either win or lose your chance to make a sale at the very outset.

For example, in a series of mail-order ads, *all with the same copy* but with different headlines, I have seen one ad outpull another by five to one. The headline was the only variable. The headline made all the difference. The reader was won or lost in the first four seconds.

In the same way, the first four seconds of your television commercial can make all the difference. You must show something or say something at the beginning that will rivet the attention of potential buyers.

2. Show a Picture of the Reward

What reward will your prospect derive from using your product or service? You should portray that reward in a picture. Or tell it in words. Or both.

Here are some rewards that have been successful in mail-order advertising:

Make money

Save money

Advance in business

Be popular

Gain prestige

Get enjoyment

Have more leisure

Gain comfort

Build better health

Get freedom from worry

Gain security in old age

3. Make Your Copy Believable

Here are tested ways to make your TV copy believable:

Include testimonials from satisfied customers.

State approval by experts. (Won the Gold Medal Award . . . Proved superior in laboratory tests.)

Tell how long your company has been in business. (Our 52nd year . . . Founded 1895.)

Give proof of popularity. (790 letters from delighted customers . . . Over 12,000 sold.)

Offer a money-back guarantee.

4. Prove It's a Bargain

Here are bargain appeals you can use that have helped TV mail-order ads pull better:

Price reduced: (Was $40 . . . now only $19.75).

Dramatize the low price: (Only $.45 a day . . . only 15 percent above wholesale price).

Give reason for low price: (Warehouse sale . . . Direct from factory to you . . . Modern equipment lowers production costs).

Build up the value of your proposition: ($5 spent may save you $500 . . . One gallon of this floorwax covers an average kitchen floor about 30 times).

5. Make an Attractive Offer

If you make an offer in your commercial, you should describe it attractively:

For example, if your offer is a free booklet, you should describe the contents.

If you offer a free sample, you should build up the value of the sample.

Offer the viewer something he can use. A travel advertiser offered a free map. A building products manufacturer offered a brochure on home repairs.

6. Make It Easy for Your Prospect to Act

Here are proven ways to induce the prospect to respond:

Offer a free cost estimate.

Offer an easy payment plan.

Offer to rent with option to buy.

Offer a free demonstration.

Offer quick information by telephone.

Offer to ship merchandise to credit card holders.

7. Give Your Prospect a Reason to Act Now

Here are some successful action-getting devices:

If the price is going up, say so.

If supply is limited, say so.

If there is a time limit, say so.

Offer a reward for promptness. Example: Free gift if you order immediately.

Use action words. Examples: Act now. Don't put it off. Delay may be serious. Order today.

In a 2,000-word mail-order ad, you can include all seven of the above elements. But in a one-minute television commercial consisting of a few pictures and sixty words of sales talk, you have to be selective. You have to select one or two essentials. Probably the most important essentials are to:

1. Stop prospects in the first four seconds.
2. Show a picture of the reward.

HOW TO USE SALES-TESTED PICTURES IN MAKING TELEVISION COMMERCIALS

When television was in its infancy, the writing of television commercials was turned over to the writers of radio commercials.

This was a mistake.

Radio commercial writers think only in words—not in pictures. And television is primarily a medium of pictures.

It turned out that the writers of print ads were better adapted to writing television commercials. They had learned to express their ideas in *both* words and pictures.

Pictures work faster than words. When you glance through the pages of a newspaper, you recognize the pictures of famous people before you have time to read their names.

Pictures are the most primitive form of communication. Pictures were the earliest messages carved on walls by our ancestors. Pictures are universal. They have no language barrier. They say the same things to all people.

I ran a split-run test of two mail-order ads in the New York Daily News—Ad A versus Ad B. The ads were identical, except that in Ad A the picture was prominently displayed at the top of the ad. The headline was printed below the picture.

In Ad B these elements were reversed. The headline was displayed at the top. The picture was placed in a subordinate position below the headline.

Result: Ad A with the picture at the top, drew 20 percent greater response than Ad B with the headline at the top.

Conclusion: The picture was a better eye-catcher than the headline.

I did a split-run test of two beauty-product ads. The ads were identical, except that in one ad the model was smiling, whereas in the other ad the same model had a serious expression. The ad with the smile pulled 25 percent better.

Pictures can be powerful in their effect. The famous philosopher Emerson was accosted by a salesman whose words were beguiling but whose face was sinister. Emerson said: "What you are, thunders so loud that I cannot hear what you say!"

Pictures, especially photographs, are more believable than words. If a photo says one thing and the words say something different, people will believe the photo.

The Need for Good Pictures

I once took a 1,500 word mail-order ad to a commercial artist to have a layout made.

"Cut 500 words so I can put in a picture," said the artist.

This was bitter medicine to a writer who grew up, as I did, in the mail-order school of print advertising, where long copy pulls better than short copy.

The artist noticed my hesitation. He repeated an old saying: "A picture is worth a thousand words."

"That is not quite right," I said. "The correct saying is: 'A good picture is worth a thousand words.'"

This incident illustrates an important point. You must use *good* pictures—pictures that show benefits—pictures that add clarity to your sales message—not just any pictures.

In print advertising, there have been successful ads that have had very small pictures or no pictures at all. Not so in television commercials. A blank screen won't do. You must show something that illustrates your story.

A Storehouse of Good Pictures

The television commercial writer who is looking for sales-tested pictures has a resource he may not be aware of.

That resource is the vast experience of mail-order advertisers who have been using print and pictures to sell merchandise for more than a hundred years.

What kinds of pictures are successful for mail-order advertisers? They are the pictures you see repeated again and again in mail-order ads, in magazines and in newspapers. If you see a mail-order ad picture repeated twice, you know it paid the first time. If you see it repeated many times, you can be sure it is a winner.

For example, take a look through *TV Guide*. What pictures are used repeatedly by the mail-order advertisers who can measure the sales results of their ads? Pay particular attention to repeated pictures. Here are some:

The book club ads show pictures of books.

The record club ads show pictures of records.

Not very imaginative. But these are the pictures that pay off—again and again and again.

More imaginative are the pictures that show the rewards of

using the product. Examples: The seed catalog ads show pictures of flowers. A mail-order ad for a book on organic gardening shows happy people piling tomatoes and carrots into baskets.

The largest categories of sales-tested pictures are:

1. Pictures of the product
2. Pictures of the product in use
3. Photos of people extolling the virtues of the product
4. Illustrations showing people enjoying the rewards of using the product

Can You Think in Pictures?

Can you translate your selling ideas from words into TV illustrations? Here is a quiz:

Suppose you were assigned to create television commercials to get recruits for the U.S. Army. What kind of pictures would you use? Here are some possibilities:

1. Soldiers on the drill field
2. A military parade
3. Pictures of famous battles
4. Photos of military heroes
5. Pictures of weapons being fired
6. Pictures of tanks
7. Pictures of warplanes

These are *not* the pictures that the Army found most effective. Millions of dollars have been spent on Army recruiting ads containing reply cards addressed to "Army Opportunities." The illustrations that get the most replies are:

1. Pictures of soldiers enjoying foreign travel
2. Pictures of soldiers learning useful skills that they can use to get ahead in their army careers or in civilian life

These pictures dramatize two basic appeals—the desire for enjoyment and the desire for advancement.

When I worked on U.S. Navy recruiting advertising, I discovered the effectiveness of these same appeals. One of the best Navy appeals is summed up in a famous slogan: "Join the Navy and see the world." And one of our most effective couponed ads had the headline: "Which of these 15 jobs do you want right now?" The ad was illustrated with pictures of sailors learning useful trades.

Examples of Sales-Tested Pictures

Here are some mail-order ad pictures that have been used time and again, with great sales success.

1. The L.L. Bean mail-order ads that appear in magazines and newspapers have been very effective in attracting customers. These ads simply show photos of shoes, shirts, pants, outdoor wear, etc. This merchandise sells itself.

2. Sears catalogs have been selling via print and pictures since 1886. They have found that the best illustrations are pictures of products and pictures of people using those products.

3. A mail-order beauty product advertiser shows pictures of beauty products and portraits of beautiful women.

4. A home study high school course shows pictures of people receiving diplomas.

5. A dress pattern manufacturer shows reproductions of dress patterns and pictures of dresses.

6. Correspondence school ads portray men and women who have been helped by taking courses.

7. RCA Music Service ads show happy, smiling people opening up packages of records.

8. Financial ads show pictures of people putting money in the bank.

9. Loan ads show people getting a loan.

10. Some mail-order advertisers show several pictures. For example, an Encyclopedia Britannica ad shows (1) a photo of the entire set of volumes; (2) a picture of the free booklet you get if you mail the coupon; and (3) a picture of a movie star saying: "I fell in love with an encyclopedia."

Television is an exciting medium to work with. Its sales effect can be great, but it is difficult to measure except in a general way. There are no split-run copy tests that can tell you the exact difference in sales results between two commercials.

Hence, there is a tendency on the part of some television commercial writers to produce commercials that are merely cute, clever, or amusing.

Copywriters who have been trained in mail-order ad writing are not likely to make this error. Their training has taught them to sell, not to be clever.

This brings to mind a remark that the Greek orator Demosthenes made to his rival orator Aeschylus. Both made speeches urging their countrymen to take up arms against King Philip. But Demosthenes' speeches were more effective.

Demosthenes said to Aeschylus: "You make people say, 'How well he speaks.' I make them say, 'Let us march against Philip!'"

Some television commercials make people say "How clever!" But the best commercials make people go out and buy the product.

A PLAN FOR TESTING TELEVISION COMMERCIALS BY DIRECT RESPONSE

There are two basic elements in every advertisement:

1. What you say
2. How you say it

This applies to television commercials as well as to all other advertising.

What you say pertains to your sales appeal. Do you talk about quality, price, popularity, value, convenience, or about some other benefit?

How you say it pertains to your method of presenting your sales appeal. For example, in your television commercials, do you let the manufacturer talk about his product? Do you let a satisfied customer praise the product? Do you show the product in use? Do you use a conversational approach such as a husband and wife talking? Or do you simply picture the product itself and let the announcer talk about it?

FINDING THE BEST SALES APPEAL

First, let's discuss *what you say* in your commercials; namely, your sales appeal. Finding the right appeal can make all the difference between the success and failure of your television campaign.

Let's assume that you have studied your product, surveyed your market, talked to consumers and reviewed your competitors' advertising. As a result, you have decided that your two most logical sales appeals are:

1. Low price
2. High quality

How are you going to decide which appeal to use? Will you produce two different television campaigns—one based on price and the other based on quality? Will you run the price campaign in one area and the quality campaign in another area? Will you run these two campaigns for six months and attempt to measure the difference in sales results?

This method of testing is expensive and time-consuming, and possibly inaccurate. The sales of your product are affected by so many variables behind your advertising.

A Better Way to Test Sales Appeals

There is a cheaper, quicker and more accurate way to test sales appeals; namely:

Test your sales appeals by direct response in print ads, and then use the winning appeal in television commercials.

Why is this method cheaper? Because, if you test print ads in a newspaper, you can test in small space and keep the cost of the test down to a few thousand dollars.

Why is this method quicker? Because in a direct response newspaper ad test, you will discover *in a few days* which sales appeal is the most effective.

Why is this method more accurate? Because you can run your test in a newspaper that offers split-run copy testing. *This is the most accurate method of testing ever invented.*

Let us say that you run your test in a newspaper with a circulation of 200,000. You can expose sales appeal A to 100,000 people and sales appeal B to 100,000 people—both on the same day, in the same newspaper and in the same position in the newspaper. This is accurate testing on an enormous scale. It cannot be equaled by any other method.

Will a sales appeal that works in a newspaper be effective in other media? Of course it will. A good sales appeal is a good sales appeal, no matter where you use it—in print media, in radio, in direct mail, on billboards and in television commercials.

How to Test Television Sales Appeals Via Newspaper Split-Runs

Step One—First you must decide what type of direct response you will use in your test. For example:

1. If your product can be sold by mail, you can include an order form in your ads.

2. If your product or service is sold by salesmen,

you can get leads for salesmen by inviting the reader to write or phone for information.

3. If you are selling a low-priced package product, you can offer a sample. You can charge for the sample or you can get increased response by offering a free sample.

4. If none of the above methods are appropriate, you can offer a free booklet about your product or service.

The important thing is to put into your test ads some sort of direct-response offer that will enable the reader to buy your product or express an interest in buying it.

Step Two—Let us say that you want to test two appeals: (a) quality and (b) price. You begin by preparing two newspaper ads—Ad A, featuring *quality* in the headline and in the copy, and Ad B, featuring *price* in the headline and in the copy.

These test ads can be all type or they can include illustrations.

What size should the ads be? They can be quarter pages. Or, they can measure as small as two columns by a few inches. The headlines should be set in big, bold type, so as to accentuate the difference in pulling power between your two sales appeals.

It is not necessary to use a coupon in these test ads. In fact, it is better to use a buried offer. The disadvantage of a coupon is that it calls attention to itself and attracts coupon clippers. On the other hand, an offer that is buried in the last paragraph of your copy gives you an exact measurement of the number of people who were sufficiently attracted by the sales appeal in your headline to read your ad through to the end.

In order to get an accurate measurement of the relative pulling power of these two ads, you should use the services of a newspaper that offers split-run copy testing. There are hundreds of such newspapers in the United States.

Do not use a geographical split-run, in which Ad A runs in the city and Ad B runs in the suburbs. Insist on a so-called "AB Split," where Ad A and Ad B appear in alternate copies of the newspaper throughout the press run. In an AB Split, each ad appears in half the circulation, on the same day, on the same page, in the same position on the page. Thus the only variable is the sales appeal you feature in Ad A versus the sales appeal you feature in Ad B. If a newsdealer has 50 copies of the paper on his newsstand, he will have 25 copies containing Ad A and 25 copies containing Ad B.

To repeat: Split-run testing is the best method of copy testing ever invented. It is cheap. It is quick. It is accurate.

Keying Your Ads

You can key your ads by inviting the readers of Ad A to write to Department A. You can invite the readers of Ad B to write to Department B.

If you use telephone response, you can use different telephone numbers in the ads. Or, you can tell readers of Ad A to ask for Miss Abbot and the readers of Ad B to ask for Miss Brown.

If you want to test more than two appeals, you can do a *series* of split-run tests in several newspapers over a period of time. I once tested thirty-six different ads with a buried offer. Some of the ads featured different sales appeals in the headlines. Some featured different ways of wording the appeals. By simply counting the replies, I was able to gather information that made it possible to build an extremely successful advertising campaign.

Testing Various Television Techniques

After you have found your best sales appeal via split-run testing, you are ready to tackle the second half of your problem; namely, *how to say it.* This requires the actual preparation and testing of television commercials because television offers qualities not found in print ads: sound and motion.

Let us say that your winning sales appeal is *quality*. How can you, in a 30-second television commercial, most effectively convey the idea that your product excels in quality?

For example, will you let the manufacturer speak directly to the audience and extol the quality of his product? Or will you use a demonstration to prove that your product is better than your competitors' products?

Your next step is to prepare two thirty-second commercials, A and B, as follows:

> 1. In Commercial A, the manufacturer speaks. He delivers a sales talk on the product.
>
> 2. In Commercial B, you use a demonstration to show the superiority of your product.

How about the offer? Suppose your offer is a sample of the product. There is not enough time in a thirty-second commercial to describe your sample and include a mailing address or a telephone number.

You can solve this problem by using sixty-second commercials instead of thirty-second commercials. This gives you an extra half minute in which to make your offer and spell out your mailing address and key number (Department A, Department B, etc.).

After your test is completed, you can drop the half minute containing the offer, and use in your television campaign only the first half of the winning commercial (thirty-seconds), in which you sell your product.

How do you test Commercial A (in which the manufacturer speaks) versus Commercial B (in which you give a product demonstration)? There is no split-run—there is no way you can divide exactly in half the thousands of television sets in a given city and run Commercial A in half the sets and Commercial B in the other half.

So you do the next best thing. You alternate your two commercials for two weeks, five days a week as follows:

First Week

Monday, Commercial A
Tuesday, Commercial B

Wednesday, Commercial A
Thursday, Commercial B
Friday, Commercial A

Second Week

Monday, Commercial B
Tuesday, Commercial A
Wednesday, Commercial B
Thursday, Commercial A
Friday, Commercial B

(*Note:* The first week begins with Commercial A and ends with Commercial A. The second week begins with Commercial B and ends with Commercial B.)

At the end of two weeks, you will have exposed Commercial A five times and Commercial B five times. By comparing the total replies from Commercial A with the total replies from Commercial B, you can tell which television technique brought the greater response: the manufacturer's spiel or a product demonstration.

How about time of day? Don't run some commercials in the morning and some in the afternoon. Select the same time of day for every commercial so that you will get the same size audience every day. For example, select a time slot just preceding a 6 p.m. news broadcast. This method was explained in detail in the preceding chapter regarding the testing of radio commercials.

SUMMING UP

The advantages of the above plan are as follows:

1. You eliminate opinion and guesswork in deciding what sales appeal to use in selling your product or service. Your decision will be based, not on theory, not on personal preference, but on the actual response of

prospective customers acting under normal conditions in a split-run copy test.

2. You also eliminate guesswork in deciding how best to present your sales appeal. You may let the manufacturer speak. Or you may show your product in use. Or you may use some other method of presentation. The important thing is that the method you choose will be the one that gets *action*—either a sale or an action that may lead to a sale.

1. ANNCR: Okay, so you've got a skill.

2. You've proved that you can beat the other guys.

3. Now where is it going to get you?

4. Now if you can learn about that,

5. maybe you can learn about computers

6. and start earning a good income.

7. West Coast Schools will teach you how

8. with expert instruction every step of the way.

9. Then before you know it their placement service could be working with you to help you find your first job.

10. Oh, the opportunities are there right now and the pay is good.

11. Now if you're short of cash for tuition, remember West Coast Schools are qualified under the federally-insured student loan program.

12. And of course they're approved for veterans.

13. So come on, get yourself a skill that really pays off.

14. Call West Coast Schools at 687-0660.

15. That's 687-0660.

Measuring Sales Results of TV Commercials

Over the years, general advertisers who cannot measure the sales results of their print ads have learned secrets of advertising success from direct response print advertisers who CAN measure sales results. In the same way, general advertisers can learn from direct-response TV advertisers. Note the direct response telephone number in the above commercial. This advertiser knows exactly how many sales each commercial gets.

1. ANNCR: Worried about a job?

2. Why not get into the exciting computer industry?

3. Technicians in this field can earn as much as a college graduate without going to college.

4. In only six months of day classes or twelve months of evening classes,

5. you can prepare for a career as a technician on Data processing equipment

6. and business machines or as a computer programmer.

7. Albert Merrill School in midtown Manhattan has trained thousands of men and women for important computer careers.

8. More than one hundred and sixty major New York firms have hired our graduates.

9. If you're worried about a job,

10. act now and get all the facts on how a student education loan can help you become a data processing technician or computer programmer.

11. ANNCR: Call or write today for a free career booklet.

12. It will be sent to men and women 17 years or older without cost or obligation.

13. Call 212-CI5-3900. Call in New York CI5-3900.

14. Or write to Albert Merrill School, 21 West 60th Street, New York. Or call CI5-3900.

What Can General Advertisers Learn from Direct Response?

Direct-response advertisers have found that they get the best results by using straight sales talks that do not attempt to be clever, cute or humorous. Persuading a prospect to spend money is serious business. Also, since you have only 60 seconds, it is best to concentrate your commercial on selling a *single idea*. In the above commercial the single idea is "How to get a better job."

1. MAN: Had enough bad news about what you shouldn't eat and shouldn't do? Ready for a breath of fresh air?

2. Then try the good news in Prevention.

3. The health magazine over 2 million families pick up each month.

4. Because Prevention tells them what they can do to help themselves look better,

5. feel better and live better longer.

6. Prevention has good news for you too. About recent health discoveries that can mean so much to you.

7. So why not try the countries fastest growing health magazine; Prevention.

8. Call toll free for a money saving free trial subscription. Twelve issues just $6.99.

9. Call now and also receive free,

10. this 72 page booklet on 'Healing with Nature'.

11. Gentler effective ways to help cope with the wide range of medical problems naturally.

12. If your first issue is not just what you want, cancel.

13. You keep the issue, keep the booklet and owe nothing.

14. Call today. Toll free, 800-648-5321.

15. That's 800-648-5321 for Prevention.

How to Keep Costs Down

Commercials used by general advertisers often cost tens of thousands of dollars to prepare. Not so with direct response commercials. The above commercial for *Prevention* magazine consists of only two low-cost elements: (1) Photos of the magazine, (2) an announcer delivering a sales talk.

1. MAN: If
    you're out of school,

2. out of work,

3. or just out for some-
    thing better.

4. Control Data Institute
    has a booklet that could
    change your life.

5. It talks about career
    opportunities
    in the exciting computer
    field.

6. And in how less than a year
    Control Data Institute can
    train you to program, operate
    and maintain computers.

7. ANNCR: Call the
    Minnesota Control Data
    Institute at 339-7771.

8. 339-7771.

1. MAN: Look through the
    help wanted ads lately?

2. When you do, you'll almost
    always see a need for computer
    people of all kinds.

3. Those ads promise super
    salaries, job advancements,
    and a chance to grow personally.

4. The best part is you don't
    have to know anything
    about computers to get
    started.

5. What it takes is computer
    processing institute
    training to put you on your
    way.

6. CPI matches their profession-
    alism

7. and knowledge to your abilities

8. and they do it better than
    anyone else. Call CPI
    today.

These Two 30-Second Commercials
Cost Little to Produce

One of the most effective forms of selling is simply a person-to-person sales talk. The above two commercials use nothing but straight selling—mainly an announcer who delivers the entire message. The cost of production is small.

1. (MUSIC THROUGHOUT)
   ANNCR: The most exciting
   gift catalog ever

2. and with just a toll free phone
   call it can be yours free from
   the Swiss Colony.

3. You've never seen anything
   like these gifts,

4. hundreds of them, half
   of them under $10,

5. many under $5, plus dozens
   with discounts from $1 to
   $5 each.

6. The Swiss Colony Gift
   Catalog,

7. free plus $12 worth of
   special TV coupons.

8. For your free copy, dial
   toll free 800-356-9000.
   800-356-9000.

Testing Various Items by Direct Response

In addition to testing copy, direct-response advertisers can test media by running the same commercial in a list of stations. Results are tabulated to determine which stations produce the lowest cost per sale. In the same way, time of day, type of program and seasonal variation can also be tested. In the above commercial for a gift catalog, seasonal variation is an important factor.

1. MAN: Ever thought about a computer career?

2. Control Data Institute, one of the world's major computer school systems,

3. can answer your questions about the placement record of our graduates.

4. Their starting salaries.

5. The qualification for entrance to Control Data,

6. and can I afford it?

7. A phone call and this booklet can help you decide if a computer career is right for you.

8. ANNCR: Call 757-3888. 757-3888.

Is Half Your Advertising Wasted?

The famous department store merchandiser, John Wanamaker said: "I know that half of my advertising is wasted, but I don't know which half." Some general advertisers have the same problem. But not direct-response advertisers. For example, if a TV sales talk such as the above doesn't work, the advertiser tests other commercials until he finds one that does work.

1. WOMAN: Here's an international Travel Tip from the American Express Card.

2. If you've got a taste for the good life, stay in style at a Sheraton showplace,

3. where everything is in the best of taste, from Damascus to Rio.

4. For reservations, call 800-325-3535. Now here's someone who's gone a long way.

5. JAMES FIXX: Do you know me?

6. When I travel with this at least if I run into trouble, I've got a place to run into.

7. The American Express Card, don't leave home without it.

8. WOMAN: The American Express Travel Tip for today was Sheraton Hotels and Inns.

A Triple Purpose Commercial

The above commercial for American Express Cards does a lot in 30 seconds. It advertises a chain of hotels where the American Express Card is welcome. It gives a free telephone number (800) for making hotel reservations. It features the famous American Express Card slogan "Don't leave home without it."

1. WOMAN: Do you want to see the latest, 2. chicest, 3. shinlest, 4. the sexiest,

5. the best in American fashion? 6. It's the Fashions of the Times. 7. A special magazine this Sunday in the New York Times. 8. After all, nobody covers the world of fashion

9. like the newspaper that covers the world... 10. ANNCR: It's a beautiful reason to get the Times delivered. 11. Call toll free 800 631-2500. In New Jersey, 800 932-0300...

Promoting Newspaper Circulation Via TV

This 30-second commercial promotes the circulation of the *New York Times* two ways: 1. The seventh panel announces "A special magazine this Sunday in the *New York Times*." 2. The last two panels offer home delivery of the *Times* and give a toll-free telephone number to call.

1. WOMAN: Hello, I hope you have a pencil ready.

2. I'd like to show you how to get this full color 48 page Shillcraft Catalog free.

3. It shows 192 lacid hook designs of beautiful things you can make yourself.

4. Luxurious rugs, elegant wall coverings,

5. lovely pillow coverings.

6. Each kit comes with full directions and everything you need.

7. This handy lacid hook, the pre-cut yarn ready to knot into the canvas,

8. and the canvas with the design marked color by color so you can't make a mistake.

9. It's as easy as tying a knot. No experience needed. You can do it even while watching TV.

10. You can get the Shillcraft Kit only by mail, they're not sold in stores.

11. So send today for your Shillcraft Catalog and these wall samples in 54 colors, all free.

12. ANNCR: To get your free catalog write Rugs, P. O. Box 7777, Radio City Station, New York, New York.

13. Once again for your free catalog write Rugs, P. O. Box 7777, Radio City Station, New York, New York.

Offering a Free Catalog Via TV

This commercial contains many good methods for getting replies. The first panel says "have a pencil ready." Panels 2 and 3 show the cover of the catalog and mention specific features; namely: "48 pages" . . . "192 designs." Panels 4 through 8 describe the contents of the catalog. Panel 10 says: "not sold in stores." In panels 11 through 13, the free offer is repeated three times and the mailing address twice.

How to make your food
taste better

• Now—for even less than a penny a meal—enjoy more meat flavor in meat . . . more chicken flavor in chicken . . . more good, *natural* flavor in *all kinds of food!* Now, discover the dramatic difference that a touch of Ac'cent makes!

For Ac'cent is the new basic seasoning that takes its place alongside Salt and Pepper. It heightens and holds the fine flavor of almost everything you cook. Ac'cent is a pure vegetable substance that adds no flavor or aroma of its own. Yet, remarkably, it brings out and intensifies the *natural* flavors already *in* foods!

Until recently, Ac'cent has been almost a trade secret of leading chefs and gourmets who have known it, used it, and praised it. Now you can use Ac'cent in your own kitchen—in your own favorite recipes—in meats, soups, chowders, fish, poultry, vegetables, gravies, salads and left-overs. Wherever you need salt, you also need Ac'cent. Use it in similar amounts—and discover how much good flavor familiar dishes *really* have!

For a free sample package of this unique seasoning, write to Dept. 1, Amino Products, 20 North Wacker Drive, Chicago 6, Illinois. Enclose a 5¢ stamp to cover mailing costs. Write for your package of Ac'cent today. Once you try it, you'll never again want to cook without it!

How to get your cooking
bragged about

• Now—for even less than a penny a meal—enjoy more meat flavor in meat . . . more chicken flavor in chicken . . . more good, *natural* flavor in *all kinds of food!* Now, discover the dramatic difference that a touch of Ac'cent makes!

For Ac'cent is the new basic seasoning that takes its place alongside Salt and Pepper. It heightens and holds the fine flavor of almost everything you cook. Ac'cent is a pure vegetable substance that adds no flavor or aroma of its own. Yet, remarkably, it brings out and intensifies the *natural* flavors already *in* foods!

Until recently, Ac'cent has been almost a trade secret of leading chefs and gourmets who have known it, used it, and praised it. Now you can use Ac'cent in your own kitchen . . . in your own favorite recipes—in meats, soups, chowders, fish, poultry, vegetables, gravies, salads and left-overs. Wherever you need salt, you also need Ac'cent. Use it in similar amounts—and discover how much good flavor familiar dishes *really* have!

For a free sample package of this unique seasoning, write to Dept. 30, Amino Products, 20 North Wacker Drive, Chicago 6, Illinois. Enclose a 5¢ stamp to cover mailing costs. Write for your package of Ac'cent today. Once you try it, you'll never again want to cook without it!

Testing TV Sales Appeals Via Print Ads

Testing sales appeals of products sold in stores is expensive and time consuming. The advertiser must spend considerable sums of money and wait months for results. And due to factors the advertiser cannot control, a sales test may not be accurate. Sales appeals can be tested via split-run in newspapers. For example the above two sales appeals for Accent Food Seasoning were tested via split-run. Each ad contains a buried offer of a sample package of Accent. The appeal "How to get your cooking bragged about" pulled 42 percent greater response than "How to make your food taste better." This method of testing takes only a few days, costs only a few dollars and gives accurate results.

17

Summing Up Success Secrets I have Learned in 50 Years in Advertising

1. The headline is the most important element in most advertisements.

2. The best headlines appeal to the reader's self interest or give news. Examples:

THE SECRET OF MAKING PEOPLE LIKE YOU

DO YOU HAVE THESE SYMPTOMS OF NERVE EXHAUSTION?

ANNOUNCING A NEW FICTION WRITING COURSE

HOW A NEW DISCOVERY MADE A PLAIN GIRL BEAUTIFUL

3. Sometimes a minor change in a headline can make a difference in pulling power. A mail-order ad for a book on automobile repair had this headline:

HOW TO REPAIR CARS

The pulling power of this ad was increased 20 percent by changing the headline to read:

HOW TO FIX CARS

4. Recasting a headline can make a big difference in response. Here is the headline of a couponed ad selling retirement annuities:

A VACATION THAT LASTS THE REST OF YOUR LIFE

Here is the headline of an ad that pulled three times as many coupons:

A GUARANTEED INCOME FOR LIFE

The losing headline attempts to be clever by calling retirement a vacation. The winning headline is a straightforward promise of a benefit.

5. Long headlines that say something are more effective than short headlines that say nothing. A book

publisher had difficulty selling a book with the title *Five Acres*. This book was transformed into a best seller by changing the title to: *Five Acres and Independence*. Another publisher had a book titled *Fleece of Gold*. The sales of the book were more than quadrupled when the title was changed to *Quest for a Blonde Mistress*.

6. Writing headlines, the copywriter should try to break the boredom barrier. "How I became a star salesman" was the headline of a successful ad for a course in salesmanship. The pulling power of the ad was increased by changing the headline to "How a fool stunt made me a star salesman."

SOME THINGS ABOUT COPY

7. Write your copy to the sixth grade level. Simple language is not resented by educated people. And simple language is the only kind that many people understand. When you read over your copy, say to yourself: "Will this be understood by my barber or by the mechanic who fixes my car?"

8. What you say is more important than how you say it. Mail-order advertisers do not use expensive artwork or fancy language.

9. Illustrations that show the product in use or the rewards of using the product or service are usually the most effective. *Examples:* In an ad for a bicycle, a picture of a boy riding a bicycle shows the product in use. In a retirement income ad, a picture of a happy couple sitting on a beach in Florida shows the reward of using the service.

10. Two forces are at work in the minds of your prospects: (1) skepticism, and (2) the desire to believe. You can do your prospects a favor by giving them evidence that what you say is true. Your client will also benefit by getting increased response.

11. Specific statements are more believable than generalities. An example of a specific statement is the famous slogan for Ivory soap: "99$\frac{44}{100}$% pure."

12. Include testimonials in your ads. Two ads for a financial publication were split-run tested in *Reader's Digest*. The ads were identical, except that one contained four brief testimonials buried in the copy. The ad with the testimonials produced 25 percent more sales. Some of the most successful mail-order ads have been built almost entirely around testimonials. *Examples:* "I was a 97 pound weakling" . . . "How I improved my memory in one evening."

13. Localized testimonials in local media are especially effective. Seven couponed ads for a public utility were tested in New Haven newspapers. One ad featured a testimonial from a New Haven woman. This ad outpulled all the others. A newspaper campaign featuring local testimonials for a packaged laundry soap raised the sales of the soap from fourth place to first place.

14. Ads that involve the reader are effective. For example, the best pulling ad for a book of etiquette showed a picture of a man walking between two women. Headline: "What's wrong in this picture?" A successful ad for a course in interior design had this headline: "Can you spot these 7 common decorating sins?"

15. Straightforward ads usually outpull "cute" ads. Two couponed ads soliciting subscriptions for a daily newspaper were tested by mail-order sales as follows:

First ad headline: "Take it from me, this is the newspaper for you." Illustration: Picture of a smiling boy offering the reader a copy of the *Los Angeles Times*.

Second ad headline: "How to get the *Los Angeles Times* delivered to your home." Illustration: None. Just headline and copy.

Results: Ad 2 outpulled Ad 1 by 190 percent.

WHAT YOU LOSE IF YOU DON'T BUY

16. When writing copy, don't merely tell your prospect the benefits he will get by buying your product or service. You should also tell him what he will lose if he doesn't buy.

17. Put your best foot forward in your copy. A copywriter asked my opinion of an ad he had written. He said, "I saved the best benefit till the end and used it as a punchline in the last paragraph."

I said, "Put your best benefit in the first paragraph. Otherwise, the reader may never get to your last paragraph."

18. Avoid humor. You can entertain a million people and not sell one of them. There is not a single humorous line in two of the most influential books in the world—the Bible and the Sears Catalog.

19. If you want to drive home a point, you should say it three times. For example, suppose you are making a free offer. At the beginning of your copy, say, "It's free." In the middle of your copy, say, "It costs nothing." At the end, say, "Send no money."

20. You can sometimes combine two successes to make a super success. For example: Seven ads for house paint were tested for pulling power. Here are the headlines of the two most successful ads:

a. "New house paint made by (name of manufacturer)."

b. "This house paint keeps white houses whiter."

These two headlines were combined as follows: "New house paint made by (name of manufacturer) keeps your white house whiter."

A campaign with this theme sold more house paint than any previous campaign.

21. Long copy sells more than short copy. The more you tell, the more you sell.

WRITE LONG, BOIL IT DOWN

22. Write more copy than you need to fill the space. If you need 500 words of copy, begin by writing 1,000 words. Then boil it down to a concise, fact-packed message.

23. You can often improve the pulling power of an ad by setting a time limit. Retail advertisers increase sales by setting a cut-off date. *Reader's Digest,* in selling subscriptions, frequently uses such phrases as, "Return this card before October 31."

24. Spell out your guarantee. The word guarantee has been used so many times that it has lost much of its force. Here is a classic example of a spelled-out guarantee:

> This is my own straightforward agreement that you can have my coaching material in your hands for 10 days examination and reading before you make up your mind to keep it. You are to be the sole judge.
>
> You can return the material for any reason, or for no reason at all, and your decision will not be questioned. Your refund check will be mailed to you in full by the very next mail. This agreement is just as binding as though it had been written in legal terms by a lawyer.

25. You should ask for action at the end of your ad. Tell the reader what you want him to do. Sometimes it pays to offer a reward for action. In selling a ten-volume world history, the Book-of-the-Month Club offered a free book "to new members who enroll at this time."

26. People who buy once are your best prospects for buying again. I used to write ads for a publisher who sold little booklets by mail for $.25 each. The people who bought the booklets were good prospects for the publisher's $5 books. And a number of the folks who bought the $5 books were later induced to buy the

publisher's $25 library. The same principle applies in fund raising. People who give once are the best prospects for giving again.

27. The copywriter's job does not begin at 9 a.m. Nor does it end at 5 p.m. His job is with him all the time. Some of his best ideas come to him while he is shaving in the morning, while he is riding on a bus, or at lunchtime, or while he is walking along the street, or sometimes in the middle of the night. He should have paper and a pencil handy at all times. He should write down ideas the minute they occur. Otherwise, some of his thoughts will be lost.

TIPS ON TESTING

28. The key to success in advertising (maximum sales per dollar spent) lies in perpetual testing of all variables.

29. Over the years, many methods for testing copy have been devised. Opinion tests, readership tests, eye camera tests, recall tests, comprehension tests, coupon tests, inquiry tests, attitude tests, etc. Most of these tests produced useful information.

30. Here is a simple test. When you write a piece of copy, put it aside and read it over the next day. You will almost always be able to improve it.

31. Another simple method is to ask somebody to read your copy aloud. If he stumbles over a sentence, say to yourself, "That's not his fault. It's my fault. I must improve the sentence."

32. If you want to get an associate's opinion of an ad you wrote, don't show him just one ad. Chances are he will try to please you by saying, "It's good." That gets you nowhere. Show him two ads and say, "Which is better?"

33. Testing ads by asking people for their opinion

is helpful. However, it can be misleading. Many will not vote for all-type ads. Most believe that an ad is not good unless it has a picture. This is not so. Some of the best-pulling mail-order ads have had no pictures.

34. In an opinion test, people hesitate to reveal their selfish motives. For example, in an opinion test of life insurance advertising, an ad with the headline, "What would become of your wife if something happened to you?" outpulled an ad with the headline, "To men who want to quit work someday." When these same ads were subjected to a mail-order sales test, the results were reversed.

HOW OPINION TESTING HELPS YOU

35. Do not discard opinion testing because it is sometimes inaccurate. Opinion testing has one big advantage over mail-order testing. You can ask the respondents why they voted for a certain ad. You can find out if the copy is understood or misunderstood. You cannot do these things in a mail-order test.

36. The best tests, if properly handled, are sales tests. Mail-order advertisers have an advantage in this respect. Every mail-order ad is a sales test. In mail order, you can test copy, media, position in media, and season—all by sales results. Hence, mail-order advertisers know a great deal about the realities of advertising. Much of this knowledge is applicable to those forms of advertising that cannot be accurately tested.

37. The most accurate test is a mail-order split-run test, in which two ads—Ad A and Ad B—are tested under identical conditions.

38. Testing copy is fun, exciting, rewarding. I recall working on ads for a finance company that offered small loans. Several of us wrote ads, and we tested them in newspapers by counting phone calls from prospects. For example, one ad would say, "Telephone this

number and ask for Miss Smith.'' Another ad would say, "Ask for Miss Miller," and so on. Thus we could tell exactly how much business each ad brought in. Then each copywriter would bet a dollar that his ad would win. Testing copy became a game we all enjoyed. It was as thrilling as betting on a horse race. We learned a lot, and the client benefited, too.

WHAT TO KNOW ABOUT ACCOUNT HANDLING

39. When you are soliciting a new account, don't tell the ad manager how bad his ads are. You may be talking to the man who wrote the ads.

40. In starting work on a new account, you are sometimes faced with the tough problem of beating the client's best ad—an ad that he has used successfully for years. How do you proceed? One way is to include in your ad every good thing in the prospect's ad, plus some good things of your own. Another way is to test—not just one new ad, but ten new ads. Your chances of finding a winner are increased tenfold.

41. Here is a philosophy you can use when your ad is competing with somebody else's ad. If your ad wins, you can say to yourself: "My experience paid off." If your ad loses, you can say: "I learned something."

Socrates used a similar philosophy in regard to marriage. He said: "If a man has a good marriage, that is a good thing. If he has a bad marriage, he becomes a philosopher, and that is a good thing."

42. Clients often tire of ads before the public does. Hence, advertisers who cannot measure sales results frequently demand a new campaign every year or so. Mail-order advertisers repeat an effective ad till it wears out. Maxwell Sackheim's famous ad, "Do you make these mistakes in English?" ran for forty years before it wore out.

SMARTEST CLIENT I EVER MET

43. Be honest. I recall serving an advertising manager who was the smartest client I ever met. I said to myself: "I can never fool this man. If I think a quarter-page ad will be more efficient than a full-page ad, I must tell him so, even though the agency makes only one-fourth as much commission. If I try to mislead him, he will see through me. After that he will never trust me." This policy of honesty paid off. It was a happy account to work on for eighteen years. After I stopped serving this man, he continued to recommend my services to other advertisers.

44. Be flexible. I used to take trips to Hartford to present new ads to the advertising manager of a large insurance company. It was a successful relationship. The ad manager became one of my best friends. We usually agreed on ads, but sometimes we disagreed. In those cases, I argued all morning for my point of view. But after lunch, I would remark: "There may be something in what you say. When I get back to my office, I'll try it your way."

45. Be diplomatic. A successful account executive said to me, "If the ad manager is in a rejecting mood, I don't show him any more new ads that day. I keep them in my brief case and show them to him some other time."

46. Don't feel bad if your client revises your ad. He will like the ad better and his revisions may improve it.

OUT OF THE MOUTHS OF BBDO

47. Bruce Barton, former head of BBDO, gave this advice: "Be polite to everybody, even the messenger. You never know when he may turn up as a client. If you are going to be mean to somebody, be mean to

the chairman of the board. He won't be around very long."

48. Get out and meet new people whenever you can. Don't spend all your time with comfortable old cronies. One time I was having lunch with a BBDO associate. A man stopped at our table. It was Roy Durstine, who was then president of BBDO. He said, "You men can't make any money talking to each other."

49. Alex Osborn, former vice-chairman of BBDO, said, "Never have an open break with anyone. The memory of the break will linger on long after the object of disagreement has been forgotten."

50. Find work you enjoy. My earliest ambition was to make enough money so I could retire at 40. But at 25, I had the good fortune to get into advertising. I never want to retire. The secret of happiness is enjoyable work, plus helping others.

INDEX